COMPUTER INTELLIGENCE
WITH US OR AGAINST US?

WILLIAM MEISEL

Computer Intelligence: With Us or Against Us?
Copyright © 2019 by William Meisel

ISBN (Print): 978-1-54398-321-0
ISBN (eBook): 978-1-54398-322-7

Table of Contents

Preface

Any author's work is colored by his past. In the case of this book, I believe it is accurate to say that I have spent most of my adult life gaining experience and insight into the subject of this book—advanced computer technology and how it impacts human society.

My undergraduate degree from the California Institute of Technology (Caltech) provided me with a strong foundation in math and engineering. I earned a PhD in Electrical Engineering from the University of Southern California. My PhD dissertation on neural networks led to several publications in the area, including "Nets of variable-threshold threshold elements," *IEEE Transactions on Computers*, July 1968. I then remained at USC as a professor of Electrical Engineering and Computer Science, teaching courses and writing the first book on machine learning, *Computer-Oriented Approaches to Pattern Recognition*, Academic Press, 1972.

After leaving USC, I started and led, for the next ten years, the Computer Science Division of a small defense company that was eventually acquired by a larger defense company. My division performed work for defense and intelligence agencies, as well as several large corporations. Most contracts utilized computer pattern recognition technology.

During the 1980s, I founded and built a venture capital-backed company, Speech Systems Inc., which developed speech recognition technology. We developed the first commercial large-vocabulary, continuous, speech-recognition system that recognized speech at the phonetic level rather than the word level, trademarked the "Phonetic Engine." The Phonetic Engine used an early form of machine learning technology to recognize spoken phonemes. (See the References section under "Meisel" for published papers on the technology.) The company developed a speech-to-text dictation product for radiologists called MedTrans. Unfortunately, at that time, the computer processing power required to support this advanced speech recognition technology was too expensive to support a practical commercial product, despite the technical achievements.

Leaving Speech Systems after ten years, I became an independent technology analyst in the use of speech and natural language technology. I created and published a monthly paid-subscription no-ads newsletter beginning in 1992. It started as *Speech Recognition Update* and changed names a few times, with the last version *Language User Interface News*. Publication of the newsletter ceased with the March 2019 issue. During this period, I edited two published books of articles on the "voice user interface."

Currently, as the Executive Chairman of the industry organization, Applied Voice Input Output Society (AVIOS), I plan the program for the *Conversational Interaction Conference* held annually. I also speak at many conferences on the commercial applications of speech recognition and natural language processing.

Over the years, I've been granted a dozen patents in computer science and speech technology, ranging from "Speech Recognition System" in 1988 to "Speech recognition accuracy improvement through speaker categories" in 2016.

I include this rather long resume to describe my extensive experience in computer science and its advanced uses, including artificial intelligence technology. This cumulative experience has given me a useful long-term perspective on the evolution of computer technology and its connection to humans, both when expectations are met and when they are not.

A challenge in writing this book is that many of the topics in themselves could be subjects for a full book. My approach is to focus on the major events and technologies that drove the evolution of computer intelligence and what those trends portend for the future of human society. One section on Algorithms provides an intuitive description of advanced methods for technically difficult tasks such as machine learning. For controversial subjects, such as the negative impacts of social media or the impact of artificial intelligence on jobs, I attempt to provide a balanced view.

I conclude this Preface with deep thanks to my editor and wife, Susan Lee Meisel, for editing that went well beyond the usual corrections of grammar. She is particularly qualified to edit this book, having edited my technology newsletter for over a decade.

Introduction

C omputer technology is embedded in modern life to an extent that was unimaginable a half-century ago. Where it will be fifty years from now is similarly difficult to predict.

The current focus on "Artificial Intelligence" (AI) has highlighted the rapidly increasing capability of computer technology, but treating AI as if it were a major change in the ability of computers is misleading. For decades, improvements in "computer intelligence" (CI)—basic computing power—has increased the range of tasks that computers can do. AI is best understood within the context of the general evolution of CI. That perspective will help us evaluate whether AI is a threat—taking jobs if not taking over. That broader view will also help us understand what is likely to come as CI evolves beyond AI.

The term "intelligence" in Computer Intelligence is *not* intended to be an analogy to human intelligence. CI is simply a convenient term summarizing, at a given time, the combination of pure computer processing power and the inventiveness of the software that uses that power.

Today's society depends on CI. Infrastructure such as the electric grids that power our homes and businesses are controlled automatically by computers and digital technology. Human communications are driven by digital networks, including the increasingly important role of mobile phones. Our dependence on computer technology is unfortunately too often made evident today when malicious cyberattacks impact business operations, our security, and even politics.

The part of computer intelligence called Artificial Intelligence certainly has had a major impact. Such achievements, however, are an *evolution*, not a *revolution*. They are driven by the long-term exponential expansion of computer power, a trend that may even be accelerating.

When computers were large devices filling a room, demanding their own air conditioning and fire suppression systems, they were at least obvious. Today, smaller versions hide within mobile phones, automobiles, TV sets, and thermostats.

Computer intelligence has long *augmented* human intelligence, providing tools that let us do things well beyond our native human abilities. Computers do arithmetic faster and more accurately than any human and have bigger and more reliable memories. We expand our intelligence with the aid of such common software as spreadsheet programs and spelling checkers in word processing programs. Computers have always been tools that expanded human abilities, and they are having an ever-increasing impact on our lives.

Looking at the evolution of computers, it becomes apparent that the core reason for the growing power of digital computers hasn't changed for decades. Faster computer processing and more memory—the hardware part of computer intelligence—seldom resulted from a fundamental new idea. Instead, improvements in computer effectiveness and power was largely driven by semiconductor chips with an exponentially increasing number of transistors (the famous Moore's Law that says the number of transistors on a chip doubles every two years).

The evolution of software languages over time is similar to hardware evolution. Fundamental principles have driven the evolution of software, driving computers from the simplest early "machine language" to today's programming languages driving complex applications. Today, the complexity itself is an issue; a major challenge is understanding and managing that complexity.

CI advances by more than the basic advances in hardware and programming languages. It also requires invention in the methodology that the software executes—"algorithms." AI techniques such as "machine learning" are an advance in algorithms. Improvements in methodology add power to CI by adding to the things it can do, not just how fast it can do them. The utility of algorithms, however, can depend on CI being powerful enough to make them practical.

This book discusses the history, current state, and future of Computer Intelligence (CI), a term this author is using to encompass the power of digital technology. CI includes the processing power of computer systems and the capabilities of the software driving them, as well as the communications technologies that enable digital systems to connect with people and each other. Digital processing today drives a wide range of products and services, such as your desktop PC, your mobile phone, the systems in your automobile, and the software inside companies that drives their operations.

With its growing impact on our lives and society, it behooves us to understand computer intelligence more deeply, both to take full advantage of the technology and to avoid potential dangers. Insights on how Computer Intelligence advanced to where it is today and where it's going can help in understanding a difficult topic. This book aims to make computer technology less mysterious and less obscure, providing a perspective to help the reader evaluate new developments. CI will impact us at an increasing rate, and understanding it will help us control its evolution.

Part I:
Computer Intelligence and its history

The story of Computer Intelligence is strongly driven by the basic trend of digital technology continually getting more computationally powerful. More computing power allows innovation in part by making it practical to use increasingly complex algorithms.

The core hardware is the chips that do the computing. Those chips have grown more powerful at an incredible rate. As noted, Moore's Law, formulated by Intel co-founder Gordon Moore in 1965, says that the number of transistors in a given area on a chip doubles about every two years, allowing the amount of computing one chip can do to double. Doubling every two years means the number of transistors will grow 32 times every ten years, to pick a time period. Moore's prediction has held up roughly for a remarkably long time. To give some perspective on where we stand currently, a single chip from Intel, the Core i7-3970X, has six processors that each can execute 3.5 billion calculations every second—a total of 21 billion calculations per second on a single chip.

An article in May 2016 in *MIT Technology Review* titled, "Moore's Law is Dead," claims current chip technology can't support the growth the Law predicts. One commentator satirized, "The number of people predicting the end of Moore's Law doubles every two years."

Chip density is, in any case, only a part of what drives the growth in available computer power today. One trend is increasing chip density through "3D" chips that stack processor slices ("dies") on top of each other, not depending on putting more transistors closer together on one die.

Another major trend is an increase in "cloud computing," where a company of any size can rent time at competitive rates on very high-powered systems accessed over the Internet. Companies using services such as Amazon Web Service or Microsoft Azure can use as much computer power as they want without the expense of maintaining a large computer center. Economies of scale for the cloud services reduces the cost of delivering that computer power.

In addition, large computer systems are integrating specialized chips, such as Graphical Processing Units (originally developed for game consoles), that can perform specialized computations more quickly than standard microprocessors and are particularly suited for today's AI. They accelerate computation in part by doing several things simultaneously—"parallel processing." The operating system of the computer center delegates appropriate tasks to this hardware.

Another trend that accelerates computer intelligence is the distribution of computing power to many devices such as smartphones. Many devices that required specialized hardware in the past today simply embed inexpensive microprocessors driven by software. A microprocessor also allows more features to be incorporated in a device, since it is a general-purpose unit. We can now carry what would be considered a powerful computer a decade ago in our pocket or purse in the form of a mobile phone.

When devices are connected to a wired or wireless network, they can call upon processing in the cloud as well as processing on the device. An important long-term trend is that processing power within those devices will increase, taking some of the load off of processing within the cloud. This sharing of the computational load between the cloud and at the "edge" further increases overall computing power.

Some computers are specifically designed to handle the most difficult computational problems. The Department of Energy spent about $500 million in 2019 to order a supercomputer called Aurora, the fastest single computer to date. It is said to be the first American machine that will reach a milestone called "exascale" performance, surpassing a quintillion calculations per second, roughly seven times the speed rating of the most powerful system built to date. Aurora will be used to analyze challenges ranging from how drugs work to the impact of climate change.

The long-term trend of computer power accelerating exponentially has continued for decades. Growth is even likely to *accelerate* due to the trends discussed. The impact of computer technology in almost all parts of society, business, and warfare will become even more pervasive than it is today.

Human evolution has always involved extending the core capabilities of our bodies and minds with external inventions. Clothing extends the limitations of our bodies to withstand extremes of the environment; it allowed early humanity to expand into new climates. Our automobiles in effect gave us motorized wheels that go beyond what we can do with our legs alone. Our telephones extend the reach of our voice.

We don't think of these extensions as part of ourselves, but we certainly depend on them constantly. Our shoes aren't part of us, but they allow our feet to tolerate hot concrete and rocky trails. At work we use tools, ranging from hammers to personal computers, to go beyond what our bodies and minds alone can do. We transfer knowledge through books and other media much more efficiently and to more people than face-to-face conversation would allow. Expanding our humanity through our inventions is the core of what has allowed humans to dominate the Earth.

Some connections with technology do almost become part of our brain. We drive a car, ride a bicycle, read, and type without thinking about all the detailed actions and processing needed to make this happen. They become part of our autonomous nervous system, embedded in our synaptic connections between neurons. We certainly didn't get these skills though evolution, yet we can often use a skill like riding a bike even if we haven't used it for years.

Computer intelligence (CI), the power of digital systems, is a tool that expands further what it means to be human. The increasing ability of computers to connect with us as other humans do—through language and images—creates a conscious interaction that uses our human senses without the adaptation required of keyboards and other such interfaces to digital systems. And mobile technology—smartphones, connected automobiles, etc.—allow that intuitive connection to travel with us and be always available.

Most tools we use and put away. Computer Intelligence will come close to being part of us.

Key CI developments

The history of computer evolution provides insights into how computer intelligence has come to play such a pervasive role in today's society and where it may be taking us. Human intelligence has always been an inspiration for the evolution of computer intelligence, and humans have always turned to tools to extend their abilities. Computer intelligence is a tool that will continue to expand human intelligence and make other tools easier to use.

Every breakthrough in CI is driven by a combination of factors—the evolution of necessary supporting technologies, cost-effectiveness, and a need that became feasible to address at the time. Major milestones in the evolution of computer intelligence reveal a steady flow of such factors. Many brilliant individuals and teams drove the advance of computer intelligence, and the milestones chosen in this section are only a part of such contributions. A common theme is that visions that showed the way required time to become viable commercial solutions.

Early computer concepts

Before digital computers, there were analog computers. The simple slide rule (Figure 1) could be considered an early analog computer.

"Digital" means that computers use a representation of data that is intrinsically limited in its resolution, one number out of a finite list of numbers—a "digital" representation. Digital computers today work with "binary" representations of numbers, representing them with zeros and ones as the only digits, as opposed to the decimal system (with ten digits) we use in most written material and in monetary transactions.

The Norden bombsight was a sophisticated optical/mechanical analog computer used by the US Air Force during World War II, the Korean War, and the Vietnam War to aid the pilot of a bomber aircraft in dropping bombs accurately. Such mechanical devices were designed for very specialized purposes, and could not be used otherwise.

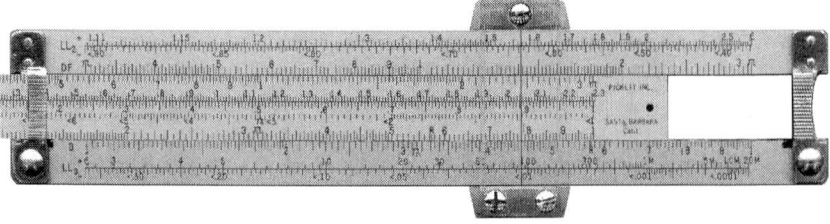

Figure 1: The Slide rule—A mechanical analog
computer, invented 1620–1630

Very early computing systems were developed using physical hardware such as gears, levers, wheels, and disks. Charles Babbage built a mechanical computer dedicated to a single category of task, his "difference engine," completed in 1822. The machine was powered by turning a crank. He announced his invention that year in a paper for the Royal Astronomical Society, entitled "Note on the application of machinery to the computation of astronomical and mathematical tables." Because the hardware had to be built very precisely, Babbage failed to get a working model.

Babbage's second effort, the "analytical engine," was designed to be programmable. Again, he never quite got it working because of the difficulty of building reliable, highly precise mechanical parts. But the concept is considered the idea behind today's general-purpose computers. The analytical engine was digital, rather than an analog system using gears, etc. It computed using standard base-10 numbers, rather than the binary representation of today's computers.

The analytical engine led to Augusta Ada King, Countess of Lovelace, the child of the poet Lord Byron, being described as the first programmer. Ada Lovelace, as she was called, was an accomplished mathematician, something seldom seen at the time for a female. In 1843, she wrote what could be described as a computer program for Babbage's analytical engine that was a specific example of how the device could be made to do a given task based on a series of instructions. The contribution was in a long appendix, called simply "Notes," for an article she translated from Italian on the analytical engine. Ada Lovelace unfortunately died at age 36.

Often in technology, a core idea is not practical at the time suggested, but is validated by later developments. This was the case with Babbage's and Ada Lovelace's insights.

Herman Hollerith made a more lasting contribution to early computers. Born in 1860, he became an employee of the US Census Bureau. He helped with the 1880 census, which, to his dismay, took almost eight years using manual tabulation.

To make the 1890 census go more quickly, he drew inspiration from the way railway conductors punched particular spots on a paper card in order to indicate traits of a passenger, allowing railways to understand things like how many children they had on specific runs. He devised punch cards about the size of a dollar bill, so that they would fit in storage designed for money. They had 12 rows and 24 columns, with the arrangement coding information gathered in the census for each individual—one card per person. Spring-loaded pins went through the holes when put in a punch-card reader, making electrical contact where there was a hole. With this mechanical counting apparatus, the 1890 census took only a year.

Later punched cards were used to load programs and data into computers. Programmers carried boxes of punched cards to a desk so that a computer operator could load the program and data.

Hollerith's contribution was timely in that it had an immediate practical use and government support. The format could then be adapted for computer input when the need arose.

Vannevar Bush, an MIT professor, was another early contributor to computer development. Starting in 1927 and completed in 1931, Bush constructed a "differential analyzer," an analog computer with some digital components that could solve differential equations with as many as 18 independent variables. The computer was thus special-purpose, rather than a general-purpose programmable computer, but showed that one could make a fairly complex computer work.

In the 1930s, Bush began developing the "memex," a hypothetical adjustable microfilm viewer. Bush expanded the concept in an essay "As We May Think," first published in *The Atlantic* in July 1945, during World War II. He expressed his concern for the use of scientific efforts in creating destruction rather than understanding. He suggested an information repository, a "memex," that would make knowledge more accessible and thus reduce what he felt was the irrationality of some human activities. Through the memex, Bush hoped to transform the increasing creation of information into a knowledge explosion. As Bush put it in the article: "Consider a future device...in which an individual stores all his books, records, and communications, and which is mechanized so that it may be consulted with exceeding speed and flexibility. It is an enlarged intimate supplement to his memory."

Today's storage of information on devices and on the Web, and the ability of search engines to find specific data within that information store, is obviously related to Bush's vision. Bush was motivated by human intelligence—"as we may think." The concept of expanding human memory was an early vision of computer intelligence being conceived as augmenting human intelligence.

Bush was a major figure in technology. During World War II, at President Roosevelt's request, he was the chairman of the National Defense Research Committee and later as the director of the Office of Scientific Research and Development, which presided over critical developments, including radar and early work on the atomic bomb. Bush's prominence brought attention to his efforts on computers and helped motivate future attention to the area.

Digital computers, once feasible, made most analog computers obsolete. The key feature of digital computers is their programmability, much easier ways to create specialized functionality than rewiring. This flexibility is emphasized by calling the control mechanism "software," as opposed to hardware.

George Boole—expressing logic mathematically

"Logic" is usually defined as the study of correct reasoning. There is certainly room for argument about what constitutes correct reasoning in a given case. Nonetheless, we understand the concept of a sequence of plausible statements leading to a specific conclusion. This type of reasoning is formal in mathematical proofs and scientific papers. Because a computer program can execute a specific series of actions, it can "reason" to the degree that reasoning is programmed as a series of steps in the computer software.

When George Boole published in 1847 a pamphlet, "Mathematical Analysis of Logic," he wasn't thinking about computers, but how logic could be expressed in mathematical form. Seven years later, he described his research in what is considered his masterpiece, *An Investigation of the Laws of Thought*, with the title highlighting his motivation to represent mathematically an element of human intelligence.

A core of Boole's methodology was the expression of "true" as the number 1 and "false" as the number 0. Expressing logic as mathematics would allow propositions to be expressed precisely. With an appropriate formula, mathematical expressions could then be manipulated in a way similar to algebra to draw conclusions. If a number of expressions were each true, the conclusions drawn from them by valid manipulation would be true. His formulation is today called "Boolean algebra." Modern software instructions perform logic operations using Boolean terminology and concepts.

Boole died at fifty. A brief obituary notice appeared in the London magazine *Athenaeum* noting *Laws of Thought* as one of Boole's principal works, and condescendingly called it a book "which sought a very limited audience, and we believe, found it."

The telegraph

Early versions of the telegraph were available in 1845, and a few years later, it was a phenomenon, with miles of wires being strung everywhere. It showed the power of the almost instantaneous transmission of information at long distances. Current economic journalist Tom Standage calls it the "Victorian Internet."

The importance of the telegraph in the context of computer intelligence is the power it showed of fast long-distance communication. It had an impact on society at the time comparable to the Internet today. That utility drove future developments in communication, a core part of computer intelligence.

Claude Shannon, switching theory, and information theory

Claude Shannon was born in 1916, and showed his mathematical abilities at an early age, with the publication of a solution to a difficult math puzzle while an undergraduate at the University of Michigan. He heard about Vannevar Bush's differential analyzer in his senior year, applied for a job with Bush, got the job, and joined Bush's team upon graduation.

The differential analyzer was controlled by over 100 relays, and Shannon's job included understanding the device and maintaining it. The experience led to insights on how George Boole's Boolean Algebra could be translated into a computing system, with switches such as relays embodying the logic. (Later, those switches would be transistors.) His insights were embodied in his master's thesis at MIT in 1938.

Shannon showed how Boole's math could be translated into hardware, thus allowing the hardware to implement "logic," to "reason" in 0's and 1's. The term "logic gate" is still applied today to a transistor circuit that executes a specific logical operation. The output of a logic gate is either 1 or 0 (True or False). When a computer executes a program, it is not just computing numbers, it is executing logic, another example of concepts from human intelligence driving computer intelligence.

Despite the obvious importance of Shannon's work on switching theory, he is best known for his insights into the meaning of information, founding what is today called "information theory." Information theory is a foundation of today's digital communications systems, and Shannon, when alive, was compared to Einstein for his insights in this area.

Shannon's interest in the area was piqued when he did work during World War II on cryptography at AT&T's Bell Labs, trying to break Nazi codes. He wrote a paper—classified at the time—on "A Mathematical Theory of Cryptography," later published. The work probably inspired what is considered his masterpiece, "A Mathematical Theory of Communication," in 1948.

Shannon applied his theory to communication systems, and felt it was perhaps being overly stretched to apply to other areas, such as physics. He wrote an editorial piece, "The Bandwagon," in a technical journal in 1956 arguing for caution in applying his ideas too broadly.

One area where his ideas apparently had relevance was in investment—"portfolio theory." According to the 2005 book, *Fortune's Formula* by William Poundstone, Shannon himself became wealthy applying this approach.

The application to communications systems was certainly of fundamental importance. Shannon's "A Mathematical Theory of Communication" described the theoretical limits on the transmission of information from a source to a receiver through an intervening channel. Such information must be coded in some way if expressed digitally (as opposed to the analog signal of classical telephony). If digital, the signal is sent as a series of "bits" (binary digits, 0 or 1). Shannon noted that, when a channel is "noisy" (e.g., electrical noise from transmitting equipment), occasionally a bit sent from the source as a 1 will be received at the receiver as a 0, or vice versa. He showed that, by using redundancy in coding information, you can reduce the likelihood of an error in the message due to noise in the channel. He showed that, with enough redundancy, the error rate for a given amount of noise can be made as low as desired.

This error-correcting ability can be understood through an example. Suppose instead of sending a series of 0s and 1s, we send 0 as three bits, 000, and 1 as three bits 111 (a "code" for each binary digit). No other group of three digits is a legitimate code. If we receive an invalid value such as 010, we can simply interpret it as 0, tolerating any one error in the three-bit group. The error rate can be made as low as desired at the cost of sending more bits.

The term "communications" in itself—originating with human-to-human conversation—suggests another case where the inspiration of human intelligence has driven the development of computer intelligence. Without technology such as the early telegraph, today's telephone, and email, human communication would be limited to face-to-face discussions, postal exchanges, or printed publications. Mobile phones, with their wireless communication, let us take our digital information and services wherever we go.

Shannon's contribution to switching theory is the most direct way he impacted computer development. But his contribution to communications is also fundamental to the computerized world we live in today. In today's economy, we are dependent on machine-to-machine communication and machine-to-human communication. We use the Internet to connect to computers in the cloud for services such as web search, ordering products, finding news and other information, and helping us get from one place to another with the additional help of global positioning systems. Computers in a "server farm" communicate among themselves through the operating system, critical to providing those web services in high volumes. And GPS satellites must communicate wirelessly with earthbound computers to give us those driving directions.

Shannon was eccentric, famous for riding a unicycle through the halls of Bell Labs while juggling balls. He also built perhaps the most useless machine ever made. It was a small wooden box with a single switch. When you turned on the switch, the box opened and a mechanical hand came out, turned off the switch, re-entered the box, and the lid closed. (Perhaps the message was to "think outside the box.")

More practically, he built a mechanical mouse that could run a maze, sensing the walls, a useful illustration of the potential of robotics. Shannon obviously had his playful side, but his systematic reasoning abilities made serious contributions to the technology supporting us today.

Ivan Sutherland

Shannon also contributed indirectly to making computers more intuitive to use. One of his students, Ivan Sutherland, wrote a doctoral thesis, "Sketchpad: A Man-Machine Graphical Communications System," in 1963. Sketchpad was a computer program that pioneered the use of a Graphical User Interface (GUI), although it was more of a drawing program than today's GUI. Sketchpad displayed graphical items like lines and arcs on the screen and allowed rotating and moving them. They could be manipulated by a pointing device (a light pen). Sutherland wrote, "The Sketchpad system makes it possible for a man and a computer to converse rapidly through the medium of line drawings."

Sutherland has been called "the father of computer graphics." The incorporation of graphics allows screens to be used for more than displaying text. This insight is obviously a major part of today's computer interfaces with humans.

The early modern computer

The ENIAC (Electronic Numerical Integrator and Computer) was invented by J. Presper Eckert and John Mauchly at the University of Pennsylvania. They began construction in 1943 and finished in 1946, partly as secret research motivated by World War II. It occupied 1,800 square feet, weighed almost 50 tons, and used about 18,000 vacuum tubes. Each vacuum tube is the equivalent of one transistor in today's semiconductor technology; a single memory chip today can have billions of transistors.

The ENIAC accepted input from an IBM punched card reader and could produce output through an IBM card punch. The output could then be printed using a specialized IBM punch card reader.

Programming it was not simple. It was done with a combination of plugboard wiring and three portable "function tables" (containing 1200 ten-way switches each). Ten-way switches were required because the ENIAC was programmed using decimal rather than binary numbers.

It is considered to be the first computer with most modern traits. It was electronic and programmable. It could "branch," that is, execute an operation based on a previous result, what is called an IF-THEN operation today. It was used for actual applications for a decade, distinguishing it from other early prototypes that were largely demonstrations.

The EDVAC and the Van Neumann model

The EDVAC (Electronic Discrete Variable Automatic Computer) was a descendant of the ENIAC proposed by Mauchly and Eckert in 1944 and completed in in 1949. It did arithmetic and stored data in a binary number representation rather than the base-10 decimal representation used in the ENIAC. Another change toward modern computers was that the program was stored in memory rather than with physical wiring that had to be re-plugged to change the program.

The EDVAC was particularly influential for its use of what is today called the von Neumann architecture, based on a 1945 description by the mathematician and physicist John von Neumann and others in a report of the EDVAC. That document describes an architecture for an electronic digital computer that separates functions (Figure 2). It uses:

- A central processing unit (CPU) that contains:
  - An arithmetic logic unit (with registers for storing data temporarily), and
  - A control unit that contains an instruction register and program counter (the latter to identify the next instruction);
- Memory that stores both data and instructions; and
- Input and output mechanisms.

The architecture may also support an external mass storage device such as a tape drive. The Van Neumann separation of function was adopted for most future computers.

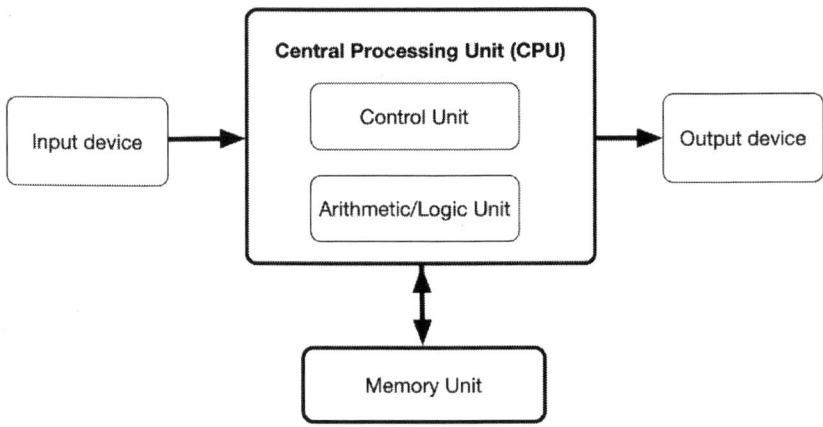

Figure 2: Von Neumann computer architecture

Douglas Engelbart, the "mother of all demos," and "Augmented Intelligence"

Douglas Engelbart was inspired by Vannevar Bush's Memex concept, in particular, and its intent to allow machines to provide humans with improved access to data. Engelbart expanded on this concept with a more general concept of letting machines improve what people can do—he called it "Augmented Intelligence." He published a long paper describing the concept in 1962 titled "Augmenting Human Intellect." The term "Augmented Intelligence" is sometimes used today to emphasize the potential role of Artificial Intelligence techniques to support human intelligence rather than replace it.

Engelbart explored this concept more deeply when he later took a job at Stanford Research Institute (SRI). He decided the key was reducing the complexity of dealing with a computer. Drawing on his experience with radar in the Navy, he envisioned a screen with graphics. A key requirement, he felt, was developing an intuitive way to interact with that screen. A research grant from the US government allowed him to explore this possibility.

Engelbart developed a pointing device to interact with the screen graphics, realizing that pointing was an intuitive human activity—another example of human intelligence inspiring computer intelligence. Inspired by the planometer, a device that measured an area by rolling around in it, he created a device with wheels that could be used to send signals to the screen to move a pointer image on the screen. The device first had a wire coming out the top, but experimentation led to the conclusion that a wire coming out the back was better. Since it then had a "tail," they called the pointing device a "mouse."

Engelbart conceived of the mouse as having ten buttons, losing sight of the value of simplicity, but his team convinced him that three buttons were enough. (Steve Jobs and Apple later reduced it to one button and eventually raised it to two buttons, the mouse so prevalent today, with its left click and right click.) The invention of the mouse is a wonderful example of the synergy of research and engineering. Engelbart's team went beyond an insightful theoretical concept to show how to make that concept practical.

In December 1968, Engelbart gave what has been called "the mother of all demos," a ninety-minute demonstration at a computer industry conference. He began by asking, "If, in your office, you as an intellectual worker were supplied with a computer display, backed up by a computer that was live for you all day, and was instantly responsive, to every action you have, how much value could you derive from that?" What he was describing and demonstrating is what we would characterize today as a "personal computer."

The live demonstration featured the introduction of the computer mouse, drag-and-drop action by the mouse, other capabilities in word processing (including features such as characterizing items on a grocery list by category, e.g., "produce"), video conferencing, teleconferencing, a collaborative real-time editor, and other more technical capabilities that play an essential part in modern computer technology. (The demo is available on YouTube; search for "mother of all demos.")

Engelbart indicated that the research was part of SRI's Augmented Human Intellect Center, emphasizing the ability for computers to interact with humans directly to help them get things done, as well as the enhanced ability for humans to interact with each other at distance. As the very name of the Center suggests, Engelbart and his colleagues were motivated by the power of using computer intelligence to augment human intelligence.

Alan Kay and Xerox PARC

Alan Kay, born in 1940, learned computer programming in the Air Force, programming a computer intended for small businesses, the IBM 1401. Later, while in college, he programmed more powerful computers.

Kay went to graduate school at the University of Utah in 1966. David Evans was a professor there, with a research emphasis on building graphical user interfaces. Evans gave Kay a copy of Ivan Sutherland's thesis on Sketchpad, inspiring Kay to work on similar ideas. Kay also attended the "mother of all demos" by Douglas Engelbart in 1968.

Kay studied how individuals could directly interact with computers, rather than submitting programs to a computer center. Kay believed that rapid progress in computer chips would allow the development of personal computers—computers dedicated to direct use by an individual with computer screens that had a Graphical User Interface. His doctoral thesis argued that a personal computer should be simple ("It must be learnable in private") and comfortable ("Kindness should be an integral part").

Kay was able to advance his vision when he later joined copier company Xerox's Palo Alto Research Center (PARC). When asked to predict future trends in a meeting there, Kay is reported to have said, "The best way to predict the future is to invent it."

Kay called the personal computer he was trying to build the Dynabook; he had previously opened a paper notebook to describe how it should look. He called the operating system Smalltalk, supposedly to reduce expectations and surprise evaluators with its effectiveness. Unlike the terminals of the day that were connected to a larger computer, he wanted it to stand alone.

There was resistance by some of Xerox's management to Kay's initial proposals, but he was able to team with other managers to build the Xerox Alto (what Kay called an "interim" Dynabook). The Alto, completed in March 1973, had a screen capable of displaying graphics, a keyboard, and a mouse. It was a large device, about the size of an under-counter refrigerator, but still considered a "personal" computer. About 2,000 copies of the Alto were used inside Xerox and distributed to research centers, providing inspiration to later entrepreneurs, but not available to the public.

Later, a Xerox group in Southern California developed the Star workstation, inspired largely by the Alto, and launched it in 1981. Of the many innovations in the Star, David Canfield Smith invented the concept of computer icons and the desktop metaphor. The user would see a desktop display that showed documents and folders, with different icons representing different types of documents. The bit-mapped display supported creating documents with both words and pictures (Figure 3), something we take for granted today. Unfortunately, it was very expensive, and the time wasn't yet right for this to become a practical commercial product.

The impact of these early efforts on today's PCs is evident. Bill Gates was quoted in 2017 in response to a question over whether Microsoft copied Steve Jobs' Apple Macintosh by using a Graphical User Interface in Windows, as saying: "The main 'copying' that went on relative to Steve and me is that we both benefited from the work that Xerox PARC did in creating the graphical interface—it wasn't just them but they did the best work...their work showed the way that led to the Mac and Windows."

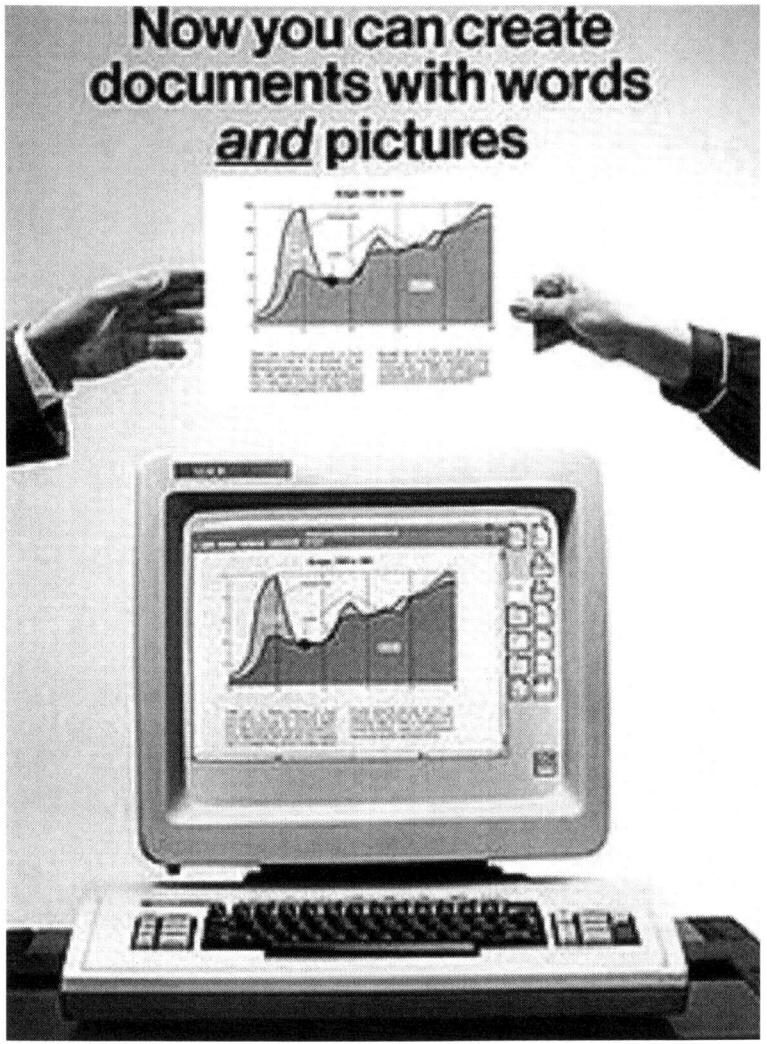

Figure 3: A Xerox ad for the Star Workstation

Perhaps Xerox's innovation, if better supported by the company, would have led to a breakthrough commercial product. One Xerox executive was quoted as saying, "The computer will never be as important to society as the copier." Xerox never created a personal computer for consumer use.

MITS Altair kit computer

Micro Instrumentation and Telemetry Systems (MITS) was a US electronics company that began manufacturing electronic calculators in 1971 and personal computers in 1975. Ed Roberts and Forrest Mims founded MITS in 1969. In 1971, Roberts redirected the company into the electronic calculator market with some initial success.

MITS then developed the first commercially successful personal computer kit, the Altair 8800, a "microcomputer" based on the Intel 8080 microprocessor chip released in April 1974. The Altair was featured on the January 1975 cover of *Popular Electronics*, leading to hobbyists buying many of the $397 kit. It was sold by mail order through ads, selling thousands in the first month. A fully assembled version was soon sold as an option. The Altair 8800 is widely recognized as the first commercially successful personal computer. This development transformed the *concept* of an affordable personal computer into a *product*.

This development did not try to emulate any aspect of the human brain. In fact, it could be considered to have made it clear that evolving from existing hardware options (a microprocessor, printed circuit boards, and standard hardware "buses" to plug them into) led to an architecture suiting the current state-of-the-art. The Altair's practical impact was motivating interest in more powerful personal computers.

Microsoft and a standard operating system

Paul Allen and Bill Gates saw the article on the MITS Altair kit and began writing a software language, later called Altair BASIC, to program the Altair that was easier to use than the "assembly language" instructions. They moved to Albuquerque to work for MITS and in July 1975 started Microsoft, with their BASIC language its first product.

Gates and Allen were friends and early computer-software enthusiasts, starting in high school. Gates also became friends with Steve Ballmer, the later Microsoft CEO, when studying at Harvard. The early programming efforts by Gates and Allen were famously characterized by intensity—long periods of concentration and little sleep.

Their version of the BASIC computer language that could program the Altair eventually spread widely through computer clubs, largely through unlicensed copies, partly based on an ethic among hobbyists that software should be free. In later years, Gates reacted to the software theft and helped establish that software was intellectual property that should be protected. Gates and Allen formed Microsoft as "Micro-Soft" in 1975, with a relatively vague goal to write software for microprocessors, believing that microprocessors would eventually bring computing to the masses.

When IBM decided to make a personal computer (PC), they turned to Microsoft for programming languages. But their biggest need was for an operating system (OS) that could manage the basic functions of the PC, e.g., managing computer memory and launching applications.

Microsoft took on the task, despite concern that the company was over-committed with existing projects. At the time (1980), Microsoft revenues were $7.5 million compared to IBM's $30 billion. Surprisingly, Microsoft was able to negotiate a deal that gave them full ownership of the resulting operating system, which was called PC-DOS (Disk Operating System). The IBM PC, unveiled in August 1981, became a worldwide standard. Other companies soon made "IBM-compatible" PCs. The trend made Microsoft the provider of the dominant operating system for PCs. The hardware and software standards created a market for application software that could address a large market, with a resulting benefit for the companies developing the applications and an increasing motivation for the purchase of PCs by companies and individuals.

The development of personal computers was driven by people like Gates and Allen who wanted direct access to computer intelligence, to use the term of this book. They apparently didn't think of the PC as somehow emulating human intelligence with its early computational limitations, but certainly did consider it a tool to *extend* human intelligence by making computer power more widely available.

Software, computer languages, and repeatable logic

A core characteristic of computer software is its consistency in performing a task. It executes logic in a repeatable way. That logic may be erroneous or contain some errors, but, because of consistency, errors can be discovered and corrected more easily.

Walter Isaacson in his book *The Innovators* quoted Bill Gates as describing his early fascination with computer software: "When you use a computer, you can't make fuzzy statements. You make only precise statements." If you are an accountant calculating tax returns, you want the software to execute steps demanded by the tax code. That code can be written and debugged to a high level of reliability, despite the logic of the program requiring long software code to describe it.

Programming languages express that logic. The basic operations of the computer are expressed in "assembly language," telling the central processing unit (CPU) each detailed step to take to execute a task. "High-level" computer languages attempt to hide this detail with more intuitive commands that are translated into assembly language. BASIC (Beginner's All-purpose Symbolic Instruction Code), developed at Dartmouth College in New Hampshire in the mid-60s, was one of the early languages. It was more readable than assembly language, using readable English-language commands such as "print," "input," "next," "if...then...else," and "end," making reading a program more intuitive.

Microsoft's Altair BASIC described the programming language as an extension of the Dartmouth language. In 1991, Microsoft introduced Visual Basic, a further evolutionary development of Basic. It included constructs from that language as well as additional commands from other languages such as "with" and "for each." The use of English words for commands, an attempt to enhance "readability" of software, has continued with later generations. The most popular languages in mid-2019 are called Java, C, C++, and Python.

Apple and the Graphical User Interface

Apple was founded on April Fools' Day in 1976 by Steve Jobs and Steve Wozniak ("Woz"). Woz designed the Apple I, and Apple released it in 1976. It used a typewriter-like keyboard and a regular TV as a screen. It was relatively inexpensive at less than $700 for the first units sold. According to Walter Isaacson's biography of Steve Jobs, the company almost wasn't able to pay for parts to deliver the first 50-unit order from Byte Shop; a phone call verifying the order was required for them to get the parts on credit. In all, some 200 painstakingly hand-assembled units were sold. If you have one today, it may be worth hundreds of thousands of dollars as an antique.

The Apple II was a more sophisticated product. It was introduced in April 1977. Those who bought one had to decide between 32,000 and 64,000 bytes of memory. (Today's models have gigabytes of memory; a gigabyte is 1,024,000,000 bytes.) The device was far-sighted, however; it supported color graphics and had slots in its motherboard for boards from other manufacturers to support functions not in the basic device.

Creativity in applications helped the limited device be a commercial success. In 1978, Dan Bricklin and Bob Frankston produced VisiCalc, the first electronic spreadsheet, first released for the Apple II. VisiCalc showed that the PC could support business applications, not just be a replacement for the electric typewriter or a game machine. Apple credited VisiCalc with the motivation behind sales of a fifth of the Apple IIs it sold. VisiCalc sold over 700,000 copies in six years, and changed the PC from a hobbyist device to a business device. Microsoft's Excel was first delivered for Apple PCs.

The Apple III had a similar hardware design, but more power. The increase in computer processing speed and memory size over time is part of the continuing increase in what is the core "intelligence" of the hardware.

But there is more to computer intelligence than memory and speed. Ease-of-use is critical, and that connection was enhanced by major developments at Apple—the Lisa and the Macintosh. A "bit-mapped" screen allowed using the screen to display graphics and images as well as text; early commercial PCs could only generate characters on the screen.

Both the Lisa and the Macintosh incorporated the Xerox PARC's Graphical User Interface (GUI) and the mouse of Alan Kay's Dynabook. Apple's Lisa was launched in 1983. It took Xerox's basic ideas and refined them significantly, with a better mouse and other improvements. Apple used the metaphor of treating the screen as a "desktop," even placing overlapping documents on the screen.

Apple then began development of its next generation PC—the Macintosh. The Lisa and Macintosh approaches to a device with a graphical interface were somewhat different. This caused some conflict within Apple, and Steve Jobs' role in the company management was reduced. This motivated Jobs to work on the Macintosh, eventually taking over its development from the original leader, Jef Raskin. Jobs unveiled the Macintosh on January 24, 1984.

The "Mac" was one-fourth the price of the Lisa, and led the rapid adoption of GUI devices. Eventually, the Lisa version was dropped, and the Mac model led the company's growth. By May 1984, Apple had shipped 70,000 units. Part of that success was due to Apple's 1984 Super Bowl ad, which positioned Apple as freeing individuals from the dominance of "Big Brother," a reference to the market domination of IBM-compatible PCs.

The effectiveness of the GUI was the driving force of the Mac, but the hardware supporting it, the higher screen resolution supported by the processing power of the Motorola 68000 microprocessor, delivered acceptable performance at an affordable price that put it truly in the "personal" range. The compact physical design was also considered part of the appeal of the Mac.

The GUI enabled the development of new types of applications such as desktop publishing, that included seeing how a final document would look on the screen. Apple's development of the LaserWriter printer further encouraged desktop creation of graphic documents, allowing both the text and images on the screen to be printed.

An early major application was Adobe PageMaker. The choice by Apple to support Adobe's PostScript format for digital documents proved a long-term advantage for both Apple and Adobe.

Apple made a critical contribution to the evolution of computers. Their innovations made the use of personal computers more intuitive and contributed to a mass market.

Microsoft and Windows 3

Microsoft was given early notice of Apple's Graphical User Interface to be in the Lisa and Macintosh, since Apple wanted Microsoft to provide its Office applications on the new devices. Microsoft realized the importance of the innovation, and began designing a new operating system to replace DOS, incorporating the GUI concept. Although Apple had required that Microsoft not develop a GUI-based OS for a period of time, that time expired even before the Lisa was introduced.

Microsoft moved in 1990 to a GUI with the Windows 3 operating system, with each "window" being able to run MS DOS applications. The combination of this continuity of applications and the support of the graphical WIMP interface (Windows, Icons, Menus, and a Pointing device) made the GUI the standard for future PCs.

Microsoft also supported the growth of Apple devices by continuing to provide Office software for the Mac. Reportedly, this took a call from Steve Jobs to Bill Gates to confirm that support for at least five more years.

Communications and networks

Early communications technologies such as the telegraph and telephone used wires connecting the end devices to transmit analog signals. Early telephony was analog, transmitting an audio signal generated by a microphone that replicated the vibrations of human speech.

Paul Baran, working at the RAND Corporation in 1960 on military applications of communications, motivated the development of digital communications using networks with multiple connecting points ("nodes"), with an emphasis on the survivability of such networks if individual nodes were disabled. A series of reports, *On Distributed Communications*, published by RAND in 1964, described "packet switching" networks for secure voice communications—sending data as small packages that could be reassembled into a complete message at the destination node.

Leonard Kleinrock at MIT promoted the approach with his publication of a paper on "packet switching theory" in July 1961 and the first book on the subject in 1964. Packet switching is the basic technology driving computer networks today.

As it became clear that the analog circuit-switched telephone network was an inefficient means for connecting computers since it was designed for voice communications, the development of digital networks accelerated. Subsequently, improvements in digital technology allowed increasing network speeds.

The very term "communications" in reference to electronic systems suggests its obvious service in helping humans communicate with each other. But a major impact on computer intelligence was in connecting computers to each other, with the Internet being an example of the result.

The Internet

A series of memos written by J.C.R. Licklider of MIT in August 1962 discussed his "Galactic Network" concept, a globally interconnected set of computers through which everyone could quickly access data and programs from any site. MIT researcher Lawrence G. Roberts continued the research, and later went to the US governments' Advanced Research Project Agency (ARPA, now Defense Advanced Research Projects Agency—DARPA) to develop the computer network concept. He put together a plan for the "ARPANET," publishing it in 1967. In August 1968, a Request For Quotations (RFQ) was released by DARPA for the development of one of the key components, packet switches that they named Interface Message Processors (IMPs).

The company Bolt Beranek and Newman (BBN) was awarded the DARPA contract in December 1968. Due to Leonard Kleinrock's early development of packet switching theory and a focus on analysis, design, and measurement, his Network Measurement Center at UCLA was selected to be the first node on the ARPANET. Doug Engelbart's project on Augmentation of Human

Intellect at SRI was the second node. In late 1969, the first computer-to-computer message was sent between the two sites. Other sites were added over the next few years, and the protocols for communication refined.

In October 1972, Bob Kahn, one of the participating researchers, organized a successful demonstration of the ARPANET at the International Computer Communication Conference, and gave the first public demonstration. One of the most important applications, electronic mail, was also introduced in 1972. The basic email message send-and-read software was developed by Ray Tomlinson of BBN in March 1972, motivated by the need of the ARPANET developers for an easy coordination mechanism.

In July, Lawrence Roberts of MIT expanded the email application by writing the first email utility program to list, selectively read, file, forward, and respond to messages. That effort established email as the main network application for over a decade, as ARPANET became the Internet.

The Internet was based on multiple independent networks, all using packet-switching to communicate with each other. The connection between independent networks was initially called "interneting," hence the name Internet. An enhanced protocol, eventually called the Transmission Control Protocol/Internet Protocol (TCP/IP), was developed to better allow the connection of independent networks. Additional software was developed to increase the reliability of the network.

The original expectation was that there would be only a few national-level networks like ARPANET. Thus a 32-bit IP address was used, where the first 8 bits signified the network and the remaining 24 bits designated the host on that network. Since the largest number that can be represented with 8 binary digits is 256, this choice limited the network to connecting 256 locations. The IP address was necessarily expanded when Local Area Networks (LANs) based on using Ethernet technology—a protocol for connecting computers within an organization that used Internet protocols—began to appear in the late 1970s, creating many more than 256 computers to be connected.

The Internet was not designed for just one application, but as a general infrastructure that could support new applications. Email was the first major application. But the ability of the Internet to support other applications was illustrated later by the emergence of the World Wide Web. Widespread deployment of LANs, PCs, and workstations in the 1980s allowed the Internet to flourish. The standardization of the Internet protocols helped foster that growth.

The Internet connected both humans and computing resources. The connection to humans through email evolved into other communication technologies, such as digital telephony. The Internet connection to computers allows using resources "in the cloud"—that is, other computers connected by the Internet.

Connections enabled by the Internet add to our individual intelligence by connecting us inexpensively to others. Many people may remember when one rushed through a "long-distance" phone call because of the high cost per minute. Today, even international calls and emails cost no more than contacting your neighbor. Similarly, the Internet allows inexpensive connections to information worldwide. The development of the World Wide Web in particular led to an explosion of access to computer intelligence in the form of informative web sites. According to Mark Meeker's 2019 Internet Trends Report, there are 3.8 billion internet users globally, more than half of the world's population.

The World Wide Web

Tim Berners-Lee made a proposal for an information management system that led to the World Wide Web (WWW) on March 12, 1989. He implemented the first successful communication between a Hypertext Transfer Protocol (HTTP) client and server via the Internet in mid-November the same year. Berners-Lee is the director of the World Wide Web Consortium (W3C), which oversees the continued development of the Web, as this is written.

The World Wide Web evolved as a collection of web sites where documents and other web resources are identified by Uniform Resource Locators (URLs, the familiar http://www.location.com/). URLs were defined in 1994 by Berners-Lee.

URLs may be interlinked by "hypertext" (click on a link and be taken to another web page). The resources of the WWW may also be accessed by typing an address into a web browser. Search engines such as Google allow typing in words describing information desired to get a list of web sites that match the words.

The ability to create records as digital words and/or pictures has allowed humans to create a repository of information and knowledge, expanding our information resources well beyond our memory and providing access to insights of other humans. The Web has made that store of information and insights inexpensively available to all, one of the clearest examples of computers augmenting basic human intelligence.

Unfortunately, the accuracy of information on the Web is not assured. The explosive growth of the Web has created disinformation as well as useful knowledge. Some companies have tried to control misuse of this resource by using AI to automatically detect misinformation or identify social media postings that, for example, show child pornography or obvious racial prejudice.

Web browsers made the information on the Web widely accessible. Mosaic, the first web browser, was developed at the National Center for Supercomputing Applications (NCSA) at the University of Illinois at Urbana-Champaign beginning in late 1992. NCSA released the browser in 1993. Starting in 1995, Mosaic was eclipsed by the browser Netscape Navigator, and by 1997 the project was discontinued. Microsoft licensed Mosaic to create Internet Explorer in 1995.

Web search

Web browsers are effective when you know the address of the web site you wish to reach. Web search engines, where you simply enter keywords or a question and are given a list of relevant web sites, has become indispensable for most other situations.

Prior to September 1993, the World Wide Web was indexed by hand. One early option was a list of webservers edited by Tim Berners-Lee and hosted on the CERN (European Organization for Nuclear Research) webserver.

More general web search was limited by computer power for a while, for example, one had to search for web site names rather than web site content.

One of the first search engines that searched deeper was WebCrawler, which came out in 1994. Unlike its predecessors, it allowed users to search for any word in any webpage, which has become the minimal standard for all major search engines since.

In 1996, Netscape made deals for web search on its browser with five of the major search engines that would rotate as the search option on the Netscape search engine page. The five engines were Yahoo!, Magellan, Lycos, Infoseek, and Excite.

Larry Page and Sergey Brin developed a web search methodology they called PageRank at Stanford University in 1996 as part of a research project about a new kind of search engine. Sergey Brin had the idea that information on the web could be ordered in a hierarchy by "link popularity," with a page ranked higher if there are more links to it on the web. Page and Brin founded Google in 1998. Around 2000, Google's search engine became predominant. The company has invested large sums in its continued improvement.

The standardization of applications

If there were a wide variety of applications using different formats, it would be difficult for individuals to exchange documents. A wide use of specific applications created a de-facto standardization of document formats and web sites.

With the wide adoption of Microsoft Office and its word processing and spreadsheet software, if you sent someone a document in Office format, the receiver could read it. Microsoft formats for such documents rapidly became an unofficial standard.

Similarly, the use of only a few web browsers has made it possible for web sites to be compatible with most browsers. The standard HyperText Markup Language (HTML) is the core of this compatibility, but browsers have some differences. The willingness of web sites to maintain compatibility with a few major web browsers has been critical to the wide use of the World Wide Web.

Learning new applications or web surfing would be much more difficult without the consistency delivered by standards and de-facto standards, typified by these examples. The consistency has been a key enabler of the growth of computer intelligence.

Business Process Automation

John Naisbitt and Patricia Aburdene, in their influential 1985 book, *Re-Inventing the Corporation: Transforming Your Job and Your Company for the New Information Society*, crystalized a change in the way businesses were run, driven by the increasing use of computers in companies. Companies had been steadily using "enterprise software" to automate business practices, but these software programs tended to be used for specific compartmentalized departments, such as the billing department. Naisbitt and Aburdene argued persuasively that companies had to be re-organized to take full advantage of computer technology.

Companies needed to organize around "processes"—for example, the series of tasks that customers went through to choose, purchase, and pay for the company's products—rather than functions like billing that are just one stage of the process. Today, that approach has been widely adopted and is called Business Process Automation (BPA). It wasn't a purely academic insight—many companies that didn't make such organizational changes are not around today. Advances in computer intelligence impact businesses as well as individuals.

Portable computing and the smartphone

The term "Personal Digital Assistant" (PDA), was used by Apple CEO John Scully at a trade show in January 1992, referring to the Apple Newton, an early version of what today would be called a tablet computer (Figure 4). It was an attempt to make computing portable. The product failed, in part because it attempted to allow handwriting on the screen as an input mechanism, and underdeveloped pattern recognition technology made that method of input unreliable. In addition, the device's low processing power limited the responsiveness and complexity of applications.

Figure 4: The Apple Newton MessagePad 2100 and the original iPhone

A convergence of technologies was necessary to make mobile phones a feasible commercial product, although the world's first mobile phone call was made in 1973 by Martin Cooper of Motorola. The phone Cooper used weighed more than two pounds (Figure 5). It could provide 30 minutes of talk-time and took about 10 hours to charge.

Mobile phones eventually got small enough and had sufficient battery life to become an important product category. That drove the expansion of cellular services to most urban areas.

The Apple iPhone, launched in 2007 (Figure 4), created the major market for mobile phones using a Graphical User Interface, with a finger as the pointing device. Such "smartphones" were connected to the Internet wirelessly, and were in effect small personal computers as well as mobile phones. Progress in screen technology, battery technology, and processing power available on a small device had crossed the tipping point that made the innovation possible.

Figure 5: Motorola's Martin Cooper makes
the first mobile phone call in 1973

Competitors followed Apple's lead, and the smartphone market exploded. Computer Intelligence became available in your pocket or purse. Smartphones expanded the impact of computer intelligence by making it portable.

Today's CI

The previous section was largely historical. Today's CI reflects the results of that evolution.

Servers and data centers

Computers can be large standalone systems, often called "mainframes," with IBM an early and current provider (Figure 6). They are typically used for applications requiring particularly heavy computing.

Figure 6: IBM z14 dual mainframe (model in 2019, about 40" wide)

Today, many applications, particularly those supporting applications accessed over the Internet, require supporting many users simultaneously. This has led to connected smaller devices—"servers"—being used in quantity. Figure 7 shows a "data center" with networked racks of servers. The computing power of such data centers can be expanded by adding servers to accommodate more simultaneous users.

The practicality of server architecture was driven by the increasing power of microprocessors, which today are much more powerful than early mainframes. Their utility in serving multiple users simultaneously also required the development of networking software that could manage such traffic.

Figure 7: Racks of computer servers in a data center

Cloud Computing

Using computers over a digital communications channel started with "time-sharing," using terminals connected by wire to a large central computer. It was introduced in the 1960s and emerged as the prominent model of computing in the 1970s. The usual way to use computers prior to that was called "batch processing"—an individual submitted a program (e.g., on punched cards), and programs were run one at a time. Thus, time-sharing required developing software that could manage multiple users. Time sharing allowed simultaneous access to computers for many users rather than submitting programs in a queue.

Today, the concept of many users sharing a computer has matured into a major option and a big business. Some companies have their own server farms. "Cloud computing" allows using powerful server farms over the Internet, with a company paying by the amount of computing it uses. The cloud-computing providers manage the computers for the companies using the service.

Amazon, Microsoft, and Google are the largest providers of cloud computing. It's a profitable business. The leader, Amazon Web Services (AWS), had revenue in the last quarter of 2018 of $7.4 billion, accounting for about 10% of Amazon's total revenue for the quarter. First-quarter

2019 spending on all cloud infrastructure services rose by 42% compared to the first quarter of 2018, reaching over $21 billion, according to Synergy Research Group.

The cloud computing trend makes increased computer intelligence more easily available to companies large and small. A company can increase the computer power it uses without a capital investment.

Cloud computing is also impacting the gaming industry. In March 2019, Google announced its Stadia gaming service. Users pay a monthly fee to play games without a game console, using any computer, smartphone, or tablet connected to the Internet. Google said it will add racks of gaming-specific chips to its cloud service.

Online shopping

In 1995, Amazon launched a website that only sold books. Led by Jeff Bezos, the company rapidly demonstrated the power of computer intelligence in shopping through a web browser, with an easily navigated web site that supported searching by subject, author, or book title, and easy purchase for delivery. The company followed up by suggesting books for readers based on past purchases.

Amazon expanded this web service into sales of other products, using similar technology to drive sales. Today, the company has added a streaming video entertainment service and grocery delivery.

A major feature driving the company's growth was its promise of fast delivery and free delivery to Amazon Prime members. The company has invested in many distribution centers to support quick delivery, which includes partial automation for order picking at some distribution centers.

The success of Amazon has generated competition and forced many companies to try to compete online as well as in stores, including retail outlets such as Walmart, which has had some success in increasing online sales. In 2018, the US Commerce Department indicated that e-commerce sales had risen to 14.3% of total retail sales.

Ride-sharing services

Ride-sharing—hailing a ride through a mobile app—is a good example of computer intelligence that enabled a new major industry. Some analysts have projected that this is the future of transportation, suggesting that many will do without cars by using a combination of such services and public transportation.

Uber was founded in March 2009 by Garrett Camp and Travis Kalanick. Uber is a major growth contributor to the "gig economy," with its use of contract workers rather than permanent employees. Other competitors, such as Lyft in the US and Didi Chuxing in China, have grown rapidly using the same model, quickly outrunning conventional taxi service.

The growth of these companies is strongly based on their use of a sophisticated mobile app and supporting software to manage its drivers. The app makes it easy for customers to summon drivers and know how soon they will arrive. The software driving the app lets drivers work whenever they turn on the driver version of the app to be directed to a pickup. Drivers can indicate where they want to go, for example, if they have delivered a customer downtown and want to return to a suburb near their home.

Artificial Intelligence

Artificial intelligence is often described as a recent major breakthrough in computer technology. As previously noted, the position taken by this book is that AI is simply a natural evolution of CI, rather than a sudden major invention. In this author's opinion, extreme views overstate its potential (e.g., that every company should have an "AI Strategy") and its risks (e.g., it will eventually take over all jobs and dominate humanity).

It is even difficult to clearly define AI. It is often described as computers and software doing tasks previously requiring humans. But this definition is inadequate. AI can be used to examine very large databases to come to conclusions that would be an impossible task for humans. For example, in 2016, Google's DeepMind group used AI techniques to reduce the amount of energy used in cooling Google's massive data center up to 40%. The AI software analyzed huge amounts of data collected by thousands of sensors in the data center (such as temperatures, power, and pump speeds). No human could even pore through so much data in a lifetime, much less see the patterns in the data that the AI methodology discovered. This is certainly not doing a task that a human previously did.

The *Wall Street Journal* reported in January 2019 on lenders using AI to process loans more quickly. The article cited an industry executive saying that employees assessing creditworthiness could only look at a limited number of variables, but AI could evaluate 2,700 borrower characteristics to determine the feasibility of a loan, allowing the company to make more, yet safer, loans. This is a typical application of AI—*doing things a human can't.*

Computers have long been used to do tasks more efficiently than humans. Most of us trust the bank statement we receive in the mail, although it most likely was never viewed or touched by human hands at the bank (even to put it in an envelope). AI is in reality just another phase of computer advances that have been occurring for decades and will continue to occur for the foreseeable future.

Some experts have attempted a broader definition of AI. Stuart J. Russell, the author of a popular textbook on AI, is quoted in Martin Ford's *Architects of Intelligence*: "An entity is intelligent to the extent that it does the right thing, meaning that its actions are expected to achieve its objectives. The definition applies to both humans and machines." Russell's definition ties intelligence to objectives, implicitly assuming that the goal of intelligence is to achieve specific objectives. Humans can obviously produce errors and still be intelligent. Thus, Russell indirectly acknowledges this by qualifying doing the "right thing" with an *expectation* to achieve an objective. This definition may not be particularly useful in distinguishing AI, however; one could argue that every computer program has an objective that it is expected to achieve.

Today computer intelligence has passed what Malcolm Gladwell would call a "tipping point" that allows an increasingly tighter connection with humans—for example, conversing with individuals using human language—and doing things we associate with human intelligence, such as distinguishing objects in images. Reaching that tipping point of computer power that makes such goals achievable might create an appropriate interpretation of what today is called AI. AI is perhaps a useful label for an *era* of CI. By characterizing Artificial Intelligence as an evolution of computer intelligence, this book does not intend to minimize the importance of techniques such as machine learning using Deep Neural Network (DNN) models—"deep learning"—that are a major methodology in AI. (Machine learning and neural networks are discussed in depth in a section of Part II.)

An article in March 2019 by the *Wall Street Journal* on the competition between the US and China in AI briefly defined AI as "algorithms that attempt to mimic human cognition." This interpretation is partly validated by the fact that DNN models were motivated by an analogy to the neurons in the human brain, and the use of the term "learning" in machine learning implies correctly an analogy to the way humans learn from a series of examples.

The basic ideas behind both neural nets and machine learning were developed in the 1950s. They have commercial impact today because CI is powerful enough to deal with very large databases and "deep" neural networks; early efforts ran into computational limitations. Once the DNNs are derived by heavy processing from the data, they can be evaluated by today's computer technology so quickly that, for example, a computer can respond in a few seconds to a voice request.

This book considers AI an evolution of the Computer Intelligence that has changed our life for decades and will continue to do so in the future. The future technology might have a different label, but the inexorable advance of computer power will continue to change society.

For example, Optical Character Recognition (OCR) technology that converts a printed document into a text file using a scanner was available in an early form in the 1970s. Today, you can take a picture of a check with hand-written numbers that you want to deposit in your bank account with your mobile phone, and the software interprets your handwriting, an advanced form of OCR that most would consider AI. In any case, the attention given to techniques that fall under today's AI label has led to a positive result—a greater appreciation of the impact CI has on our lives and the importance of fully understanding that trend.

The 2018 Turing Award, known as the "Nobel Prize of computing," was given to Yoshua Bengio, Geoffrey Hinton, and Yann LeCun—sometimes called the "godfathers of AI." They were recognized with the $1 million annual prize for their work in developing deep learning. "There was a dark period between the mid-90s and early-to-mid-2000s when it was impossible to publish research on neural nets, because the community had lost interest in it," LeCun has noted. "In fact, it had a bad rep. It was a bit taboo." When computer power had reached the point where the technique was practical, the researchers were able to show its power by improving the accuracy by 40% over previous techniques on a standard image recognition problem called ImageNet.

As AI has become considered a major breakthrough, its definition has sometimes been stretched. Some things attributed to AI are simple statistics. For example, a company like Amazon can place things in a large warehouse based on how often they are ordered, with frequently ordered items more easily accessed. Those simple statistics are implemented through computer technology, but probably shouldn't be considered AI—more complex models such as neural networks aren't required for this task. This specific example comes from an article in a magazine that *did* call that use of statistics part of AI, typical of the vagueness of the concept.

One reason the term Artificial Intelligence (AI) has been assumed to be a major change rather than a natural evolution is that it has been claimed to be a threat to humanity by luminaries such as Elon Musk, Bill Gates, and the late renowned physicist, Stephen Hawking. Elon Musk has said that AI research is "summoning the demon" and that "AI is more danger-ous than nuclear weapons." A *Newsweek* report on a conference in 2017 quoted Hawking as providing a more balanced, although equally troubling, assessment: "Computers can, in theory, emulate human intelligence, and exceed it. Success in creating effective AI, could be the biggest event in the history of our civilization. Or the worst. We just don't know. So, we cannot know if we will be infinitely helped by AI, or ignored by it and side-lined, or conceivably destroyed by it."

In 2015, Gates wrote: "I am in the camp that is concerned about super intelligence. First the machines will do a lot of jobs for us and not be super intelligent. That should be positive if we manage it well. A few decades after that though, the intelligence is strong enough to be a concern. I agree with Elon Musk and some others on this and don't understand why some people are not concerned."

Those concerned about AI getting "too smart" are not necessarily arguing that killer robots will roam the earth wiping out humans, as in some science fiction thrillers. They are in part concerned about computers taking over more and more jobs, until AI creates a social and economic crisis. This issue is a valid concern, and will be discussed extensively in Part III of this book.

When the concern is closer to the science-fiction concept of computers dominating human society or even destroying it, these warnings are often coupled with a qualification that recognizes that current AI technology must evolve beyond today's limited methods into "Artificial General Intelligence" (AGI) before this becomes a real threat. AGI is even more poorly defined than AI.

Many who are concerned about the danger of AI are not thinking about some specific techniques of AI being a threat, but are concerned about the increasing capability of computers to do complex tasks that humans couldn't attempt without computers. In that sense, the concerned parties are perhaps using "artificial general intelligence" to refer to what I am simply considering the continuing advance of "computer intelligence." But to the degree that AGI refers to computer intelligence taking on such things as consciousness and ego—which might require growing up in a human body—the term is not constructive.

The term "Artificial Intelligence" tends to humanize computers. A computer is a tool. It can do some things better than humans. But so can a hammer. A hammer is much better at driving nails than a bare hand, but no one has claimed that hammers will make hands obsolete. A computer similarly does some things better or faster than humans without being a threat to replace humanity.

The major technology driving AI in its present form is "machine learning," which, based on example data, can adapt a mathematical model to best achieve a goal such as recognizing one pattern from another, e.g., distinguishing images of dogs from images of cats. More specifically, the mathematical model that has driven the most impactful applications is the aforementioned "deep neural networks" (DNNs). Machine learning using deep neural nets ("deep learning") will be discussed in more detail in a later section, but a key characteristic is that the DNNs are very complex models and require substantial computational resources to derive the numbers that define a specific DNN.

The methods of using machine learning and neural networks have been around for decades, but the computational power to make them effective has only been available fairly recently. As early as 1943, W.S. McCulloch and W. Pitts published an article, "A logical calculus of the ideas immanent in nervous activity," that described how human neurons could be viewed as implementing logic similar to Boolean algebra. Later work examined the possibility of using neural models for logical operations or pattern classification. But it took computer intelligence passing a tipping point to make it practical to optimize large neural networks. The availability of those computing resources has encouraged experts to make important *improvements* to those core technologies, making them increasingly effective.

Natural language understanding

One specific technology usually included under the label of AI is natural language understanding. The use of human language to interact with computers has reached a maturity where many of us talk or type to computers every day, a breakthrough enabled in part by advances in deep learning technology. The technology allows a closer connection between humans and machines—people using familiar speech or text to interact with a digital system. The phenomena of computers being able to handle human language effectively is a major breakthrough that allows such advances as talking with Apple's Siri, Google Assistant, and Amazon's Alexa.

The benefit of this human-language interaction includes being able to use language to interact with computers intuitively. The basic goal of such technology is to allow a user to interact with a digital system with the simple instruction: "Just say or type what you want." Using voice interaction can also allow a hands-free, eyes-free voice interface when necessary, e.g., for safety reasons in automobiles.

In general, most products, services, and computer software today get increasingly complex with added features and connectivity to the cloud. What used to be intuitive because there were relatively few functions in an application or operating system has become increasingly confusing as options multiply. For example, changing a station on a car radio and reducing the volume were essentially the same in every car. Most people getting into an unfamiliar car today might have trouble just turning on the entertainment, much less selecting from the many entertainment options available. A conversational system can reduce this frustration.

A Harris Poll survey published in December 2018 found that the majority of consumers are comfortable interacting with AI solutions for customer service, and that, in some cases, AI is actually preferred over human interactions. When asked about AI capabilities that enable positive customer experiences, 85% think 24/7 availability is useful. The same percentage also cited the advantage of connecting directly to a virtual assistant, instead of going through a menu of recorded choices. About 79% of consumers said that AI solutions provide positive customer experiences when they enable consumers to interact conversationally—as if talking to a human—instead of forcing them to use "robot speak."

Home devices with speech recognition

Speech recognition and natural language processing made possible the launch of Amazon's Echo in June 2015, a speaker with several microphones. The device includes a cloud-supported digital assistant Alexa. One could command Alexa at a distance from the Echo, waking the assistant up by preceding each command with the name "Alexa." This pioneering device created a new category of connection to computer intelligence, answering questions, playing music, and controlling connected home devices. Amazon indicated in May 2019 that there are now "more than 60,000 smart home devices that can be controlled with Alexa," supported by "7,400 unique brands."

Furthermore, Amazon made Alexa available directly to other providers of connected home devices. By including a microphone, additional software, and a network connection, the device could use Alexa in the cloud without requiring an Echo in the house.

Other major players launched competitive versions, including Apple's HomePod and Google Home. Chinese company Huawei launched the AI Cube in China. With the AI Cube's ability to control up to 64 devices, Huawei apparently expects almost every device in the home to have the ability to be controlled through a home network.

China's Baidu launched several versions of its Xiaodu series smart speakers. Xiaodu smart speakers are integrated with iQiyi's AI projection technology, which supports a voice-controlled video experience. Xiaodu, like the US-based smart speakers, supports skills from outside companies. In mid-2019, the Xiaodu Skills Open Platform counted more than 32,000 developers and over 2,000 skills.

Sales of smart speakers in China in the first quarter of 2019 grew by more than 500% year-on-year, according to research from Strategy Analytics. This lifted *global* Q1 sales to 25.9 million, a 168% increase over the same period in 2018.

DNA and bioengineering

Machine learning is being used as one tool in genetic engineering, with our growing knowledge about DNA and how to modify it. Drew Endy, who is doing research in this area, emphasized the almost frightening potential of genetic engineering at an October 2018 conference on the subject. He spoke of "reimplementing life in a manner of our choosing" and shaking off the constraints of evolution. Machine learning can help model the effects of changing specific DNA sequences.

Internet of Things

"Internet of Things" (IoT) is a term coined about 1999 that describes the fact that many devices today have computing capabilities of some sort (and possibly sensors) and are connected to the Internet. Categories of some devices can communicate over a network among themselves to act as a group.

The Internet of Things includes items in homes such as security systems or doorbells that can be monitored through an app on a smartphone. It includes industrial systems with networked sensors to give an integrated view of a factory environment for monitoring and control.

The IoT is simply a continuing expansion of devices with an Internet connection. The IoT results from the cost of an internet connection and computing on the device dropping sufficiently to allow easily adding such a connection.

The term is sometimes defined by its potential impact. For example, the web site Techopedia said, "IoT describes a world where just about anything can be connected and communicate in an intelligent fashion. In other words, with the Internet of Things, the physical world is becoming one big information system." Cisco, which builds networking equipment, has stated, "The IoT links objects to the Internet, enabling data and insights never available before." Research firm Strategy Analytics reported in May 2019 that the number of devices connected to the internet reached 22 billion worldwide at the end of 2018.

SAS, a company that provides tools to analyze data, defined IoT on their web site (as of April 2019) as requiring devices that can sense their environment: "The Internet of Things is the concept of everyday objects—from industrial machines to wearable devices—using built-in sensors to gather data and take action on that data across a network. It may be a building that uses sensors to automatically adjust heating and lighting, or production equipment that alerts maintenance personnel to an impending failure. Simply put, the Internet of Things is the future of technology that can make our lives more efficient."

The healthcare community considers the trend sufficiently important that they have coined the variation IoMT (Internet of Medical Things). IoMT is a connected infrastructure of medical devices, software applications, and health systems and services. IoMT connects people (patients, caregivers, and clinicians), data (patient or performance data), processes (care delivery and patient support), and enablers (sensors, connected medical devices—such as wrist bands and mobile apps) to deliver improved patient outcomes more efficiently.

IoT isn't a well-defined concept, but defines a trend that is of some importance. The trend is another way computer intelligence can allow us to monitor and control "things." It can allow more efficient industrial processes or systems. It makes possible trends that can have important societal implications.

A downside of the IoT is that devices can be used in cyberattacks as attackers or can be attacked themselves since they are connected to the Internet. In 2016, consumer devices such as digital cameras and DVR players were infected with software called Mirai and used in a "denial of service" attack on Dyn, a company that many other companies use to handle internet traffic. Those devices simulated real traffic to Dyn with repeated calls from each device. The attack bombarded Dyn with so much traffic that it collapsed, bringing down sites including Twitter, the Guardian, Netflix, Reddit, CNN, and many others in Europe and the US.

In addition to being used in this way, devices on the IoT can be directly attacked. To take an extreme case, CNN reported in 2018:

> The FDA confirmed that St. Jude Medical's implantable cardiac devices have vulnerabilities that could allow a hacker to access a device. Once in, they could deplete the battery or administer incorrect pacing or shocks, the FDA said. The devices, like pacemakers and defibrillators, are used to monitor and control patients' heart functions and prevent heart attacks.

The vulnerability in this case occurred in the transmitter that reads the device's data and remotely shares it with physicians.

Wearables

Wearables are devices that can be placed on the body or clothing. They include connected smartwatches, fitness devices, and earbuds. As a trend, they add options to the availability of computer intelligence wherever we are, often with a connection to smartphones.

Smartwatches are a growing category. Smartwatches have a screen, allowing them to constantly display more than just the time, with the ability to switch screen formats (Figure 8). One of the first was the Samsung Galaxy Gear, introduced in September 2013. Apple launched the Apple Watch in April 2015. According to research from Strategy Analytics, global smartwatch shipments reached 12 million units in the second quarter of 2019.

Figure 8: Apple Watch Series 4

Fitbit released its first wearable around 2009, largely for activity tracking. The company's products are usually worn on the wrist.

An example of earbuds is Apple's AirPods, smart earphones with a microphone that connect wirelessly to Apple devices and integrate with Siri through voice commands. Similarly, Google's Pixel Buds give users voice access to Google Assistant.

"Smart glasses" provide another option for displaying information. The visual option is a translucent display on part of the glass.

The entertainment explosion

The simultaneous expansion of fast Internet connections, either wired or wireless, and of computer servers in the cloud capable of quickly finding and delivering requested entertainment choices, has revolutionized our consumption of entertainment. Streaming audio/video in particular lets one watch a movie or series or listen to music or other audio at one's leisure "on-demand" and on portable devices.

The on-demand option makes a huge selection possible. The range includes classic movies and movies that never make it to a theatre. You can binge-watch old episodes of a TV series or create your own on-demand option by recording a broadcast show with a digital video recorder (a recording that allows fast-forwarding through ads).

Search functionality eases finding a show or film of interest. Entertainment sources let you select music you like and create or use playlists. While you're watching or listening, you can have more control—pause the entertainment whenever you like to do something else.

This is so common now that we almost forget the restrictions that existed not that long ago. Wait until a movie is in a theatre near you, go at a specific time, perhaps get your popcorn before the show starts, and take what seats are available when you arrive. Movie theater attendance in the US and Canada in 2017 fell to its lowest point since at least 1992.

Shorter entertainment choices have flourished. YouTube and similar services allow viewing short videos.

In India, entertainment options drive smartphone purchase and use. According to India's telecommunications regulator, subscriptions for mobile-broadband services more than doubled between the end of 2016 and the end of 2018, from 218 million to 500 million. A low-end phone costs about 3,500 rupees ($50), a substantial amount for a typical villager, but they have become a priority purchase. Competition between providers has lowered service costs significantly. Indians now use nearly three times as much data on their phones as Americans for a fraction of the cost. According to *The Economist*, as of November 2018, the average cost of one gigabyte of mobile data in the US was $12.37; in India, it was $0.26.

Entertainment options include educational programs. For example, relevant to some of the themes in this book, the excellent PBS series on the brain is available on many services. And, if you have a special interest, from repairing cars to cooking to painting, you can usually find a resource to advance your knowledge in that field on YouTube or elsewhere.

And relatively new "podcasts"—specialized digital audio shows you can listen to at any time—have grown as an option. eMarketer estimated in mid-2019 that US podcast ad revenues had grown from $106 million in 2015 to $417 million in 2018, heading to over $1 billion in 2021.

"Augmented reality" (AR) technology, delivered with special goggles that immerse the user in a 3-D experience, is another developing option. Apple offers ARKit, its software development toolkit for AR, and Google's its competitive ARCore. In a 2019 update, Apple noted that, by understanding body position and movement as a series of joints and bones, a developer can use motion and poses as an input to the AR experience. Apple also announced human inclusion, meaning that AR content realistically passes behind and in front of people in the real world, making AR experiences more immersive.

There are business applications for AR. When some Walmart store workers want to apply for a higher-paying management role, the company fits them with a virtual reality headset to see if they are the right candidate for the job. They can see how workers respond in virtual reality to an angry shopper, a messy aisle, or an underperforming worker.

These fundamental changes in entertainment, driven by advances in computer intelligence and communications, have expanded jobs that require creative talent.

Blockchain

Blockchain is best known as the mysterious technology behind the "cryptocurrency" Bitcoin. Blockchain is a highly secure platform that makes it very difficult to fake transactions or to create new Bitcoin currency once the cryptocurrency is launched. Blockchain, in effect, can regulate crypto-currency so that Bitcoin has a limited supply—a manufactured scarcity. Just as gold is valuable because there is a limited supply and you can't make more, Bitcoin could then be considered valuable. Many transactions are conducted in Bitcoin, and it changes value relative to other currencies depending on perceived value.

Cryptocurrency can be used for any set of transactions where reliability and resistance to fraud or hacking is critical, but the largest impact is in enabling transactions in other than a national currency and one which is accepted in all countries. It has been claimed that it is popular with users who want to "launder" ill-gained profits.

More generally, blockchain is a continuously growing digital file of encrypted transactions called "blocks" that are distributed across a network of computers. Each transaction is recorded on multiple computers at different locations, so that the transactions can be verified, and can't be changed in any single place.

In addition to user data, each block contains an index, a timestamp, a list of transactions, a "proof," and the "hash" of the previous block. A hash is a fixed-size number derived from any size data, in this case created by the data in the previous block. Because each new block will contain a hash of the previous block, blockchains can't be changed without destroying data. If a hacker were to corrupt an earlier block in the blockchain, all subsequent blocks would contain incorrect hashes, and the corruption would immediately invalidate the records affected. Blockchain can be used for any set of transactions where reliability and resistance to fraud or hacking is critical.

Intelligence at the "edge"

Most AI services, such as natural language understanding and speech recognition, are executed in the cloud today, thus requiring an Internet connection for devices such as smartphones or home speakers that use the services. This creates continuing costs for companies providing the devices, since they must continue to support cloud computing to make the devices work. The services fail when an Internet connection is not available. Further, there are potential issues of privacy when all transactions pass through a wired or wireless network.

An important long-term trend is doing more complex computing in the device—on the "edge" of the network, using the network less. Doing more on the device reduces the computing required in the cloud.

An example of this trend is software announced by Sensory, Inc., in May 2019. The company announced the first full-feature release of TrulyNatural, the company's embedded (on-device) large-vocabulary, speech recognition platform with natural language understanding. The company claimed more than 50 people-years of development and five years of beta testing behind the development. The company said the solution was ideal for home appliances, IoT, set top boxes, automobiles, and more. The embedded technology could be used for some tasks that didn't require the most complex processing, with the more complex tasks that require large updated databases, such as song selection, defaulting to the cloud.

5G wireless networks

The broadly used cellular network powering mobile phones as of 2019 is called the fourth generation of such technology (4G). It has driven the use of mobile phones and provided accessibility to cellular service through large towers powering the service (Figure 9).

Cellular companies are promoting a transition to the fifth generation (5G). 5G operates in a different frequency band and can provide faster data transmission speeds. In current development, 5G is reaching speeds that are twenty times faster than 4G, offering download speeds of up to 600 megabits per second compared to 4G's typical 28 megabits per second. Such speeds could increase, for example, the downloading of video entertainment.

5G requires more densely spaced cell tower transmitters because the new frequency declines in power more quickly with distance from the tower. However, 5G transmitters are smaller than 4G transmitters and can be put on existing structures such as telephone poles (Figure 10).

Figure 9: 4G cell tower

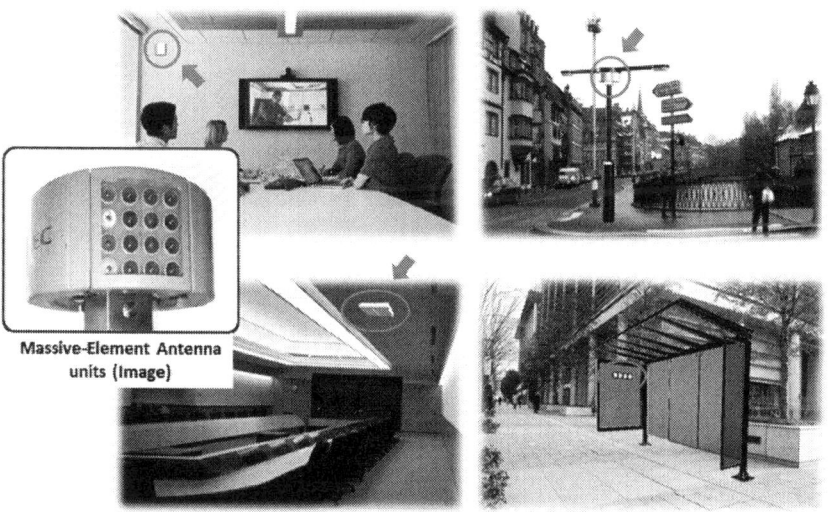

Figure 10: Small NEC 5G antenna (Source: NEC)

The transition to 5G faces hurdles. It will require new mobile phones capable of using the frequency. The June 2019 edition of the Ericsson Mobility Report forecasts 1.9 billion 5G subscriptions by the end of 2024. (Ericsson builds 5G equipment.)

Having more transmission units means that the technology is more precise in locating phones using it, raising some objections on privacy grounds. And, since 5G frequencies don't penetrate buildings and other structures as well as 4G, more transmitting units may be required to guarantee reception. There have also been some complaints by homeowners about new 5G units being placed in locations near their homes. Thus, cellular providers may potentially have at least initial difficulty placing enough units to create the full coverage to which mobile phone owners are accustomed.

International political issues complicate a transition to 5G. Huawei, a Chinese company, is a major supplier of 5G hardware. The US government argues that Huawei would have to obey a Chinese government order to use the devices to spy on users of 5G service and has placed barriers to its use in the US. The US Bureau of Industry and Security (BIS) of Department of Commerce announced in mid-May 2019 that it was adding Huawei Technologies and its affiliates to the Bureau's Entity List, barring US companies from transferring technology to the Chinese vendor without a special license from the US government. The Department's announcement said, "This action stems from information available to the Department that provides a reasonable basis to conclude that Huawei is engaged in activities that are contrary to US national security or foreign policy interest."

The government action prompted Google to limit its support for Android running on Huawei smartphones, forcing Huawei to depend on the Android Open Source Project and do without Google services on future smartphones. Facebook announced that, similarly, it will no longer allow its apps to come pre-installed on mobile devices made by Huawei. ARM, a provider of chips critical to the manufacture of most smartphones, suspended its work with Huawei.

Huawei has repeatedly refuted allegations it would spy for its government or that it had installed backdoors, arguing that no evidence has been produced to support such claims. The company issued a report pledging to never cooperate with spying or espionage. The issue has become part of trade negotiations at this writing.

Such issues lead to predictions that the deployment of 5G may be slower than anticipated; however, the eventual faster data transmission would tighten the connection between humans and computer intelligence further. A report in early 2019 by Ericsson found that six in ten smartphone users in large cities reported facing network issues in crowded areas and were willing to pay more for 5G service.

Self-driving vehicles

Many companies are pursuing the objective of cars and trucks that drive themselves, using complex sensors and software. Currently, self-driving cars are usually tested with a driver that can take over. The vision is that such vehicles could make services like Uber and Lyft profitable, and perhaps reduce traffic congestion by letting fleets of on-call vehicles serve us quickly, eliminating the need for personal vehicles, at least in crowded urban areas.

Semi-autonomous driving is currently available in some vehicles today, such as the Tesla Model 3 with an Autopilot feature. The driver is supposed to be aware, and take over if a difficult situation arises. The system has failed in a couple of well-publicized fatal accidents. Despite the obvious issues, this product category marks a substantial expansion in the type of task with which we may be trusting computer intelligence.

Quantum computing: The next breakthrough in computer intelligence?

The current generation of computer technology uses semiconductor chips. Early digital systems used individual transistors; those evolved into "integrated circuits" (ICs, chips with many transistors on them). The complexity of such chips has grown exponentially over time, allowing faster computing and more complex programs.

Quantum computing is often posited as the next generation of computing. It uses a different type of computing element, based on the behavior of particles at the smallest level—quantum physics. The predictions of quantum physics have been validated repeatedly, leading experts to say that the theory is valid, despite the strange behavior it predicts. Richard Feynman, Nobel prize winner in physics, said simply, "If you think you understand quantum mechanics, you don't understand quantum mechanics." Feynman suggested at one point that the best way to compute the outcome of an event controlled by quantum effects was to use a computer with quantum elements, and let it simulate a system to make predictions. He did not suggest how to build such a computer, and no one followed up with the idea at the time.

Interest in quantum computing rose in 1994 when mathematician Peter Shor described a way a quantum computer could factor very large numbers (that is, describe them as multiplications of "prime" numbers—2, 3, 5, 7, 11, ...—that could not be further factored). This factoring had the potential to do things such as breaking encrypted communications, the coding of which could not otherwise be broken by any computer using current technology. Shor's clever algorithm in part motivated growing research into quantum computers. The number of papers on quantum computing has exceeded 1,000 annually since 2012.

Quantum computers are research projects today. The most optimistic predictions of experts are that fully useful systems will exist in 5-10 years, with less optimistic experts predicting 20-30 years. One researcher, Mikhail Dyakonov, has said that even the larger number is overly optimistic, and he says in an article that he is among the minority who believe quantum computing will not be available for the "foreseeable future."

Despite Feynman's warning, we can attempt to understand the difference between conventional computing and quantum computing. The integrated circuits used for conventional digital processing handle binary digits, 0 and 1. Quantum computing can be thought of as using computing elements that store data, not as firm 0s and 1s, but as values that have a certain probability of being 0 or 1 (quantum bits, or "qubits").

A basic problem with quantum computing is that, because of its prob-abilistic nature, it will often generate erroneous results "by accident." To get a result that is highly likely to be correct, one might have to do the same computation more than 100 times and take the most common result to have high confidence in its accuracy. This characteristic significantly reduces the theoretical efficiency of quantum computers.

Dyakonov estimated that solving interesting problems would require 1,000-100,000 logical qubits. He said that even the lower number implies that "A useful quantum computer needs to process a set of continuous parameters that is larger than the number of subatomic particles in the observable universe." At this writing, Intel has created a 49-qubit chip, IBM a 50-qubit chip, and Google a 72-qubit chip.

Quantum computing currently requires extreme refrigeration. The cores of D-Wave quantum computers operate at -460 degrees F, near absolute zero Centigrade.

Perhaps the question is partly a question of what one views as the useful scale of quantum computing. An IBM web site in March 2019 said:

> Over 50 years of advances in mathematics, materials science, and computer science have transformed quantum computing from theory to reality. Today, real quantum computers can be accessed through the cloud, and many thousands of people have used them to learn, conduct research, and tackle new problems.

> Quantum computers could one day provide breakthroughs in many disciplines, including materials and drug discovery, the optimization of complex systems, and artificial intelligence. But to realize those breakthroughs, and to make quantum computers widely useable and accessible, we need to reimagine information processing and the machines that do it.

A Perspective

The evolution of computer intelligence has been accelerated rapidly by improvements in the core hardware and software. The remarkable achievements celebrated as Artificial Intelligence are but one step in this steady increase in computer intelligence.

Many of the giant steps in computer intelligence, such as the Graphical User Interface, depended in part on the inspiration and hard work of individual visionaries and teams. The visions weren't evident at the time, and it is hard to predict the next vision.

Predicting future technology innovations is difficult in part because the usual "necessity is the mother of invention" doesn't seem to be the driver of major technology innovations. More often, "invention is the mother of necessity." Something like email or smartphones is invented, and a large number of individuals decide that the innovation is something they must have, although they never realized the necessity until the invention was available.

Many of the advances in computer intelligence depended on individual insights into how to accomplish software tasks efficiently and make computers more effective. Defining the underlying way to accomplish a task is independent of the software that executes the task. The underlying methodologies invented to accomplish those specific tasks efficiently are called "algorithms."

Part II:
Algorithms—The core of Computer Intelligence

The evolution of computer intelligence includes progress in what the software does as well as how fast it does it. An unambiguous specification of the steps required to complete a specific task—specified independent of the software that implements the steps—is typically called an "algorithm." Algorithms are fundamental to computer intelligence. They enable the application of a systematic and "logical" way of thinking to a task.

A grammar checker in a word-processing program is a form of algorithm that will call your attention to wording it considers ungrammatical. For example, the grammar checker in a word-processing program might suggest changing a singular noun to the plural form. Such software utilizes a series of grammar rules that can be written independent of the specific software code. Once that algorithm—that collection of rules—is defined, it is translated into software to allow its use.

Algorithms are reliable to the degree that they address the intended purpose. Specification of the algorithm as a mathematical formula or a series of logical steps allows review of the logic without dealing with computer code. If the logic is expressed in mathematical form, the math must be valid as well. An algorithm should provide a correct result, assuming the logic is correct. If the logic is only valid most of the time, as is the case with a grammar checker, the algorithm is useful to the extent it is correct often enough to be useful.

In addition to the logical process expressed, algorithms addressing a specific problem are not all equally effective or efficient. Suppose the problem is to find the shortest traffic route between two locations. One algorithm would be to list all possible routes in the local area, calculate the distance for each route, and pick the shortest route. That list-every-option approach is obviously inefficient. For example, some routes overlap, and it's not necessary to recalculate the distance of a given partial route for every route that uses it.

Dynamic Programming

An example of a category of algorithm is the work of Richard Bellman (1920-1984), a mathematician that published 619 papers and 39 books. His invention of "dynamic programming" is an algorithm based on a fundamental idea that can be stated in words, the "principle of optimality," as he called it. As such, it provides a good example of the logic behind an algorithm that distinguishes it from the specific equations and computer code that implement that logic.

Dynamic programming is a class of algorithms that describe an approach to optimizing a series of decisions (a "multi-stage decision process") leading to a goal. Finding the best driving route, for example, is a series of decisions at every possible turn.

The general applicability of Bellman's analysis is suggested in the Preface to his book, *Dynamic Programming* (1957), where he indicates which chapters are most relevant to mathematicians, economists, statisticians, engineers, and operations analysts. Later he became interested in applying math to health research and founded the journal *Mathematical Biosciences*. He was awarded the Medal of Honor from the Institute of Electrical and Electronics Engineers (IEEE) in 1979 "for contributions to decision processes and control system theory, particularly the creation and application of dynamic programming." His work is embedded in many parts of computer science and engineering today.

Bellman bases a number of his mathematical analyses on his "Principle of Optimality":

> An optimal policy has the property that whatever the initial state and initial decision are, the remaining decisions must constitute

an optimal policy with regard to the state resulting from the first decision.

A policy that specifies a series of decisions is "optimal" if that series of decisions produces the best result as measured by a specific criterion. The goal of the map routing problem—the criterion being optimized—is to minimize the distance traveled or the travel time.

A process like a series of turns in a given mapped area requires a number of decisions over time. Each decision puts the system in a new "state," e.g., a car at a specific intersection on a specific road with a different set of turn options than if another decision had been made in a previous "state." The result of this series of decisions can be measured, e.g., the total travel time.

The principle of optimality can be restated in terms of the routing problem. If you are at any specific turn decision on the optimal route (the shortest route), the remaining route must be one you would get if you were to analyze the map from the current point to obtain the optimal route from that point to the destination. Otherwise, the point you are at couldn't be part of the best route. It turns out that such a straightforward observation can be interpreted mathematically to create efficient algorithms, in this case, finding the optimal route much more efficiently than listing all possible routes. One does so by working backward from the destination and retaining the optimal route at any point reached as one moves "backwards." This approach saves a lot of computation relative to listing all possible routes and measuring them.

Bellman was a remarkable mathematician, but he never wrote a line of computer code. Creating algorithms is very distinct from the skill of programming.

Contributions by researchers such as Bellman to addressing difficult tasks efficiently improve our experience with digital systems every day. What is called "Artificial Intelligence" and "machine learning" today is a continuation of this tradition.

Machine learning and deep neural nets

The methodology driving much of what is called Artificial Intelligence today is modeling the implications of very large datasets using what is called a Deep Neural Network (DNN, sometimes shortened to "deep neural *net*"), one of the most important algorithms in computer intelligence today. The DNN model itself, as the name suggests, is inspired by a simplified model of how the human brain employs deep layers of interconnected neurons (Figure 11). The "deep" in Deep Neural Network simply implies that there are many layers between the input and output. (In a human brain, the layers of neurons are not so nicely organized.)

A DNN model that summarizes the implications of a large dataset is derived by using another class of algorithms called "machine learning," which generalizes *labelled* examples in the dataset. Each example is labelled by the class of thing it of which it is an example. If the DNN is learning to distinguish images of dogs versus cats, for example, the examples are labelled either "dog" or "cat." Finding a good DNN using machine learning is often summarized as "deep learning." The use of the word "learning" suggests an analogy with how humans learn to distinguish patterns by being exposed to many examples where the pattern class is known.

Suppose the problem was to distinguish printed letters in a scanned document by examining an image of each letter. In figure 11, the input values at the bottom of the diagram would be the values of the pixels in an image of a letter. The number of outputs of the neural net, shown at the top of the figure, would be the number of letters being distinguished. For example, the first output could be designed to be "1" if the model concluded the image was lower case "a" and "0" if not (the 1 for true and 0 for false suggested by George Boole). The machine learning would do its best to create a model where only one output at a time was 1, with that output correctly corresponding to the letter in the image. If no outputs were 1, or more than one output was 1, that would reflect uncertainty, perhaps because of faulty printing or a font that wasn't in the examples.

A specific DNN model is derived using a database with many labelled examples of the classes of things being distinguished. Once a good model is derived, it can be used to classify new examples in a way that is consistent with the data that was analyzed to create that model. The derivation doesn't need to be repeated; the resulting model can be evaluated fairly quickly.

Machine learning finds the best-fitting DNN model by slowly improving its predictive accuracy by trial-and-error. If a small change in the parameters describing the DNN makes the predictions better on the labelled data, that change is kept; if the small change in the model makes the prediction worse, a different change is tried.

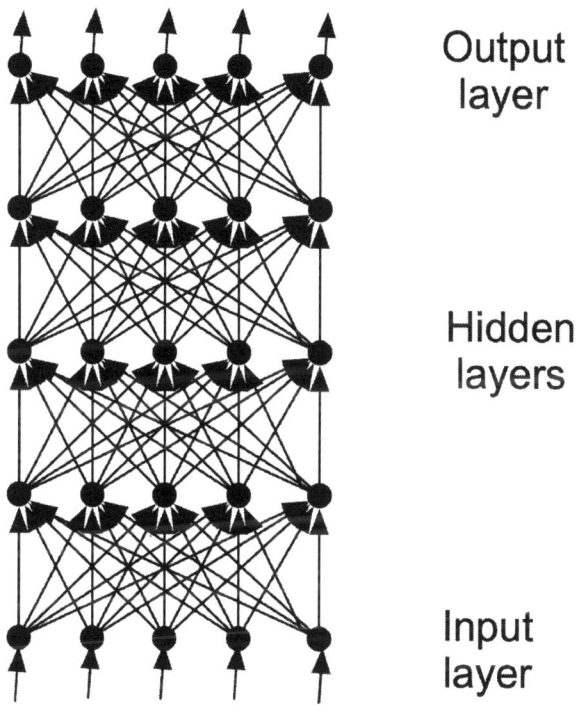

Output layer

Hidden layers

Input layer

Figure 11: A Deep Neural Network: Each dot is a mathematical function considered a simplified description of the behavior of a single human neuron in the brain.

A category of machine learning algorithms that work by a evaluating a series of small changes in this manner are sometimes called "steepest descent" or "gradient descent." Similar to finding the lowest point in a valley by climbing slowly down a mountain by always stepping down, the objective is to find the lowest value of a criterion being minimized, e.g., the error rate in classifying labeled examples. Instead of trying a random direction, one "looks ahead" to see which direction will take one down the farthest in a single step, with adjustments to avoiding getting stuck on a "ledge."

The mathematical approach in the case of deep learning is more sophisticated than this over-simplification. In a landmark 1986 paper, David E. Rumelhart, Geoffrey E. Hinton, and Ronald J. Williams showed how an algorithm called "back propagation" could use the concepts of steepest descent with an efficient method specifically tailored to neural nets.

Deep learning can require significant computing power. That computational load is what deterred DNNs being widely used until the cost and time required for the computing to find optimal DNNs crossed a practical "tipping point." Once the best DNN is derived in a specific application, the result can be used efficiently. It may take hours of computer time to *learn* to recognize the letters of the alphabet, but, once learned, the *recognition process* can be very efficient, making a decision in a fraction of a second.

Much simpler models than neural nets have long been used in CI for predicting outcomes based on data. For example, FICO credit scores are based on a statistical analysis of how reliable people with certain histories and characteristics have been in paying their bills.

Neither data-based pattern recognition techniques nor neural nets are new. For example, my book, *Computer-Oriented Approaches to Pattern Recognition*, published in 1972, was an early description of using labelled data in a pattern recognition algorithm that was implemented as software on a general-purpose computer. A neural net was a known modeling option in the mid-60s. As noted, the key optimization algorithm, back propagation, was developed in 1986. The technology has had a major impact recently because computing power has reached a point where it is practical. Continuing improvement in computer processing power and memory will make it applicable to a growing number of problems.

Processing human language

Innovations in algorithms have made real what once was formerly only a subject of science fiction—talking to computers. Computer scientists have struggled for decades to give computers the ability to deal with human language. Today, algorithms that let us speak or text in "natural language" with digital systems are a rapidly improving part of computer intelligence.

Technologies required to maintain a computer-human voice conversation include (a) speech recognition, (b) natural language processing (NLP) to "understand" what the human is saying or typing, and (c) voice response. Text-to-speech synthesis is required to speak back an answer that comes from a database in the form of text. All of these technologies have gone beyond the tipping point of usability and affordability fairly recently. When interaction is texting rather than speaking, the NLP can be applied directly to the text without the speech recognition component.

The "personal assistants" such as Apple's Siri, Google Assistant, and Amazon's Alexa are examples of voice-based conversational options. Automated conversations with companies by talking or typing in human language are available through customer service channels. These channels include customer service telephone lines, chatboxes on web sites, messaging services such as Facebook Messenger, and applications on mobile phones.

The goal of Natural Language Processing technology is to discover the "intent" of a user request. The NLP must also identify any data in the request that is required to fulfill the intent. For example, a spoken or typed request to a bank may be "Transfer $200 from my savings account to my checking account." The *intent* is to transfer money between accounts. The needed *data to complete the request* are which account to *transfer-from* and which to *transfer-to*—in this example, "savings" and "checking" respectively. In an example of a longer conversation, if the user said, "Please transfer $200 to my checking account," and there were several other accounts, the NLP would need to be able to trigger an inquiry as to which account to transfer from.

Speech recognition has been slowly improving for decades. Large-vocabulary speech recognition systems required for most applications today start by attempting to recognize the basic *sounds* of speech—"phonemes."

Anyone who has learned to read "phonetically"—"sound it out"—is familiar with the concept of the sounds associated with letters.

This is a difficult task, since phonemes are brief sounds whose audio signature is affected by the phonemes around them. The major improvement in recent years has been to use deep neural networks trained on many examples to distinguish phonemes.

One of the issues in recognizing phonemes is that they are not clearly delineated, as are letters on a typed page. Where phonemes start and end is part of the recognition process. A technique called Hidden Markov Modelling (HMM) has been a successful method of finding potential boundaries for many decades. The core mathematics of Markov models was developed by Russian mathematician Andrey Markov about 1906.

The phonemes have to be translated into words, essentially by using a dictionary with phonetic spellings of the words to help in converting the sounds into words. This is in effect a reverse version of the dictionary we use to learn how to pronounce a word; a phonetic dictionary lists all the words that sound like a series of phonemes identified in the speech recognition process.

An additional difficulty in deciding the appropriate interpretation of a sequence of phonemes is that some words sound exactly the same, e.g., "to," "two," and "too." Simply looking up the phonetic sounds in a dictionary isn't the full solution.

A "language model" uses the context of other words in the sentence to resolve this ambiguity. One version of a language model is a table of the probabilities of words occurring together, created using simple statistics over a large body of text. For example, "too much" is much more likely than "to much" or "two much," while "two cats" is much more likely than "to cats" or "too cats."

Called "statistical language models," such models significantly improve recognition because they use context to help understand what was said. Statistical language models "understand," for example, that the more accurate transcription is "went downtown" than "went down town."

In a given application, the text from which these probabilities are generated could be specific to an application, such as transcribing medical dictation. In such cases, the automated system can understand medical terminology much better than a layman.

Deep neural networks have improved both the recognition of phonemes and the power of language models. With the use of DNNs derived by machine learning from labelled data, researchers at Microsoft and Google have reported word recognition accuracy of about 95% on a relatively difficult problem of people carrying on an unstructured telephone conversation. Humans listening to the same speech were no more accurate; so, at least for this standard test, one can say that computer speech recognition has achieved parity with humans.

Understanding natural language is a less mature technology, but advancing rapidly. Some simpler NLP tasks can be addressed using a search for "keywords" or "key phrases" derived for specific applications, such as looking for "transfer" or "account balance" in a request to a bank. The most impressive results again come from DNNs.

Speech recognition and natural language processing technology using deep learning will continue to improve rapidly because machine learning is driven by data. As the DNNs are used in applications, data is generated that can then be used to improve their performance. As performance improves, users are likely to use the application more often, generating more data. This virtuous cycle will drive continuing improvement of a given application.

Similar language technology can also translate *between* languages. Google Translate is a free service that translates words, phrases, and web pages between English and over 100 other languages—an example of the state of a difficult technology.

Similar core technology can also be used to help understand "big data" in voice or text files. By finding documents or parts of documents that pertain to a specific subject, a version of natural language processing can help with search results or simply understanding what categories of information are available in a large database. One commercial example is software that analyzes calls into a customer service line to understand why customers are calling or if agents are following required procedures.

These human language processing capabilities support the increasingly important capability for users to hold a text or voice conversation with a digital system, essentially a new user interface option supplementing or replacing the familiar—but increasingly overburdened—Graphical User Interface. Conversational interaction can ease dealing with a complex digital system.

Just the answer, please—Answering technology

One of the key aspects of computer intelligence today is finding information. Web search is a critical feature of web browsers, allowing one to type in keywords and get a list of web sites that might provide an answer. Although Web search today is being improved by the use of deep learning, getting a list of relevant web sites as a result of a search doesn't provide a direct answer. Instead, the search typically provides links to web sites the user can examine further to look for an answer.

One of the least developed parts of computer intelligence at this writing is the ability of computers to distill the huge amount of information available on the Web and within companies into concise answers to questions— let's call it "Answering Technology" (AT). AT can be particularly critical to the effectiveness of voice-only interfaces, where the lack of a screen makes providing a long list of options impractical. Even when a screen is available, the user would prefer an answer, not a research project.

AT can address two major goals:
- What is the best answer to a question posed in natural language?
- To what degree can the computer consider the validity/truth of that answer?

Stating a question fully can give more information than the typical list of keywords in a web search. For example, a web search for "pepperoni pizza" produces links to pizza outlets and recipes while a typed inquiry, "How many calories are in a slice of pepperoni pizza?" at this writing, using Google search, produced the answer "380 calories" at the head of a list of web sites.

Some inquiries will have controversial answers or issues relating to the accuracy of information being accessed. Thus, an additional capability of measuring the accuracy or controversial nature of the answer would be valuable. The technology for doing so would have to be invented.

AT is not the same as NLP in conversational applications. The goal of NLP in such cases is to understand the user's intent and can indicate what information is desired, but determining an appropriate answer is a separate task. When the answer comes from standard database software, e.g., a bank customer's account balance, finding the answer is "a simple matter of software." When the answer is buried in a number of unstructured documents, however, it often currently requires a human to create an answer database.

Google is beginning to address the issue of providing more immediate results of its web search, using underlying "knowledge graphs" to summarize information about some inquiries in the form of a "knowledge panel" or "cards" (Figure 12). The knowledge graph in Figure 13 illustrates that concept.

In April 2019, Google updated its Google Assistant on Android phones to provide knowledge panels in response to more requests. One can, for example, ask for "Events in Mountain View" and receive a list of upcoming events. The cards have been updated to include more visual results, such as a stock price graph in response to a stock quote inquiry.

An example of available AT technology was described as of May 2019 on the Google cloud services web page. Under the heading "Document Understanding AI (Beta) – Digital Transaction Management," Google said in part:

> In domains like contracts and real estate agreements, *Document Understanding AI* extracts insights from thousands of stored documents in order to perform semantic question answering, clustering, and classification...This solution enables companies to digitize, classify, and extract knowledge—such as form fields, text passages, tables, and graphs—from thousands of documents. It helps to organize and store knowledge graphs and other extracted data for easy search, query, consumption, and actionable insights...[The] solution scales document management across multiple industries—such as finance, legal, and healthcare—for custom entity extractions and representation in a knowledge graph.

Albert Einstein

Theoretical physicist

Albert Einstein was a German-born theoretical physicist who developed the theory of relativity, one of the two pillars of modern physics. His work is also known for its influence on the philosophy of science. Wikipedia

Born: March 14, 1879, Ulm, Germany

Died: April 18, 1955, Princeton Medical Center at Plainsboro, NJ

Education: University of Zurich (1905), ETH Zürich (1896–1900), MORE

Spouse: Elsa Einstein (m. 1919–1936), Mileva Marić (m. 1903–1919)

Children: Eduard Einstein, Hans Albert Einstein, Lieserl Einstein

Quotes

View 7+ more

Imagination is more important than knowledge.

If you can't explain it simply, you don't understand it well enough.

Two things are infinite: the universe and human stupidity; and I'm not sure about the universe.

People also search for

View 15+ more

| Isaac Newton | Eduard Einstein Son | Stephen Hawking | Nikola Tesla | Elsa Einstein Spouse |

Figure 12: A knowledge panel by Google for the search "Albert Einstein"

Figure 13: A knowledge graph of how author Ayn Rand
relates to other historical figures (Source: Github)

Earlier work planted the seeds for today's knowledge graphs. In 2007, William Tunstall-Pedoe and colleagues created a website called True Knowledge intended to offer one-shot answers to all kinds of questions. The programmers attempted to create a comprehensive knowledge graph, which in their case was a giant treelike structure. At its base was the category "object," which theoretically encompassed every single fact. Moving upward, the "object" category branched into the classes "conceptual object" (for social and mental constructs) and "physical object" (for everything else). The higher up the tree you went, the more refined the categorizations got. The "track" category, for instance, split into categories that included "route," "railway," and "road." The tree swelled to tens of thousands of categories, comprising hundreds of millions of facts. Creating and maintaining something that attempts to categorize all human knowledge (and adapt to new terms and knowledge) is obviously a challenging—if not impossible—task.

In 2010, Google acquired Metaweb, a startup that was creating an ontology called Freebase. Two years later, the company unveiled the Knowledge Graph previously mentioned, which boasted 3.5 billion facts. That same year, Microsoft launched what would become known as the Concept Graph, which grew beyond 5 million entities. In 2017, Facebook, Amazon, and Apple all acquired knowledge-graph-building companies. To help automate the process of creating and updating knowledge graphs, researchers have begun designing autonomous systems that crawl the web for answers, stocking ontologies with new facts faster than any human could.

Knowledge graphs are one approach to providing a database that can be used to provide answers to questions posed in natural language. But they provide a resource, not a full solution.

The objective of creating answers from large data sets is sometimes addressed in part by companies under the heading of "analytics." For example, some companies can take the recorded customer service calls that most companies store, convert them to text, and "cluster" them into similar calls to help companies understand why customers are calling. By understanding what customers are asking, companies can develop Frequently Asked Questions databases with answers for agents or automated systems.

Some companies are specifically trying to address AT. For example, Equals 3 has software called Lucy that they describe on their web site:

> There is finally a technology for organizations struggling to manage and leverage their vast sums of information. Lucy reads and learns all of an organization's accumulated knowledge across all the different places the information lives. She takes written reports, PPTs, PDFs, videos, audios, graphs, datasets and learns them like an expert. Ask Lucy for what insights you're looking for and she will do more than point you to the sources with answers. She delivers the specific answer unit within the relevant assets.

noHold, a company with tools and a platform that supports specialized digital assistants, has developed Module 1000, a tool to develop digital assistants that is particularly designed for companies with thousands of products. One of the challenges companies face when managing so many products is how to deliver effective support for each customer regardless of the product they purchased without straining resources and budgets. Module 1000 extracts content supporting the digital assistant from existing documents such as product manuals and logged customer service session scripts. The company's CEO Diego Ventura summarized the challenge in a statement:

> When dealing with thousands of product lines, possibly in multiple languages, it is key to be able to capitalize on existing content. It is unrealistic to create specialized content for each of the thousand products, just to make sure it works for the Virtual Assistant.

In an update to its Edge web browser announced in May 2019, Microsoft added a new feature called Collections, which Microsoft says will allow users to collect, organize, share and export content they find online more efficiently, integrated with Microsoft Office. Rather than getting specific answers directly, this approach organizes data on a particular subject, making it easier to find a specific answer.

Answer Technology may require humans checking answers that were automatically generated for their relevance and accuracy or picking the best in a list of possible answers, making human intelligence part of the answer-generating process. Perhaps this is an area where evolving computer intelligence will create jobs rather than replace them.

Robotic process automation (RPA)

Companies use computers to automate many business processes. Some of this automation relies on software packages such as databases where a company stores business information for quick access. Computer intelligence long ago replaced most filing cabinets full of paper documents.

Sometimes achieving a business task involves a "process," a series of actions controlling multiple software tasks to achieve a specific goal, perhaps accessing a particular software application multiple times or using a series of different applications. When such a process is automated so that it doesn't require an employee recalling multiple steps, but reduces it to one operation, it is sometimes called "business process automation" (BPA). BPA developed by software developers and business planners have made companies more efficient for decades.

A relatively new way of creating BPA that doesn't require human design has been called "robotic process automation (RPA)." The term does not imply the use of physical robots. Instead, it is a software solution that is analogous to a robot that learns, a form of machine learning.

In one version, a skilled worker uses a Graphical User Interface on a PC to go through a series of steps to accomplish a task, and RPA software observes the steps. For example, the task may be receiving email containing an invoice, extracting the relevant data, and typing that data into an accounting database and/or ordering system. The RPA software can then repeat that process by emulating the human without direct use of the GUI. The tasks are typically repetitive tasks that humans dislike; one commentator said that "no one has a degree in cut-and-paste."

RPA is possible in part because of the continual evolution of computer intelligence. For example, as developers of software packages realized that those packages would be accessed by other software, not just humans using a direct interface with the software packages, they added Application Programming Interfaces (APIs). APIs are features of a software package that allow it to be controlled by other software by using a well-defined format. This has become a standard practice and a trend that makes RPA practical with much less programming effort.

In 2018, Forrester Consulting surveyed 100 decision makers at the managerial level from core business lines to evaluate how RPA affects employee engagement. The survey found:

- 66% said RPA restructures existing work, enabling employees to have more human interactions;
- 60% said RPA helps employees focus on more meaningful strategic tasks; and
- 57% said RPA reduces manual errors.

The decision makers also agreed, however, that poorly managed RPA efforts can exacerbate existing fears of automation in the workforce.

Blockchain

Blockchain is a relatively new technology—Internet-based software that securely stores information. Rather than being controlled by one entity, blockchain is spread across multiple computers and records data in a way designed to ensure that the information cannot be inappropriately changed or corrupted. By decentralizing data and protecting the way it is manipulated, blockchain promotes security and the safe sharing of information.

Blockchain is best-known as the technology behind the cryptocurrency bitcoin, providing a secure environment that keeps track of who owns how much bitcoin and prevents the "manufacturing" of new bitcoin. Bitcoin itself is an interesting case of something that was created entirely by software—software that guaranteed a limited supply. Like precious metals, the very scarcity seems to have given it value. In April 2019, one bitcoin was worth over 5,000 US dollars. It rose from almost nothing to over $19,000 in December 2017, then experienced a long decline.

A number of other blockchain cryptocurrencies have since been created. Some have an established value, but logic would seem to suggest that there must be a limit to how much wealth you can create by simply manufacturing a new currency. It has been said that cryptocurrencies such as bitcoin are used by criminals to launder illegally gained money because it is hard to trace users; some analysts argue that such use is a major reason cryptocurrencies retain value.

One disadvantage of the technology is that it remembers all transactions with multiple copies; thus, the data in an application can grow rapidly and eventually create problems with high storage demands. This growth and the distributed platform can also cause the response of blockchain software to slow over time.

In addition to cryptocurrency, applications taking advantage of blockchain technology include:

- Secure storage of *healthcare records.*
- A *decentralized authentication system* which aims to replace logins and passwords with SSL certificates stored using blockchain. (SSL, Secure Sockets Layer, is the standard security technology for establishing an encrypted link between a web server and a browser.)
- IBM's blockchain-based *Food Trust network* designed to improve the way food is traced from farm to grocery store. The network can help validate claims such as that food is "organic." The Albertsons chain is one of the users with its 2,300 stores across the US.
- Tracking *financial transactions* to combat fraud and assure compliance with regulations.
- A platform for *government operations.* Thirty government departments in Dubai formed a committee dedicated to investigating opportunities across health records, shipping, business registration, and preventing the spread of conflict diamonds. Samsung is creating blockchain solutions for the South Korean government for public safety and transport applications.
- Tracking *real-estate transfers.*
- Kodak's blockchain system for tracking *intellectual property rights and payments* to photographers.
- Recording and tracking *royalties for musicians.*

An Internet of Things World survey found mixed attitude among professionals about blockchain. While 29% of IoT leaders said that they don't currently see a benefit of leveraging blockchain in their organizations, another 29% reported their belief that blockchain could help with Internet of Things security.

A Gartner November 2018 report, "Predicts 2019: Future of Supply Chain Operations," noted that there are few successful deployments of blockchain projects in supply chains, with "initiatives failing to match the initial market exuberance that will lead to disillusionment and buyer fatigue." Gartner also predicted that, by 2023, "90% of blockchain-based supply chain initiatives will suffer blockchain fatigue for lack of strong use cases." The report suggested that applications should be a good fit to the technology and be driven by need, not just a desire to adopt a well-publicized new technology.

Some companies, however, are providing platforms integrating blockchain with their core products. In mid-2019, Salesforce announced Salesforce Blockchain, which combines blockchain with the company's Customer

Relationship Management software. The company has built tools that allow building blockchain-based applications with less expertise.

The role of algorithms

Algorithms are the intelligence behind many computer applications. Algorithms are implemented as software code, but the methodology behind them is independent of specific software code. Without the inventiveness of algorithms, many of the applications that we take for granted today and will see tomorrow wouldn't be possible.

Part III:
How CI changes society

We take for granted the increasing role of computer intelligence in our lives, with frustration when our Internet connection fails and panic when we think we've lost our smartphone. We often count on GPS services for navigation, with hardly a thought of the satellites and communications systems and map data required to support those services and to make navigation services available on a mobile phone. Global Positioning Satellites even require using Einstein's theory of relativity to correct for the time distortion caused by the satellite's high speed. Without the correction, the clocks in each GPS satellite would get ahead of ground-based clocks by about 45 microseconds per day and increasingly misinterpret ground locations.

We don't think anything of taking as many photos with our smartphone as we want. We forget the days when one had to have a specialized camera and film plus the expense of developing that film. If you wanted to share a photo with a relative far away, you had to mail a physical copy. Today, you post it on Facebook, attach it to an email, or send it from your mobile phone.

We can access the assets of the Web whenever we want with web browsers and search engines. Short videos—often created by non-professionals—are available on services like YouTube or TikTok. In 2018, YouTube was the world's second biggest search engine with more than 1.8 billion people registered on the site, watching five billion videos daily.

Changes in the broadcasting and entertainment industry are occurring at an increasingly rapid rate. News is available as quickly as events occur. We can watch streaming video of some US congressional hearings. Services are available to watch and pause movies or TV series whenever convenient. Companies including Netflix, Apple, Amazon, AT&T, Disney, and Comcast are getting into streaming video that enables watching movies or series on demand, often an unlimited number for a monthly fee.

The companies are both producing and licensing content. In the year through May 2019, AT&T, Comcast, and Disney spent $215 billion in total on acquisitions of, respectively, Time Warner ($104 billion), Sky (a European broadcaster for $40 billion), and much of 21st Century Fox ($71 billion).

This trend is driven by Internet speeds that are fast enough to let someone immediately watch a streamed video show. Software to search for and choose shows from a display, using a TV remote, a PC, or a smartphone, makes it easy to use these services. Computers in the cloud supporting those services provide enough computing power to allow a rapid response.

Many more of our daily activities are now interwoven with computer intelligence. Through an app on a smartphone, we can get a ride to a specified destination. A huge selection of products can be ordered and delivered quickly and efficiently through online shopping sites.

Cashiers scan bar codes at the grocery store checkout counter, rather than typing prices on price tags into a register. The store computer system knows immediately what is being sold and what products should be reordered to keep shelves stocked. Some stores are testing systems that watch shoppers with cameras and keep track of what the shoppers picked up, so that they can just walk out of the store without checking out.

Our social connections with other humans have expanded through computer intelligence, including wireless communications. "Asynchronous communications," such as text messages and email, allow us to carry on conversations extended over time, addressing the latest message when time allows. We can include links to web sites easily in our messages. Social media allows a more permanent documentation of what we are doing as we do it, letting our friends and family view aspects of our lives at any time.

Microprocessors and other semiconductor chips drive software in almost all devices and products, whether computers, mobile phones, automobiles, or clocks. Internet connections provide access to an increasing number of services in the cloud. CI will be an increasing part of our lives.

Communicating with computers using human language

A particularly important part of the evolution of computer intelligence is the ability to deal with digital systems in human language ("natural language"), as noted earlier. Speech recognition and natural language processing (NLP) technologies allow dealing with computers using a skill that humans have long honed to communicate with one another. Interacting with digital systems by speaking or texting does not require mastering a user manual. The user manual in practice can be simply, "Say or type what you want in the context of this application."

Natural language interaction with digital systems has gone beyond the level of accuracy that is necessary for it to be useful and widely adopted. The technology has progressed beyond the tipping point of practical utility and is continually improving.

There are limitations. The interaction of a company-specific digital assistant may be limited by the context of what a company does. Don't ask the mobile app of a bank to provide a weather forecast.

The importance of this trend is that it makes the increasing power of computer intelligence easily accessible, instead of a potentially frustrating experience. The familiar Graphical User Interface (GUI)—with its icons, menus, folders, and pointing device, is becoming overburdened, particularly on the small screen of a smartphone. We are being forced to deal with too many features and options, with too many choices and clicks required to finish a task. Interacting using human language can make computer intelligence seem more of a partner, a "digital assistant."

Examples of that progress are the general digital assistants including Apple's Siri, Google Assistant, and Amazon's Alexa. These "personal assistants" allow interacting with your smartphone or a digital device (such as a smart speaker) by simply saying what you want. Samsung has a version, Bixby, for its Android smartphones, providing an alternative to Google Assistant that makes Samsung less dependent on Google. China's Tencent Holdings has Xiaowei, a digital assistant for its messaging service WeChat, helping the service's billion-plus users with tasks such as playing music and hailing a ride. The personal assistants are handling an increasing variety of tasks, offering a list of relevant web sites if they can't deal directly with a request.

The long-term intent of the general digital assistants is to not restrict the context. They will answer questions, perform tasks such as reminding you of an appointment, and contact almost any other company for its services if that company has provided a compatible specialized digital assistant supporting its services.

Examples of what you can say to Alexa illustrate this diversity. After saying, "Alexa," one can make requests such as the following:

- Play "Hello" by Adele.
- Tell me a pet joke.
- What's my news briefing?
- What is 340 times 43?
- Is it going to rain tomorrow?
- Give me a *Game of Thrones* quote.
- What is the tallest mountain?
- Read my Kindle book.
- When do the NBA playoffs start?
- Play the *Stuff You Should Know* podcast on iHeartRadio.
- What does the word 'congruent' mean?
- How do you cook a turkey?
- Convert one pound to ounces.

The Echo is always listening for the "wake-up word" Alexa, using software *in the device* rather than software in the cloud. Once it hears "Alexa," it records the following request and sends a digital representation over the Internet to Amazon computers. The computers convert the speech to text, interpret it using natural language processing, find an answer (if it is something Alexa can deal with), convert the answer (which is usually in text form) to speech using text-to-speech synthesis technology, and then send that audio back to the Echo device, which plays it. This occurs in seconds, despite all the computation and data transmission required—an impressive example of the rapid progress of computer intelligence.

Microsoft offers the digital assistant Cortana, which it seems to be making more specialized for managing software applications. There are other specialized versions, such as Dragon Drive from Nuance Communications, designed to be installed by automobile manufacturers in vehicles to allow hands- and eyes-free operation of car functions such as entertainment or temperature control.

The general digital assistants are a major strategic and competitive imperative for the companies involved. For example, Amazon said in April 2019 that it had 10,000 employees working on Alexa and versions of its Echo home devices. Alexa is also available on other platforms than the Echo, including Internet-connected devices such as thermostats from other companies. Google Assistant isn't just available on Android-based devices—you can download it as an app to an Apple iPhone running Apple's operating system iOS and use the Google Assistant instead of Apple's Siri. The Echo is available for under $100 at this writing, and digital assistants are free applications on a smartphone.

Large companies are investing heavily in adding features to their digital assistants. Samsung enhanced its Bixby personal assistant with the Bixby Marketplace in July 2019 for users in the US and Korea. The Bixby Marketplace allows users to browse and add services known as "capsules" to enhance their Bixby experience. The initial capsules include Google Maps, Spotify, iHeartRadio, NPR, Yelp, and more (Figure 14).

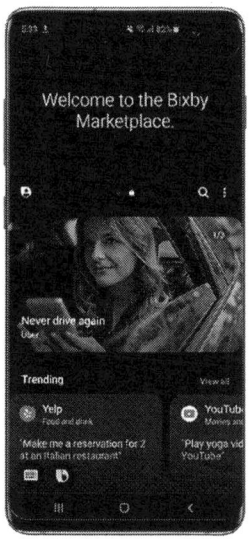 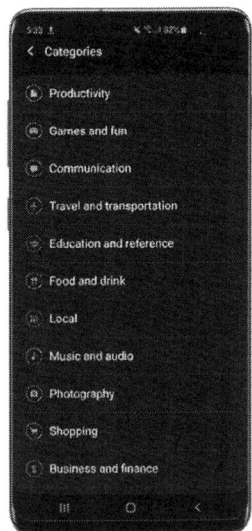 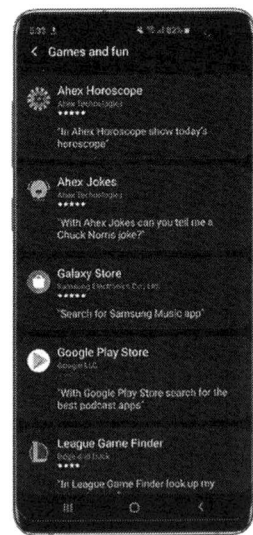

Figure 14: The Samsung Bixby Marketplace (Source: Samsung)

Why do these major companies invest so much in digital assistants? In part, to create a closer connection with you, and perhaps sell you something or advertise to you. But more strategically, they realize that, in the long run, general digital assistants will be major portals to web services and applications. They can be an alternative to classical web search, with the obvious long-term business opportunities that implies. Google's advertising revenues for its web search were $32.6 billion in the fourth quarter of 2018 alone.

Companies continue to upgrade the general digital assistants. For example, in May 2019, Google announced that Google Assistant can now deliver answers and respond to requests up to ten times faster than the previous version. Users can now fluidly switch between tasks and toggle across apps without having to say "Hey Google" before every request. Google Assistant was also upgraded to better understand the difference between requesting an action, like a command to "send an email to Fred," and the user dictating the message for transcription. Android phones will get a "driving mode" activated by saying "Hey Google, let's drive," launching a screen with info for driving and voice control.

In a Google demonstration of these new capabilities at a conference, the presenter asked Google Assistant to bring up her photos, and then to show only those photos with animals. She tapped one and said, "Send it to Justin," which dropped the photo into a messaging app. She then said, "Set subject to Yellowstone adventures," and the assistant understood that it should put "Yellowstone adventures" into the subject line, not transcribe what was spoken into the body of the message.

Google is also expanding the assistant's understanding of personal references, the company said. If a user says, "Hey Google, what's the weather like at Mom's house," Google Assistant will apparently understand that "Mom's house" refers to the home of the user's mother, look up her address, and provide a weather forecast for her city.

Such updates illustrate the continually increasing capabilities we can expect from the general digital assistants. Eventually, our favorite assistant will be an essential companion. Like a friend, it will come to know us well if we allow it.

Speaking is perhaps the most efficient form of communication with digital systems, yet text messaging has become a popular form of communication. Text communication with automated systems is thus expanding rapidly. For example, Facebook Messenger allows sending text messages to a company, and "chatbots" allow typing a message for automated customer service on a web site.

In order to be available through channels such as these, companies must build their own independent—company-specific—digital assistants. A company-specific digital assistant could be reached through the general digital assistants. It can alternatively be accessed directly through a customer-service telephone line that simply answers a call with "Please say why you are calling." A company assistant may also be accessed through an app downloaded to a smartphone or, as mentioned, through a chatbox on the company web site.

Companies often give these digital assistants a name. Bank of America, an early adopter of the technology, calls its digital assistant Erica. The company announced in mid-2019 that, after the first year of use, Erica had completed over 50 million client requests for over six million users and was being engaged by an average of more than 500,000 new users per month. Erica is also proactive, notifying customers of such things as upcoming Bank of America credit card bills and third-party electronic bills and helping to schedule payments. In the long run, all companies will be expected to provide a branded company digital assistant available through multiple channels, *just as you expect a company to have a web site today.*

The company digital assistants are going beyond customer service. Today, companies are beginning to recognize a customer who contacts them is an opportunity that should be addressed, rather than, for example, keeping a customer service call as short as possible. After answering questions such as the status of a flight, a Lufthansa digital assistant asks customers where else they might want to travel, and gives information on tourist destinations in Europe serviced by the airline. Platforms specifically supporting conversational ads are available; IBM, for example, has an interactive ad service.

The distinction between customer service and advertising (or, more generally, marketing) will blur over time. Any contact is an opportunity to engage the customer, and can be treated as such when the contact can be automated at minimal cost. Interactive ads have the potential to engage a customer much like entertainment and games.

As an example of this trend, audio-streaming service Spotify announced in May 2019 that it will be launching voice-interactive advertisements. The ads encourage the listener to say a verbal command in order to take action on the ad's content. Initially, the audio ads will direct listeners to a Spotify playlist or a podcast.

While the use of company digital assistants to interact with *customers* is a major trend, the technology can also enable company *employees* to interact with internal "enterprise" software or company operations. Companies use a wide range of software designed to manage operations, and many of those software packages require input from employees and/or provide data to employees. A conversational interface to enterprise software can make it more efficient for employees to use the software. Specialized digital assistant platforms are available for some specific enterprise activities, e.g., supporting the human resources department in answering common employee questions.

The automobile is a special case where a voice option seems necessary for safety. The AAA Foundation for Traffic Safety estimated in 2019 that the average American spends 51 minutes per day in their car. Car companies are competing with companies like Apple and Google for control of this potentially lucrative marketing channel, adding the ability to pay for gas, coffee, or entertainment through vehicle systems.

For example, BMW wants to connect directly with their drivers, not simply connect them to a smartphone. They've launched a specialized digital assistant that is installed in the car, developed in a partnership with Microsoft. BMW customers could, for example, make an appointment at their preferred BMW dealership by talking with the personal assistant—a conversation that might start with a reminder that service is due and finish with the system arranging the appointment.

The maturing of natural language processing also impacts applications that don't engage in a conversation. For example, a call to a customer service center is often introduced with a warning that the call will be recorded. This huge database of recorded calls can reveal insights into why customers are calling, new problems that have developed with a product, agents that don't follow required procedures, and more. Historically, managers selected a very small subset of these recordings to review, hoping essentially that a small sample will be revealing. Today, language-processing software can transcribe all the voice calls, analyze the resulting text to discover trends, and flag problem calls for management review. Some available software even detects emotion in the conversation, e.g., an angry customer.

A hundred years ago, the British philosopher Alfred North Whitehead wrote in his book *An Introduction to Mathematics*, "Civilization advances by extending the number of important operations which we can perform without thinking about them." The intuitive connection between humans and computers through language is as close as we can come to a direct connection with computers without wiring them to our brain. Today, there is sometimes frustration when the computer doesn't understand, but continuing R&D will reduce those occasions.

CI in Healthcare

An astounding number was reported in 2017. US healthcare costs had reached $3.5 trillion, 17.9% of gross domestic product! By comparison, healthcare costs were just $27.2 billion in 1960, 5% of GDP. That translates to an annual healthcare cost increase from just $146 per person in 1960 to $10,739 per person in 2017. In 2018, a family of four paid an average of $28,166, an increase of $1,222 from 2017, including the average cost of health insurance paid by employers and employees. Deloitte's 2019 Global Health Care Outlook estimated that global health care expenditures will continue to rise at an annual rate of 5.4% through 2022. US Medicare spending grew 4.2% to $706 billion in 2017. By 2020, retiring baby boomers are expected to drive Medicare and Medicaid costs to 24% of the budget.

These are just a few of the statistics that indicate the growing burden of healthcare costs on individuals, companies, and governments. The large and growing expenditures are improving overall health, but the US is not getting as good a return on that investment as some other countries. The Organisation for Economic Cooperation and Development (OECD) has compiled data on dozens of health outcomes and process measures. Across a number of these measures, the US lags behind similarly wealthy OECD countries. In some cases, such as the rates of mortality, premature death, and disease burden from any cause, the US is also not improving as quickly as other countries. Deloitte said that, when compared to ten developed countries, the US ranks last in overall health care performance, highlighted by per capita spending that is 50% greater than the next country and last place in rankings of efficiency, equity, and healthy lives.

One attempt to reduce (or at least understand) this issue involves more accessible healthcare records. While some medical offices still work with paper documents and file folders, medical records are increasingly being computerized. In 2016, the US Office of the National Coordinator for Health Information Technology released data briefs on Electronic Health Record (EHR) adoption and interoperability based on the American Hospital Association's annual survey. According to one brief, 96% of non-federal acute care hospitals have adopted a certified EHR system, up from 71.9% in 2011, the year a federal EHR incentive program launched. Adoption of basic EHR functionality between 2008 and 2015 rose from 9.4% to 83.8%. This adoption included about 80% of small, rural, and critical-access hospitals implementing a basic EHR. EHR systems help healthcare organizations maintain accurate records and assure proper follow-up care. They also potentially provide a source of research data on healthcare outcomes.

EHRs and other computer software changes how care is provided, documented, and reimbursed. A 2017 paper by L.N. Dyrbye and colleagues published by the National Academy of Medicine confirms the benefits of such software, but expressed concern that more than half of physicians are experiencing substantial symptoms of burnout and that nurses report a similarly high prevalence of burnout and depression. Work process inefficiencies such as computerized order entry, the burden of administrative/clerical activities, and documentation requirements are cited as key contributors to burnout.

Nuance Communications is an example of a company providing speech recognition and natural language processing tools that help healthcare providers and organizations operate more efficiently and effectively, reducing the administrative load of EHRs and making their use more effective. One set of Nuance products uses speech recognition to transcribe a report from a doctor who may be examining a radiology image or dictating notes on a patient visit. The tools can then analyze the dictated notes to fill in the fields in Electronic Health Record software. Even though the doctor needs to check the accuracy of the computer analysis, the automation significantly reduces the fraction of time doctors spend with the computer.

One example cited by Nuance is the use by the University of Rochester Medical Center (URMC) of the Natural Language Processing capabilities of Nuance's software to support the URMC's Backstop tracking program at six of its hospitals. The URMC Backstop program helps ensure patients with radiology findings receive their recommended follow-up care in a timely manner. URMC improved patient outcomes and reimbursements for the organization by using Nuance software. The results included a 29% increase in the completion of recommended examinations that would otherwise have been missed and a reduction of diagnoses being delayed by 80%. This example shows how computer intelligence can both provide physicians and nurses more time in their day, helping to reduce burnout, and improve healthcare outcomes as well.

Constance Lehman, MD, PhD, chief of the breast imaging division at Massachusetts General Hospital (MGH) and a professor of radiology at Harvard Medical School, speaking at the 2019 World Medical Innovation Forum, provided an example of computer intelligence providing improvements in radiology diagnosis. She said AI has the potential to address one of the most significant challenges in mammography—reducing the variation in results from clinicians studying the same image.

"Some structures in the body lend themselves well to precise measurements, which makes it easier to see when changes occur. But in other areas, radiologists are looking at very subtle patterns of tissue structure," she explained. "Mammography is probably one of the most extreme examples of that. We look for differences in texture and shading in the normal healthy glandular tissue, not specific structures, and every mammogram is like a unique fingerprint for every woman."

Dr. Lehman developed a deep learning tool that is more accurate than doctors at identifying individuals at high risk of developing breast cancer. In a confirming result, a computer running AI software at a contest in 2018 in Beijing defeated two teams of doctors in accurately recognizing maladies in magnetic resonance images (MRIs).

Consulting firm Deloitte has created DeloitteASSIST, a patient communication solution that uses speech recognition and natural language processing to enable patients in a medical facility to request assistance without the need to press a button. They speak their request to the device, and nurses are alerted to their need. Other AI techniques prioritize and route requests to the appropriate resource (orderlies, patient support assistants, volunteers) to meet the patient's needs.

Over one billion people globally, or 15% of the population, live with some sort of disability, and that number is expected to rise as people live longer. In 2018, Google introduced a set of accessibility apps called Live Transcribe and Sound Amplifier, aimed at the 466 million people in the world who are deaf or hard of hearing. Those apps leveraged Google's speech-to-text technology to transcribe conversations in real time, allowing individuals to see the text of what was being said.

At the Google I/O conference held in May 2019, Google expanded its accessibility services. Google CEO Sundar Pichai said, "Fundamental AI research which enables new products for people with disabilities is an important way we drive our mission forward." The company described three new projects: to improve computers' ability to understand impaired speech; to use on-device speech recognition and text-to-speech conversion to help anyone who can't hear or speak hold a phone conversation; and a device that allows activating Google Assistant without speaking by pressing a button. Google also said that it was building out a bigger dataset of voices to train its technology, so that Google Assistant and other voice interfaces can better understand those who have nontypical speech patterns.

Using digital assistants such as Alexa in healthcare can create privacy concerns. Laws such as the Health Insurance Portability and Accountability Act (HIPAA) require that health-care companies and their contractors take steps to keep patient information confidential and prevent tampering.

Amazon announced in April 2019 that it was working with companies such as health insurance provider Cigna, diabetes management company Livongo Health, and major hospitals to develop features for Alexa to help patients while supporting the privacy law. Such applications could do tasks such as schedule urgent-care appointments, track when drugs are shipped, check health-insurance benefits, or speak blood-sugar results.

Innovative health applications will continue to be introduced. For example, the issue of assessing concussion in football has highlighted the need for an immediate and more accurate assessment method to identify brain injuries. Mindsquare and AppTek announced the development of a mobile device that can conduct a cognitive test where speech patterns are analyzed in real time using AppTek's technology. AppTek's speech processing technology captures fluctuations in tone, utterances, and volume of speech. The data collected is then assessed in real time and compared to a previous baseline study. Once this data is compared, medical providers are given the information to help determine if there is a brain injury.

Deep learning is increasingly used in healthcare research. For example, S. Joshua Swamidass, a professor at Washington University, discussed at the Early Drug Discovery Symposium in April 2019 how recent advances in deep learning can model bioactivation pathways with increasing accuracy, giving us deeper understanding of why some drugs become toxic and others do not.

At the end of 2018, CompanionMx launched a mobile mental-health monitoring system called Companion, developed with funding from several government agencies. With Companion, patients who are being treated for depression, bipolar disorders, and other conditions download an app and create audio logs on their smartphones. The patients are asked to regularly talk about how they're feeling, and the information is transmitted to AI software for analysis. Using emotion detection technology developed by Cogito, CompanionMX analyzes patients' voices along with certain behavioral data for changes in mood or behavior. For instance, Companion monitors smartphone activity to see if the patient is withdrawing from contact with others. Caregivers can then reach out if they see indications of a problem.

The growing role of computer intelligence is making healthcare more effective, a key social and economic issue.

Addressing global challenges

In 2015, all 193 member countries of the United Nations ratified the 2030 "Sustainable Development Goals" (SDG), a call to action to "end poverty, protect the planet and ensure that all people enjoy peace and prosperity." The first of 17 goals (Figure 15), for example, is: "By 2030, eradicate extreme poverty for all people everywhere, currently measured as people living on less than $1.25 a day."

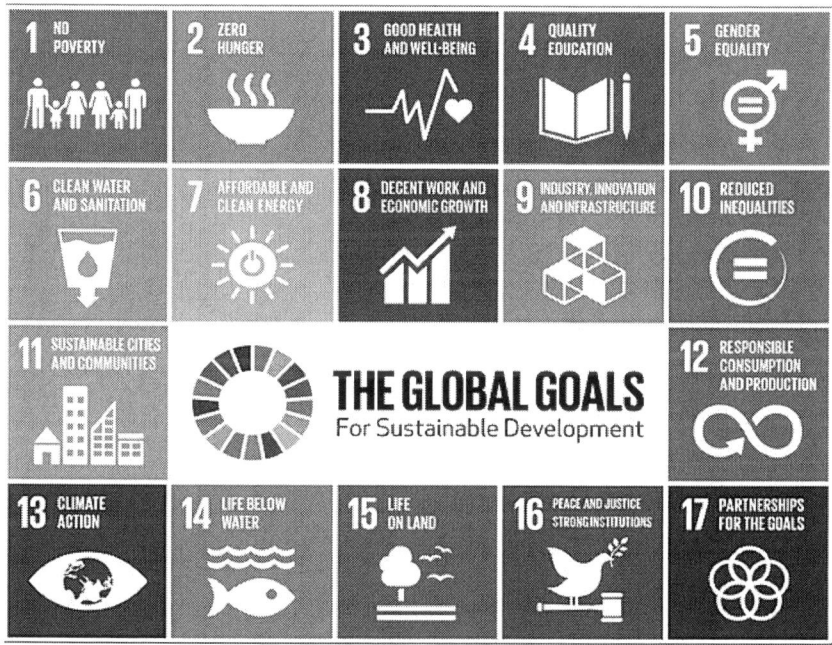

Figure 15: UN Goals (Source: United Nations)

The UN emphasized that Science, Technology, and Innovation (STI) will be critical to the pursuit of these targets, particularly through their contribution to increased productivity and thus improved economics. Artificial intelligence and machine learning are expected to be major contributors. A recent study by the McKinsey Global Institute estimated that AI could add around 16% to global output by 2030, about $13 trillion. McKinsey predicted that the resulting annual increase in productivity growth could substantially surpass the impact of earlier technologies that have fundamentally transformed economies and society—including the steam engine, computers, and broadband internet.

An article posted by the United Nations Development Program and written by three experts from McKinsey Global Institute indicated that AI could help in all 17 categories. "Good Health and Well-Being" is a major category that can benefit, as indicated by the previous section. For example, more than 400 million people worldwide afflicted with diabetes could in theory be detected by an AI-enabled wearable device that is said to detect potential early signs of diabetes through heart rate sensor data.

Since mobile phones are widely deployed in developing countries, they could become health advisors, even interacting by voice for illiterate users. The UN article noted that a camera on a mobile phone could potentially help millions of rural dwellers who have no easy access to dermatologists distinguish between a benign skin lesion and melanoma. Along with Good Health, the authors expect the other areas to be most impacted by AI are Peace and Quality Education.

Reading forms the basis of most learning activities in the classroom. Yet, according to UNESCO, 175 million children globally lack even basic literacy skills. And, even in countries with well-established public education, teachers in early grades may struggle in classrooms with widely disparate levels of reading abilities, in some cases because the language of instruction is a second language for the student.

Computer intelligence can help by letting students practice reading independently. For example, Irish company SoapBox Labs announced a partnership with Microsoft in March 2019 where Microsoft will make available in its Azure cloud computing service SoapBox's speech recognition for children's voices. The speech recognition technology can support automated reading and language learning software to rapidly advance a child's literacy skills. A PC or connected device listens as a child reads aloud, assessing pronunciation and responding appropriately. The companies plan a pilot project in Ireland.

Conversational technology is already being used internationally, helping residents with government and charity services:

- The *Medical Concierge Group, Uganda*, has a Facebook Messenger chatbot that provides free triage and care advice for health symptoms.
- An AI chatbot application launched by the *Dubai Electricity & Water Authority* (DEWA), "Rammas," speaks English and Arabic and can take requests such as paying utility bills. It is available on the DEWA website, IOS and Android phones, and Facebook, using Google natural language processing technology.
- A chatbot on the web site of the *Government of Maharashtra, India*, provides 1,400 services managed by the state government. The Right to Services Act of 2015 mandates that citizens should be able to access information regarding public services through digital platforms. Devendra Fadnavism, Chief Minister of Maharashtra, said, "Technology is the only way we can scale governance and fulfill the aspirations of our young population."
- A Facebook messenger chatbot, Gov.sg, launched by the *Ministry of Communications and Information (MCI) of Singapore* helps locals and visitors to more easily locate information about the government's agencies, news, press releases, workforce, and policies. In particular, it can identify and track the status of complaints regarding lapses in public services.

Confronting issues created by computer intelligence

The increasing role of computer intelligence in society is driven by its benefits. But that same trend creates problems, some obvious and some controversial. These concerns have become a major societal issue.

Too much "screen time"

Individuals spend increasing amounts of time with their "screens"—PCs, smartphones, television, game consoles, etc.—and with the applications they deliver, especially social media. Some experts are concerned that screen time is reducing face-to-face social interactions and that too much screen time is unhealthy.

Historical alternatives to face-to-face communication have also led to warnings. Using writing to preserve and distribute human thoughts was criticized by Socrates, who died in 399 BC. He famously warned that writing would "create forgetfulness in the learners' souls, because they will not use their memories."

When the printing press gave us wide access to the ideas and stories of others, both for education and entertainment, warnings were sounded that individuals were being overwhelmed by data. A respected Swiss scientist, Conrad Gessner, wrote a book in the mid-1500s stating that the overabundance of information generated by the printing press was both "confusing and harmful."

Jumping ahead to the 20th century, radio and TV generated concern that children wouldn't do their homework. Media historian Ellen Wartella noted, "Opponents voiced concerns about how television might hurt radio, conversation, reading, and the patterns of family living and result in the further vulgarization of American culture."

New technologies have long generated concerns when introduced that seem largely overstated in perspective. Or perhaps the concerns were correct, and simply created a new societal baseline.

Screen time today can involve interacting with computers directly, e.g., playing games with them or surfing the Web—activities that don't involve any direct contact with others. Screen time can, however, be an interaction with other humans with a screen as an intermediary through social media or digital communications.

Social media can be broadly defined as websites and applications that enable users to create and share content or to participate in social networking.

The use of social media is a major trend that can include email and smartphone texting, as well as applications such as Facebook and Twitter.

Facebook and Twitter are examples of communication that is relatively passive and not intended for specific contacts; that is, one creates a post for others to read at their convenience if interested. Other social media, such as email and texting, are direct contacts with specific individuals, and can make the recipient feel that a response, even if not immediate, is required. Dealing with social media can seem like a duty and be very time-consuming.

Tristan Harris is the director and a co-founder of the Center for Humane Technology and previously worked as a design ethicist at Google. Harris has been warning about the addictive nature of technology for many years. In South Korea, the government even pays for social media addiction therapy. Harris notes that most technology is designed to keep users involved; after all, that is the basis of the success of many products and social services. He has said, "Technology is holding the pen of history right now. Every major election, and the culture of a new generation, is being written by who? Are they waking up and saying to themselves: I want to create a culture where we take pictures of ourselves all day?"

At a conference in April 2019, Harris gave an example of abuses of social media. He quoted a former Google engineer, who works at his Center, saying that YouTube, part of Google, automatically recommended videos by Alex Jones, an American radio show host and far-right conspiracy theorist, to users 15 *billion* times. Jones, for example, has claimed on videos that the Sandy Hook Elementary School mass shooting in December 2012—where one individual shot and killed 20 children between six and seven years old and six adult staff members—was "completely fake" initially and later that "no one died," presumably trying to minimize it because the tragedy led to a call for gun control laws.

Marc Benioff, co-CEO of Salesforce.com, said in 2018 that social media should be regulated like tobacco. He asked Tristan Harris of the Center for Humane Technology to speak to his 40,000-person workforce in February 2019 "because this is a call to arms, and everyone needs to hear him now." Harris has called on the industry to responsibly examine the effect of their technology on the human brain and behavior. He believes technology can be re-focused to strengthen society instead of causing divisions and making distraction an impact of technology.

Aza Raskin, co-founder of the Center for Humane Technology with Harris, is another critic focusing on technology tending to be addictive. He has said that social media is designed to capitalize on teen insecurities, driving them to keep checking their smartphones to avoid missing out. A statement by the Center encouraged "technology creators to approach innovation to protect a deeper understanding of our basic human nature and focus on benefitting rather than 'downgrading' humanity."

Facebook has made some changes to get people out from behind their computer screens and meeting up in person. One such product announced in April 2019, called Secret Crush, gives Facebook users in some countries, as a part of Facebook's Dating service, a way to indicate which of their Facebook friends they're romantically interested in and get notified if the feeling is mutual, with neither's identity revealed unless both state an interest in the other. Facebook has also revamped its Events tab to make it easier to find nearby events. Of course, both enhancements require more use of Facebook.

Mark Carrier, in his book *From Smartphones to Social Media* on how technology affects our brains and behavior, notes that there is very little scientific evidence of negative effects on sociality, noting, for example that, one-third of all romances in the US start online. Carrier also notes that it is hard to prove the common claim that playing violent games translates to real-life behavior. But he says that there is "credible scientific evidence to support connections between social media use and negative emotions, and connections between social media use and poor academic performance."

One difficulty in quantifying impacts of digital device use is the difficulty of finding valid data. It is hard to measure the level of digital device use and the resulting outcome for enough individuals to establish statistically valid conclusions.

Research showing a negative impact includes a 2018 research paper by Melissa G. Hunt, Rachel Marx, Courtney Lipson, and Jordyn Young at the University of Pennsylvania, which examined the impact of overuse of social media and the "fear of missing out" on loneliness and depression.

After a week of baseline monitoring, 143 undergraduates at the University of Pennsylvania were randomly assigned to either a group where Facebook, Instagram, and Snapchat use was limited to 10 minutes per platform per day, or to a group that used social media as usual for three weeks (recording their use).

The limited use group showed significant reductions in loneliness and depression over three weeks compared to the control group. Both groups, however, showed significant decreases in anxiety and fear of missing out over the baseline, suggesting a benefit of self-monitoring even when use wasn't limited.

Whatever the psychological effect of dealing with social media, it can certainly waste time dealing with unwanted issues. Spam emails or marketing calls to smartphones can take more time in examining them and deleting them than we want to spend. Even to "unsubscribe" takes time (when such an option is even offered), and one wonders how often the request is honored or simply results in your email address being sold to another spammer. And "phishing" emails that impersonate a company you might deal with in order to get your password or other data can force you to waste time going to the company web site directly to check if there is a problem, even if you don't make the mistake of clicking on the link in the email or downloading an attachment.

If you have been frustrated by spam phone calls, you can partly blame automation. Computers can make the calls and transfer the ones that show interest to agents. For example, one machine in China costs only about $450 and can make 5,000 calls a day.

China's Alibaba showcased a solution that most of us would love. They programmed an automated system, a bot named Husky, to answer calls and engage the telemarketer in conversation, imitating a human and wasting *their* time. Among other things, the bot keeps reassuring the telemarketer, "I'm interested."

Looking at history, many of these concerns seem overstated, typical over-reactions to new means of communication. It's not common in the current era to worry about all the books that have been published that one hasn't read; and we don't typically worry that we spend too much time reading. Modern resources such as web sites and email invitations to discussions or talks can encourage getting together face-to-face. Perhaps, over time, individuals will become more discerning and companies will provide better tools to help us focus our attention on what we want to know. We can hope society is better at adapting to change than we fear. On the other hand, CI has made screens a major source of news and opinions, with some negative results.

Disinformation and objectionable content

Early in the life of the Internet, there was great hope that the new technology would democratize sources of information and ideas, with positive results. One result was indeed the use of the medium to organize protests in authoritarian countries, but soon the authorities began using that vehicle to identify and punish critical voices and to overwhelm individual voices with government propaganda. The battle was one-sided, given the resources of a government versus individuals.

Nuala O'Connor, CEO of the Center for Democracy and Technology and the former chief privacy officer in the US Department of Homeland Security, was interviewed by the *Wall Street Journal* in November 2018. She summarized a basic issue of the evolution of the Internet succinctly:

> Its greatest contribution is also its greatest threat. The greatest thing the internet has done is to allow for the elevation of the individual voice: the dissident, the stay-at-home mom, whichever person who wasn't formerly heard in the public square. Yet because everything is now on the same playing field, hate speech is on the same level in your daily life. As industrial companies had a duty of care to clean up and to not harm the environment, what is the duty of care that internet companies have to not pollute the informational or social environments of the communities they're serving?

An example of the problem was highlighted in an Oxford University study published in May 2019 that analyzed junk news during the EU parliamentary elections. They carefully defined junk news and found that, for news in the English language, junk news was four times more likely to be shared, "liked," or commented upon than news from reliable sources.

The terms "junk news" and "fake news" have historically been used interchangeably to describe news that could be verified as untrue. President Trump changed the meaning of "fake news" when he used it to describe news of which he simply didn't approve, some of which could be objectively proven true. Singer and Brooking's book *Like War: The Weaponization of Social Media* characterized the change in the meaning of "fake news": "even the term used to describe untruths went from an objective measure of accuracy to a subjective statement of opinion."

A survey by analytics firm UM in May 2019 indicated that 46% of internet users worldwide believe most of the news they see online is "fake," rising to 54% in the UK. Just 8% of internet users globally believe that three-quarters or more of the information they get from social media is "true." This book will use the term "junk news" for news that actually has no basis in fact, usually presented to intentionally mislead the reader.

Junk news can be used to advance specific issues, e.g., to promote or attack a particular politician or political party. But much of it is motivated by financial gain. A sensational headline that draws a lot of traffic to a web site, for example, can also draw ads, generating revenue for that web site from automated systems because of that traffic.

Jestin Coler is an example of a business publishing junk news designed to draw readers to many web sites. At one point, Coler had about 25 web sites. Advertising on the web sites created revenue for Coler.

One of Coler's most popular items told the false story of an FBI agent and his wife who, amid an investigation of Hillary Clinton, had died in a suspicious murder-suicide, claiming the news came from a real-sounding but fake newspaper, the *Denver Guardian*. In a ten-day period, 1.6 million readers were drawn to the site that had posted the story. On Facebook, the sensational headline would be glimpsed at least 15 million times.

A particularly strange case that showed the power of relentless junk news was the "Pizzagate" claims spread by Twitter (#pizzagate), promoted by right-wing activists (including Jack Posobiec) once it surfaced in a junk-news article. Arising in the final days of the 2016 US election, the hoax claimed

Hillary Clinton and her aides were involved in satanic worship and under-age sex trafficking at a particular DC-area pizza parlor, Comet Ping Pong. Perhaps adding the specific location was intended to make the posting seem more like real news. There was no connection to reality.

Edgar Welch was one recipient of the news. On December 4, 2016, he burst into the pizza place with an AR-15 assault rifle, intending to rescue the underage victims. When all he found was terrified people eating pizza and cooks massaging dough, he confusedly surrendered to police. Welch pleaded guilty in March 2017 to assault and a federal firearms charges and was sentenced to four years in prison.

Polls after the election found that nearly half of Trump voters believed that the Clinton campaign had participated in pedophilia, human trafficking, and satanic ritual abuse. Posobiec, who originally spread the story through a tweet, tweeted more junk to defend himself: "Nothing to suggest man w/ gun at Comet Ping Pong had anything to do with #pizzagate."

As noted, the motivation to create junk news is often not ideological, but simply to make money from ads. Advertisers don't want their ads placed near controversial content, but many sites are attracting ads to a web page from automated systems that place ads based on keywords on the page. In May 2019, White Ops and the Association of National Advertisers estimated that $6.5 billion was lost to such ad fraud in 2017 and that ad fraud in 2019 would cost $5.8 billion. Those numbers translate into revenue for junk-news sites.

Social media and information sources such as Facebook and YouTube (part of Google) have come under criticism for not doing enough to prevent or remove postings with objectionable content or misinformation. One person's "objectionable content" may be another's "news," so the distinction isn't necessarily easy, but some content is clearly objectionable. The issue of freedom of speech comes into play when companies decide what is objectionable, so that making decisions on such content is politically sensitive as well as difficult.

An example of content that was posted against the public interest is live video coverage of the Christchurch mosque shootings, two consecutive attacks at mosques in Christchurch, New Zealand, on March 15, 2019. The Christchurch killer wanted his massacre publicized and live-streamed it on Facebook. Parts soon appeared on YouTube, showing many different segments of the attack, published by many separate individuals who viewed the original Facebook video posted by the killer. Others shared links to the videos, raised their visibility, and created viral growth in viewing.

Many such mass killings are created by individuals who most likely want publicity, even publicity for what is essentially a "suicide by cop." Getting that publicity amplified through social media can incite others with a similar mindset. While such attacks are clearly valid news coverage, minimizing identification of the attacker and not showing the violence itself—in order not to provide an incentive to other deranged individuals—would appear to be in the public interest.

YouTube didn't want to provide the gory video of the Christchurch massacre and didn't want to provide the killer with the publicity he desired. YouTube employees found various versions of the video and used it to train machine learning to find similar cases of the video. Initially, YouTube had thousands of employees reviewing videos that were likely to be from the Christchurch rampage surfaced by the machine learning, but they couldn't keep up with continued new postings. The company finally decided to simply block all candidates found by the machine learning software. This particular episode is typical of both the difficulty in preventing clearly objectionable content from being posted and the need for automated computer intelligence to at least reduce its impact.

Facebook responded to that incident in May 2019 by announcing new restrictions on who can use Facebook Live. Users who have previously violated Facebook rules by posting objectionable live content would lose their live privileges for a period of time. The incident led to Facebook, Twitter, Microsoft, Google and Amazon signing up for the "Christchurch Call" in May 2019 to address the spread of extremist content. The initiative's web site summarized:

> The Christchurch Call is a commitment by Governments and tech companies to eliminate terrorist and violent extremist content online. It rests on the conviction that a free, open and secure internet offers extraordinary benefits to society. Respect for freedom of expression is fundamental. However, no one

has the right to create and share terrorist and violent extremist content online.

In June 2019, a statement signed by all members of the Group of 20, including the US, at a summit in Osaka, Japan, demanded that operators of online content-sharing platforms, such as Facebook and Twitter, step up efforts to ensure violent terrorism-related imagery can't be streamed or uploaded. The declaration was proposed by Australia following the Christchurch attack.

Junk news can also be delivered by paid ads. Facebook pledged in March 2019 to eliminate paid ads promoting false claims of the danger of vaccines. Ten weeks after that pledge, an article in the *Wall Street Journal* on May 31, 2019, described many examples of such ads still appearing on both the Facebook platform and Instagram app (Facebook owns Instagram). These included ads from an antivaccination group that claims unethical doctors conspire to hide the harm vaccines do to children. Facebook and Instagram's automated systems recommended similar content to those who view such an ad or searched for information on vaccines. The same issue of the *Journal* reported that the number of measles cases in the US hit its highest level in 25 years by May 2019, according to the Center for Disease Control and Prevention.

In February 2019, pedophiles were found swapping notes in the comments section of children's videos, pointing out parts they liked. The videos themselves were innocent, and YouTube couldn't simply block the videos. YouTube has since disabled comments on most videos that feature children. Quickly finding the many videos posted that "feature children" could only be done by an automated system.

Advances in computer intelligence can be misused to create computer-generated "deepfake" videos, a concern in general, but particularly for the 2020 election. Powerful new AI software has made it easier to create convincing fake videos, making it easier to fabricate someone appearing to say or do something they didn't really say or do. Images of President Obama saying something he didn't have been posted. Individuals have found their faces pasted onto pornographic videos online.

In June 2019, the *Washington Post* described the phenomenon with the headline: *Top AI researchers race to detect 'deepfake' videos: 'We are outgunned.'* The article described (1) the tools available that allow almost anyone to create the fakes; and (2) the difficulty of quickly detecting such fakes before they propagate over social media. Even relatively simple distortions of true videos can cause havoc: A video of House Speaker Nancy Pelosi was simply slowed down to make it seem she was slurring her speech—the video was viewed more than three million times, according to the *Post* story. The article also highlighted a further complication: "The dividing line between a parody protected by the First Amendment and deepfake political propaganda may not always be clear-cut."

The US House Intelligence Committee held a hearing in May 2019 in which AI experts discussed how such deepfakes could evade detection and leave an enduring psychological impact. Rep. Adam Schiff, who chairs the committee, said at the time, "I don't think we're well prepared at all. And I don't think the public is aware of what's coming."

In an example of how computer intelligence may help, researchers have designed automatic systems that can analyze videos for indications of a fake, including even how a candidate's real-world facial movements, such as the angle they tilt their head when they smile, relate to one another. But such methods have limited effectiveness.

"Forensic" methods can look for inconsistencies in in a video in lighting, shadows, and camera noise. Researchers are said to worry that the technology for creating deepfakes is getting better faster than their detection capability.

Two startups, TruePic and Serelay, are developing technology that stamps videos and photos as they are taken so that modified versions can be detected as such. This doesn't work until the technology is installed, and can't work on images already in existence. The technology can perhaps have an early impact in documenting the video from security cameras.

The major Internet companies said in an announcement that they will address the general issue of false and objectionable content in part by identifying such content, including R&D on how to do so. The companies have said they will share information and tools to help each other identify such content. They also announced the ambitious goal of working collaboratively to provide greater support for relevant research in order to detect and address the root causes of extremism and hate.

Despite good intentions, critics claim that the core problem is that the real goal of the providers of social media is increasing the use of their channels; their software encourages remaining in their world. eMarketer estimated US marketers will spend over $29 billion on programmatic video—video ads that are displayed automatically to people based on characteristics of the web site being visited or preferences of the visitor.

YouTube's algorithm for recommendations and its user interface are engineered to maximize "watch time," and can encourage watching a series of videos on a given subject, controversial or otherwise, once one video on that subject is viewed. A senior executive said in 2017 that recommendations drive 70% of the site's viewing. YouTube has since changed the company's algorithms to include "satisfaction" with the videos in their recommendations to try to reduce negative effects. Facebook has been similarly criticized, particularly after it was identified as a major target of Russian hackers during the 2016 election.

Companies and individuals trying to be "popular" on social media can pay for automated services that simulate individuals and increase the popularity of messages or posts by their actions. Instagram is apparently one company trying to counter such practices with a planned message that "Using Apps to Gain Followers Isn't Allowed," with a plan to compensate in rankings for users apparently benefiting from such apps.

Facebook reportedly considered eliminating political ads completely, but decided against an outright ban. Perhaps the decision reflected the difficult issue of deciding what was a "political ad," with the danger of Facebook's decisions appearing to be biased in some way.

Illustrating the difficulty for companies trying to police their users, Reddit, a news and discussion forum, quarantined a popular pro-Trump user group on its platform in June 2019 after some members threatened violence against both law-enforcement officers and public officials. A spokeswoman for the quarantined group said threats of violence are a violation of its user policies, emphasizing the difficulty of characterizing a full group by individual posts. In the same month, President Trump reiterated his view that

Facebook and other tech giants are biased against him and his followers, illustrating the controversial nature of companies silencing specific sources or postings.

In May 2019, Facebook published its third Community Standards Enforcement Report, a report on its activities to reduce malignant content for the Q4 2018 and Q1 2019. The company reported metrics across nine policies within their Community Standards: (1) adult nudity and sexual activity, (2) bullying and harassment, (3) child nudity and sexual exploitation of children, (4) fake accounts, (5) hate speech, (6) regulated goods (such as drugs), (7) spam, (8) global terrorist propaganda, and (9) violence and graphic content. By examining a sample of content *not banned*, the company estimated that:

- For every 10,000 times people viewed content on Facebook, 11 to 14 views contained content that violated the company's adult nudity and sexual activity policy;
- For every 10,000 times people viewed content on Facebook, 25 views contained content that violated the company's violence and graphic content policy; and
- 5% of monthly active accounts are fake.

Facebook listed the amount of fake accounts it acted on, which includes removing content, applying a warning screen, or disabling accounts. Facebook disabled 1.2 billion accounts in Q4 2018 and 2.19 billion in Q1 2019, citing an increase in bad actors using automated systems that created large volumes of accounts at one time.

Facebook has longstanding policies against illicit drug and firearms sales. In the summer of 2018, the company began trying to use AI to identify content that violates their regulated goods policies. In Q1 2019, Facebook took action on about 900,000 pieces of drug sale content, of which 83.3% were detected by AI. In the same period, Facebook took action on about 670,000 pieces of firearm sales content, of which 69.9% were detected automatically. The company said that, by catching more violating posts proactively, the technology lets their team focus on spotting the next trends in how bad actors try to skirt Facebook's detection.

Facebook also said in May 2019 it will stop paying commissions to employees who sell political ads. The change was driven in part by revelations that Russia purchased spots to influence the 2016 elections.

The company also indicated how much was detected by Facebook's systems before someone reported it; this metric typically reflects how effective AI is in a particular policy area. In six of the policy areas Facebook included in their May 2019 report, they proactively detected over 95% of the content they eventually took action on before someone reported it. For hate speech, Facebook now detects 65% of the content removed before outside reports, up from 24% just over a year ago. In the first quarter of 2019, Facebook took down 4 million hate speech posts. The company indicated it is continuing to invest in technology to expand its abilities to detect this hate content across different languages and regions.

Timothy Cook, Apple's chief executive, rebuked his Silicon Valley peers in a speech to European officials in October 2018, criticizing them for building a "data industrial complex" in which our personal information "is being weaponized against us with military efficiency." He said "rogue actors and even governments" have used our data against us "to deepen divisions, incite violence and even undermine our shared sense of what is true and what is false."

Cook criticized how some unnamed companies deliver personalized news feeds that lead to "confirmation bias," serving up "news" that reinforces our prejudices, rather than providing alternative views. "Your profile is then run through algorithms that can serve up increasingly extreme content, pounding our harmless preferences into hardened convictions," he said. "If green is your favorite color, you may find yourself reading a lot of articles—or watching a lot of videos—about the insidious threat from people who like orange."

Cook didn't mince words: "We shouldn't sugarcoat the consequences. This is surveillance. And these stockpiles of personal data serve only to enrich the companies that collect them."

Part of the difficulty of controlling poor or objectionable content is that "clickbait"—sensational headlines—is effective. A headline that says, "You won't believe what Pelosi said about vaccination," will probably gain more clicks than one that says, "Is vaccination safe?"

In May 2019, Facebook made changes in its algorithm for promoting pages to reduce the effect of clickbait. Facebook announced it has updated the News Feed ranking algorithm to incorporate data from surveys about who you say are your closest friends and which links you find most worthwhile. The hope is that the change will give preference to pages that make people feel satisfied with the choice.

The Google News Initiative (GNI) was formed in March 2018 to help news organizations adapt to the Internet era. Philipp Schindler, Google's chief business officer, described GNI as deepening Google's commitment to helping the news industry cope with challenges to their business models from digital transformation. It provides funding for some initiatives in the area, and guidance on tools to adapt to a new era in news delivery. In launching GNI, Google indicated that one major focus will be on combating the spread of online misinformation, especially during breaking news situations. On the technology front, Google said it is working to improve the tools to separate content from authoritative sources from content by purveyors of misinformation and inaccurate content.

The company is taking a similar approach to content on YouTube, including highlighting content from verified sources in a separate "Recommended" list. Google said it will also work on empowering news organizations through technological innovations such as machine learning and natural language processing tools.

Perhaps the strongest motivator for companies that derive their revenues from advertising to address these issues would be a revolt of the advertisers, some of whom have found their ads being placed through automatic systems next to objectionable content they don't want to be associated with. Marc Pritchard, chief brand officer of Procter & Gamble (P&G), a major advertiser with annual revenue of $67 billion, spoke at an Association of National Advertisers conference in April 2019. He said that trying to retrofit platforms designed for social communication for advertising wasn't working. He said, "Rather than calling for endless retrofitting and clean-up...it's time to invest our brainpower into an ecosystem that builds in quality, civility, transparency, privacy and control from the very start." He added that P&G will only buy media from places where content quality is "known, controlled, and consistent with its values...It's not acceptable to have brands showing up where opioids are being offered, illegal drugs are promoted, abhorrent behavior is present, or violence is seen."

Advertisers can drive some reform. But the best solution would be for individuals to consider the source. If one sees a sensational headline, rather than just clicking on it, one can go directly to a source known for quality journalistic standards to see if the news referred to in the headline is there, perhaps with a more modest presentation. Before the "democratization" of the World Wide Web and social media, most news sources had standards for verification of news items, and news was filtered by editorial oversight and a desire to maintain a reputation for reliability. If something was an opinion, it was typically labelled an "editorial" or "opinion."

Unfortunately, some news sources have become politicized to the extent that their view of stories is considered by many to have a specific political or philosophical bias. Perhaps an independent non-profit organization could offer news sources certification with a label if the sources labeled articles or videos with standardized labels such as "news," "opinion," "rumor," or "debatable." "Rumors" would be items where the primary news source is credible, but the news organization couldn't find either independent verification or contradictory sources. "Debatable" are items where the source is questionable or there is conflicting evidence. News sources that did not provide those labels for articles would not be certified by the independent organization. The certifying organization could periodically audit news sources to see if the labels displayed by the source were accurate. That independent organization could also provide a channel for individuals to report junk news on certified sites. If advertisers *required* such certification for a site where their ads were displayed, junk news sites might be denied monetary compensation.

In March 2019, Mark Zuckerberg, founder and chief executive of Facebook, wrote an opinion piece in the *Washington Post* discussing approaches to regulations dealing with the issue of reducing misuse of social media and cyberattacks. Zuckerberg recommended the creation of third-party bodies to set standards governing the distribution of harmful content and to measure companies against those standards. "Regulation could set baselines for what's prohibited and require companies to build systems for keeping harmful content to a bare minimum," he said.

Facebook made changes to its handling of political ads, requiring advertisers in many countries to verify their identities before purchasing such ads. It also has a searchable archive that shows who pays for ads, what other ads they ran, and what audiences saw the ads. But Zuckerberg said that deciding what constitutes a political ad isn't always easy. "Our systems would be more effective if regulation created common standards for verifying political actors," he said. On standards for the ads themselves, he said, "We believe legislation should be updated to reflect the reality of the threats and set standards for the whole industry."

Zuckerberg also indicated that controls are necessary when information moves between applications, e.g., when people use Facebook to sign into another service or site. He said this also needs common standards. Facebook supports a standard data transfer format and the open-source Data Transfer Project (DTP). DTP is a collaboration of organizations (including Facebook, Google, and Twitter) committed to building a common framework with open-source code that can connect any two online service providers, enabling a seamless, direct, user-initiated portability of data between the platforms.

Difficulties in defining "harmful" means governments will develop different standards. The result could be a web that looks different depending on your location, despite its foundation as a worldwide standard. For example, at this writing, the *Chicago Tribune*'s and *Los Angeles Times*' websites don't comply with the EU's General Data Protection Regulation on privacy, so there's no access to those web sites from Europe.

The best we can do, perhaps, is show alternative points of view and let the consumer of the information come to their own conclusions. Unfortunately, the way we consume information today often leads to the aforementioned "confirmation bias"—automated systems present links that support previous clicks and reflect our point of view, and that reinforcement makes us all the surer that our bias is correct.

Hacking

Computer intelligence has provided us with services we want, but the increasing complexity and power of such services has led to vulnerabilities. Hacking—breaking into government, company, and individual computer systems through a flaw in the software or exploiting individual carelessness— is an increasing problem. Hackers can attack individual accounts for criminal activities, such as stealing personal and financial information. Ransomware can disable a company's computer operations unless a ransom is paid.

In one particularly bad case, a Chinese national and an unnamed co-defendant were indicted by the Justice Department in May 2019 on computer hacking charges related to breaching large US businesses. The indictment included the 2015 theft of data from health insurer Anthem Inc., the US's second-biggest health insurer. In that case, hackers broke into a database containing personal information for about 80 million of Anthem's customers and employees, including data like social security numbers, addresses, and employment information.

Several individuals were accused in a four-count indictment of working for what prosecutors described as "an extremely sophisticated hacking group operating in China." In addition to Anthem, the hackers are accused of breaching at least three other unnamed US businesses. That indictment didn't claim the hack was backed by the Chinese government.

Some very large companies, which should have the resources to defend their data, have admitted deep penetration of information that affects the financial security of their customers. For example, in November 2018, Marriott announced that 500 million accounts had been hacked, the second-largest data compromise behind the hack of Yahoo in 2013 that exposed three billion accounts.

In September 2018, Facebook announced that due to a vulnerability in its software, nearly 50 million accounts were hacked. The hack allowed an attacker to steal access tokens that would provide entry to people's personal accounts. In addition to those accounts, Facebook reset the accounts of another 40 million users as a "precautionary step."

"We face constant attacks from people who want to take over accounts or steal information around the world," CEO Mark Zuckerberg wrote at the time. "While I'm glad we found this, fixed the vulnerability, and secured the accounts that may be at risk, the reality is we need to continue developing new tools to prevent this from happening in the first place."

No less than the US National Security Agency has been hacked. A group known as the Shadow Brokers in August 2016 claimed to have gotten into the NSA systems and downloaded NSA's spy tools. The group provided examples and have since sold the spying tools to whoever will pay for them. In March 2017, WikiLeaks published 8,761 documents allegedly stolen from the CIA that contained extensive documentation of alleged spying operations and hacking tools.

In another example, the city of Baltimore's computer system was hacked in May 2019, preventing the use of many city services for weeks. Among other impacts, it was difficult to close purchases of property because the city's database of liens on specific properties could not be accessed. The motive was ransom; the attackers demanded money to restore the computers. The city did not pay the ransom, noting that, in addition to not wanting to encourage such attacks, that the hackers could leave the software in place to re-activate at any time. In July 2019, Baltimore was still struggling to recover, and estimated that recovery costs would be at least $18.2 million—a combination of lost or delayed revenue and direct costs to restore systems.

The *Wall Street Journal* reported on July 18, 2019, that Microsoft found through its AccountGuard detection service that suspected nation-state hackers attacked political campaigns 781 times. The majority of attacks were reportedly by Russia, Iran, and North Korea. China was said to be part of the attacks, but on a lesser scale. Other attacks by these actors were against business and personal accounts, almost 10,000 customers of Microsoft's AccountGuard service.

Two hospitals in Ohio and West Virginia were forced to turn away emergency patients in November 2018 after their computer systems were crippled in a ransomware attack. The hospitals could not process incoming emergency patients, forcing them to divert those requiring medical treatment to other local hospitals. These attacks can threaten lives.

In May 2017, a strain of ransomware called WannaCry attacked Windows-based systems around the world with targets that included public utilities and large corporations. The ransomware temporarily crippled National Health Service hospitals and facilities in the United Kingdom with some health consequences. The WannaCry cyberattack was stopped within a few days of its discovery with emergency patches released by Microsoft. The attack was estimated to have affected more than 200,000 computers across 150 countries, with total damages ranging from hundreds of millions to billions of dollars. In December 2017, the United States, United Kingdom, and Australia formally asserted that North Korea was behind the attack.

In May 2019, security firm Armison reported that WannaCry continues effectively unabated, with at least 3,500 successful attacks per hour globally. The company's research estimated that 145,000 devices worldwide continue to be infected, noting that "a single WannaCry infected device can be used by hackers to breach your entire network." A primary reason WannaCry persists is an abundance of unpatched older Windows versions in the healthcare, manufacturing, and retail sectors. As an indication of how hard it is to avoid such vulnerabilities, Microsoft warned in May 2019 that it had patched a Windows vulnerability that would allow an attack similar to the WannaCry attack, encouraging users to upgrade so that they couldn't be hacked.

The Privacy Rights Clearinghouse and Department of Health and Human Services cited 148 hacks of healthcare organizations in 2018, leading to 6.9 million individual records exposed. The *Wall Street Journal* reported in May 2019 that hospitals were pressing device makers to improve security and disclose safety features in light of the attacks.

Another vulnerable system is Smart TVs. At a security conference in August 2019, security researcher Pedro Cabrera showed how modern TVs—and particularly Smart TVs that use the internet-connected HbbTV standard implemented in much of Europe other parts of the world—remain vulnerable to hackers. He even illustrated how a drone flying over a home with such a TV could be hacked wirelessly to display content sent from the drone.

While the ideal solution in cybersecurity is simply to prevent exploitable bugs, experts agree that this is basically impossible for nontrivial code. Risk can be reduced through techniques that address some aspect of the threat:

- *Malware detection:* Known software viruses can be identified by searching for specific code, in essence a "fingerprint." Methods that could identify malware when a fingerprint is not available include reviewing behavior of the protected software for evidence of unacceptable runtime activity typical of malware. Some malware detection is said to employ machine learning to identify bad code on the basis of examples.
- *Use of proven software modules:* Software modules with reusable code for specific tasks can be improved over time by fixing any detected weakness. Reusing, rather than re-inventing, such code, could improve robustness.
- *Runtime software controls:* Software in the system running an application can be used to check for activity that is suspicious. This technique is sometimes called runtime application self-protection (RASP). It relies upon understanding what kinds of activity are likely to be malicious, either by human insight and experience or machine learning.
- *Software review and scanning:* When source code for an application is developed, it is typically reviewed for poor practices or specific vulnerabilities. This is time-consuming and costly when done by individuals, so automated code-scanning tools are used. Most such tools focus on avoiding poor software practices. Good practices can at least improve the quality of the software and thus, hopefully, the ability to avoid vulnerabilities or find vulnerabilities quickly if it is hacked.
- *Software process maturity:* Security experts have suggested that, rather than directly inspecting software for evidence of malware or vulnerabilities, reviewers should examine that software's development process. This depends on the observation that good code has tended to come from well-trained developers working with quality tools in modern, well-organized development environments, while exploitable code comes from sources without these qualities.

Edward Amoroso, the CEO of TAG Cyber and a Distinguished Research Professor in the New York University Tandon School of Engineering's Computer Science Department, suggested that computer intelligence could be a partial solution in a 2018 article:

Deep-learning advances are especially promising for software security. This is because the improved efficiency and massive parallelism that characterize the approach are perfectly suited to the large number of combinations that must be examined in typical software execution. We might hope that deep-learning algorithms would be a superior way to review code for unused execution paths, dead code, logic errors, race conditions, and the like.

AI ethics

Computer intelligence is very powerful, and as it gets increasingly more powerful, companies can potentially use it in ways that violate the ethical standards of society. For example, information can be pieced together from diverse sources to learn more about individuals than they want to be exposed.

Ideally, companies will voluntarily adhere to ethics guidelines when using AI, such as incorporating appropriate human oversight of AI applications. One would think that ethics should guide use of *all* technologies, but the capabilities of AI and the difficulty of understanding how AI makes its decisions has led to particular concern.

The European Union published guidelines for trustworthy AI in April 2019. According to the guidelines, trustworthy AI should be lawful, respecting all applicable laws and regulations; ethical, respecting ethical principles and values; and technically robust while "taking into account its social environment."

The EU guidelines put forward a set of seven key requirements that AI systems should meet in order to be deemed trustworthy:

1. *Human agency and oversight:* Proper oversight mechanisms need to be ensured, which can be achieved by involving humans in the process or putting a human in control.

2. *Technical robustness and safety:* AI systems need to be resilient and secure. They need to be safe, ensuring a fallback plan in case something goes wrong.

3. *Privacy and data governance:* Besides respecting privacy and insuring data protection, there must be policies and procedures

that ensure the quality and integrity of the data and prevent illegitimate access to data.

4. *Transparency:* Humans need to be aware that they are interacting with an AI system, and must be informed of the system's capabilities and limitations.

5. *Diversity, non-discrimination, and fairness:* Unfair bias must be avoided. AI systems should also be accessible to all, regardless of any disability.

6. *Societal and environmental well-being:* AI systems should benefit all human beings, including future generations. Their social and societal impact should be carefully considered.

7. *Accountability:* Mechanisms should be put in place to ensure responsibility and accountability for AI systems and their outcomes, including auditability. Moreover, a route for redress of failures should be ensured.

The broadness of the statements could possibly be criticized. An organization could say they support the goals without actually doing anything specific.

Many of these considerations would seemingly apply to any software. Shouldn't any software be subject to oversight (e.g., privacy issues) or be "robust" and "safe"? Why should AI have a particular obligation to promote societal and environmental well-being any more than other software? The distinction is apparently that the major AI technique of deep learning produces results that can't be as easily examined as standard computer code. If the data has a bias, the deep learning model will reflect it. If that is the core concern, then the issue of "explainability" of a Deep Neural Networks's conclusion in a given case, discussed in the next section, may be a more focused area that can be addressed.

The goal of understanding the implication of a prediction made by computer intelligence could apply to many techniques not considered AI. The Institute of Electrical and Electronics Engineers (IEEE), a key engineering organization since 1963, formed the *IEEE Global Initiative on Ethics of Autonomous and Intelligent Systems (A/IS)*. In July 2019, the group released *Ethically Aligned Design (EAD): A Vision for Prioritizing Human Well-being with Autonomous and Intelligent Systems,*" a 291-page report on A/IS issues created by over five hundred people over three years. The report takes a broader view that applies to any autonomous system—software that takes action without human intervention—although the reference to "intelligent systems" suggests that AI motivated the effort. The report summarized its goals:

> Autonomous and intelligent technical systems are specifically designed to reduce the necessity for human intervention in our day-to-day lives. In so doing, these new systems are also raising concerns about their impact on individuals and societies. Current discussions include advocacy for a positive impact, such as optimization of processes and resource usage, more informed planning and decisions, and recognition of useful patterns in big data. Discussions also include warnings about potential harm to privacy, discrimination, loss of skills, adverse economic impacts, risks to security of critical infrastructure, and possible negative long-term effects on societal well-being... The analyses and recommendations in EAD1e are offered as guidance for consideration by governments, businesses, and the public at large in the advancement of technology for the benefit of humanity.

The ideals of ethics guidelines are admirable, but the devil is indeed in the details. The difficulty in formalizing such guidelines is illustrated by Google's effort in early 2019 to create an ethics board, the Advanced Technology External Advisory Council (ATEAC), composed of members outside Google. It was founded to guide "responsible development of AI" at Google. The eight-member board was to meet four times in 2019 to consider concerns about Google's AI program, including how AI can enable authoritarian states, how AI algorithms can produce differing outcomes, and whether to work on military applications of AI.

Google cancelled the plan within a month or so after its composition because of conflicts over the Council's membership. Thousands of Google employees signed a petition calling for the removal of Heritage Foundation president Kay Coles James from the Council over her comments about trans people and her organization's skepticism regarding climate change. The inclusion of drone company CEO Dyan Gibbens reawakened old divisions in Google over the use of the company's AI for military applications. The dynamics led to the resignation of one Council member and another refusing to resign, despite complaints, while implying other board members had worse problems. Google issued the statement:

> It's become clear that in the current environment, ATEAC can't function as we wanted. So we're ending the council and going back to the drawing board. We'll continue to be responsible in our work on the important issues that AI raises, and will find different ways of getting outside opinions on these topics.

Specific CI issues such as harmful content on web sites are more specific and can be addressed with focused efforts. In April 2019, the UK disclosed in a policy paper that it plans to create a regulator to enforce a new legal obligation for companies including Facebook and Google to take "reasonable and proportionate" action on illegal or potentially harmful content published on their platforms, including child exploitation, false news, terrorist activity, and extreme violence. The regulator would have the power to issue civil fines for failures to do so. The government indicated that it intends to refine the regulations and turn them into law.

"The era of self-regulation for online companies is over," said Jeremy Wright, the UK's digital secretary, in remarks accompanying the proposal rollout. In addition to very large fines, Wright said that the government was looking at holding individual company executives and directors liable.

Google issued a long document on "Perspectives on Issues in AI Governance," partly in response to such actions. The document says:

> To date, self- and co-regulatory approaches informed by current laws and perspectives from companies, academia, and associated technical bodies have been largely successful at curbing inopportune AI use. We believe in the vast majority of instances such approaches will continue to suffice, within the constraints provided by existing governance mechanisms (e.g., sector-specific regulatory bodies).
>
> However, this does not mean that there is no need for action by government. To the contrary, this paper is a call for governments and civil society groups worldwide to make a substantive contribution to the AI governance discussion.

The Google Perspectives document highlights where government has a crucial role to play in clarifying expectations about AI's application on a particular context. The document indicates that these include "explainability standards, approaches to appraising fairness, safety considerations, requirements for human-AI collaboration, and general liability frameworks."

A Google report notes that other technologies have required oversight—for example, research in genetic engineering, nuclear technology, and space exploration. Some, like genetic engineering, were addressed by self-regulatory international guidelines and others by international agreements. Both approaches have been largely successful in these areas. However, there have been important failures in some areas, as would be expected with international agreements/guidelines with weak enforcement mechanisms and the potential for simple deniability of violations. Despite the difficulty of establishing such guidelines, Google warns: "If the world waits too long to establish international governance frameworks, we are likely to end up with a global patchwork that would slow the pace of AI development while also risking a race to the bottom."

Trying to impose vague or even specific ethical standards on AI projects would certainly slow or even cancel some AI projects for companies trying to adhere to those standards. Companies, such as those in some countries less concerned about ethics, would thus have a competitive advantage. Kai-Fu Lee, in his book *AI Superpowers*, highlights the competition between China and the US in this area, and warns of China's advantages in having less regulation and accountability.

China, for example, has an inherent advantage in that privacy concerns are not an issue. The country monitors its citizens for its own purposes, and has no problems collecting large databases to power machine learning. For example, the average Chinese Internet user spends half of his or her time online in WeChat, a Chinese application that has the features of many other social media and messaging platforms familiar to Western users. The Chinese government, however, apparently monitors WeChat, judging from some government prosecutions that were based on what an individual said using the service.

Former Deputy Secretary of Defense Bob Work, speaking at the AFCEA's Artificial Intelligence and Machine Learning Summit in March 2019, said of the DoD's work in AI, "If we're going to succeed against a competitor like China that is all-in in this competition—I mean they are all in, from the top leadership down to the commanders in the field—we're going to have to grasp the inevitability of AI and adapt our own innovation culture and behavior so that AI has a chance to take hold." Work said the DOD needs "small plays" going on departmentwide, "substantial, sustained experimentation using these technologies, widespread applications being applied by the services across all operating domains."

Explainability

Techniques such as deep learning result in models that make predictions based on analyzing data, essentially a statistical approach, where it is difficult to explain how a decision was made. A similar statement about statistics in general is that they can show a *correlation* between factors—simply that they often occur together—without it being true that one *causes* the other. Concern arises when one uses methods that summarize the implications of data to make important decisions, e.g., which potential employees to interview, without being able to explain how that decision was made.

Google has noted in a blog posting that deep learning's lack of explainability isn't unique—humans can have difficulties in explaining a decision based on experience, e.g., "an oncologist may struggle to explain the intuition that leads him or her to believe they fear a patient's cancer has recurred." Google notes that an AI system coming to a similar conclusion can go beyond a doctor asking a patient to trust their experience because *the AI could provide 100 examples of similar cases that led to the empirical decision.*

This simple insight from Google is fundamental, and hasn't received the attention it deserves. Showing actual examples that were similar to the specific data that led to a conclusion provides a strong counterargument to concerns over the explainability of empirical techniques such as deep learning. There are CI methods that could be used to find a number of similar cases to the one an algorithm has labelled—similar cases where the outcome is known. Human intuition and pattern recognition skills are well suited to deciding if the examples are persuasive or appear to be a data error or some sort of anomaly.

Computer intelligence is well-suited to finding such similar cases, since it can search the multi-dimensional space of features defining a pattern for other examples of the pattern in the data set "near" the case of interest. Since the examples that the AI learned from are labelled by outcome, one could see if all the similar cases had the same outcome or if some did not. Using the intuition of a human expert to understand what caused the difference could provide some confidence in the prediction. In the case of a medical image that was classified as showing a cancerous tumor, the results of a follow-up biopsy or later developments for many of the similar cases might be available.

While the similar-case approach to understanding can be used to help understand the AI's decisions in a particular case, it can also be used by computer researchers to detect issues with a specific machine learning model. Issues that could impact the validity of a model include data-labelling errors, use of input variables that shouldn't be included, and over-fitting the model to "outliers" (highly unlikely cases or data errors). Perhaps one ethics guideline for AI use in cases *where an error creates significant risk* should be a panel of experts looking at examples similar to a significant number of prediction cases *prior to mass deployment.* Such examination could help detect systematic errors before the machine learning model is used and would increase confidence in an autonomous system.

Researchers at Google Brain have developed a different approach to explainability called "Testing with Concept Activation Vectors" (TCAV) that allows a user to ask a black box AI how much a specific, high-level concept has played into its decision-making. For example, if a machine-learning system has been trained to identify zebras in images, a person could use TCAV to determine how much weight the system gives to the concept of "stripes" when making a decision. TCAV was originally developed for machine-learning models trained to recognize images, but is said to also work with models trained on text and certain kinds of data visualizations such as EEG waveforms.

A "What-If Tool" developed at Google for TensorFlow, a popular machine learning framework, provides an interactive visual interface for exploring model results without the need for writing any further code. The What-If Tool lets developers change a specific input variable (e.g., gender) to see how changing that variable would affect a specific decision.

Privacy

Applications such as Facebook and Google search have long retained significant information about individuals to target ads. Advances in CI make that data collection more effective. Concern about how that data is being used and protected by Internet companies is becoming a major privacy issue.

The revelation that Cambridge Analytica had harvested the personal data of millions of people's Facebook profiles without their consent, and used it for political purposes, was a major political scandal in early 2018. The scandal has been described as a watershed moment in the public understanding of how personal data can be misused. The news precipitated criticism of Facebook's policies in handling customers' data. Compounded with the extensive misuse of Facebook by Russia to affect the 2016 election, the issue generated calls for tighter regulation of tech companies' use of data in general.

Companies' can also violate privacy in their marketing to proactively contact customers using information about them. The following examples show how CI can be used to target customers:

- Amazon tracks each customer's viewing and purchase history to find products to recommend, resulting in some 35% of sales coming from those recommendations.
- Netflix recommends shows based on each viewer's preferences, demographics, and watch history. Seventy-five percent of what people watch comes from recommendations.
- The TechCrunch chatbot tracks the articles each person reads and delivers new articles based on that history.
- Facebook characterizes its users in order to target ads to those most likely to be interested.

Pew Research in January 2019 surveyed a representative sample of Facebook users about how they had been characterized. For example, about half of Facebook users are assigned a political "affinity" by Facebook. Among those who are assigned a political category by the site, 73% say the platform's categorization of their politics is very or somewhat accurate, while 27% say it describes them not very accurately or not at all accurately.

Facebook privacy practices were investigated by the Federal Trade Commission. The package of penalties for Facebook's past privacy scandals in a mid-2019 settlement includes a record-breaking $5 billion fine and government oversight of its business practices.

At the annual Facebook F8 Conference in April 2019, Mark Zuckerberg, Facebook CEO, emphasized a new emphasis on privacy. "I believe the future is private," he said. "At the end of the day, this isn't just about building some new products, it's a major shift in how we run this company."

Facebook made changes in the priority of news and other posts to deemphasize those posts that were labelled popular simply because users had in some way indicated those posts were more relevant to them. As Facebook explained it, "We've begun surveying people on Facebook to ask them to list the friends they are closest to. We look at the patterns that emerge from these results, some of which include being tagged in the same photos, continuously reacting and commenting on the same posts and checking-in at the same places. We then use these patterns to inform our algorithm." The objective is apparently to make it more difficult for those outside the users' friends and groups to insert unwanted posts. A difficulty with such an approach is that if all the friends share the same views, such selectivity amplifies confirmation bias.

Speaking at the Aspen Ideas Festival in June 2019, Zuckerberg endorsed federal privacy legislation and greater regulation of political advertising. He said that "Regulation and a robust democratic process is the best way to handle some of these issues," but that companies couldn't wait for government action.

Apple has made privacy a marketing feature for its products, creating additional focus on the issue. An Apple ad claimed, for example, "What happens on your iPhone stays on your iPhone." Despite that claim, applications downloaded from the Apple Store at that time did have features that communicated information back to the company providing the app.

But at its developers' conference in May 2019, Apple announced it would enhance privacy in an upcoming version of the iPhone operating system. The company said it would provide a random email address for logging into an app, avoiding an individual having to provide their actual email address. The practice would limit the tracking of data to data gathered *within* the app for that user, since that data could not be associated with outside data labelled with the user's actual email address.

A tool that reduces privacy is "cookies." Cookies are data crumbs left on your computer or smartphone when you use a browser and visit a specific site. That site leaves information in your browser, so that, if you return to the site, it knows what you did in previous visits. This can be used to streamline your experience, but also to trigger targeted marketing, and thus has created privacy concerns. Some sites will ask permission to leave a cookie; others may simply tell you they use cookies, leaving you the option of accepting the cookie or leaving the site.

Google was expected to roll out a dashboard-like function in its Chrome browser that will give internet users more information about what cookies are tracking them and offer options to avoid or erase them. Apple's Safari and Mozilla's Firefox restricted by default most tracking cookies in 2017 and 2018, respectively.

Google announced actions to enhance privacy at a company conference in May 2019. People can now enable "Incognito Mode" in Google Maps and YouTube, so that the places you search and navigate won't be linked to your account. Privacy and security settings have been moved to a more accessible place in a Google account, with the most relevant controls appearing first. People can now choose to have their search data deleted after a certain number of months.

The speech recognition accuracy of digital assistants is enhanced by using voice data collected from customers. An anonymous speech snippet that a user said to Amazon's Alexa or Google Assistant (after waking up the assistant with a keyword like "Alexa" or "Hey Google") may be listened to by contractors and labelled with what was said. Customers' speech provides labelled data for machine learning to process. Google said in a blog in July 2019 that it used language experts globally to listen to only 0.2% of "audio snippets" taken from the Google Assistant to better understand different languages, accents, and dialects. The blog entry said, "This is a critical part of the process of building speech technology, and is necessary to creating products like the Google Assistant."

While some media outlets have tried to make this recording and labeling of commands to a personal assistant a headline issue of privacy violation, the chance that the brief recording of a specific utterance contained sensitive information *and* that that information could somehow be associated with an individual—*and* that the labeler is motivated to misuse this data—seems vanishingly small. A privacy tradeoff is endemic to today's use of human language to interact with digital systems. The technologies are trained on speech and language data, and the use of that data benefits all users to the extent it improves the accuracy and flexibility of those technologies.

The use of home speakers like the Amazon Echo or Google Home that are very visible listeners has perhaps made the privacy issue more obvious. As a technology analyst, this author has repeatedly been asked if such devices are always listening or could be hacked to spy on the user. I sometimes note that a mobile phone has a microphone (and a camera!) and is almost always with us, yet doesn't get much attention as a potential target for privacy invasion.

Amazon in May 2019 added the ability to delete voice records by saying commands such as, "Alexa, delete everything I said today." However, the capability to do so has to be enabled in the Alexa app on a smartphone, which probably means that most people won't bother, and, if they do, often forget to use the command. Since Amazon could provide an option to delete all voice records automatically after a specified period of time, it's apparent that those records are important to Amazon in improving its technology. Since users benefit from technology that can understand and respond to a request more accurately, the issue will continue to be a tradeoff between privacy and benefits.

In May 2019, Microsoft announced new privacy controls for its updated Edge web browser. Users will be able to choose between "Unrestricted," "Balanced," and "Strict" settings, which Microsoft says will allow users to limit how third parties track a user across the web.

The European Union's General Data Protection Regulation (GDPR) applies to any company collecting personal data from a citizen of the EU. It codifies and unifies data privacy laws across all EU member countries. Personal data is defined as any information related to a natural person that can be associated directly or indirectly with that person. It represents one of the clearest efforts by governments to avoid misuse of personal data in an age of computer intelligence.

Enforcement of GDPR went into effect May 25, 2018. In the year since that date, European data protection authorities indicated that almost 90,000 separate data breach notifications were received from organizations attempting to comply with the GDPR by meeting its reporting requirements. About 145,000 complaints and inquiries have been additionally lodged by concerned citizens.

In January 2019, Google was fined 50 million euros by French authorities for collecting personal data from users without providing an adequate level of transparency on how that data would be used to personalize advertisements on the platform. Under the provisions of the GDPR, organizations must get valid consent to use personal data for every specific use of that data—no blanket consents are allowed.

In October 2018, in an interview with the *Irish Times*, Sridhar Ramaswamy, who ran Google's advertising division at the time, indicated his concern about the future of online advertising. "Overall, I think that advertising has had a positive impact," he said. "But it is clear today that there are also a number of concerns about user trust and that is a pretty significant problem. Trust has become a slippery point, a big issue. When it comes to data, people are unsure about how their browsing data is being used. They have become annoyed by experiences of ads that follow them around the internet...It is a big problem and something that the advertising industry needs to think about." Ramaswamy has since left Google.

Smaller companies have also been fined for privacy issues. In March 2019, a Polish data processing company was fined 220,000 euros for searching the internet for publicly available personal data and then using that data to contact over 90,000 individuals for promotional purposes, a violation of the GDPR since the use of that data was not authorized by the individuals. About 12,000 of the contacted individuals complained about the activity.

In December 2018, a Portuguese hospital was fined 400,000 euros for allowing its staff to use bogus accounts to access patient records. The hospital had records of 985 registered doctor profiles while only having 296 actual doctors on staff. While the motive for the violation seemed to be a matter of convenience for staff and not malicious intent, the authorities still ruled that the violation was willful and blatant.

Roslyn Layton, a visiting scholar at the American Enterprise Institute, issued a critical assessment of the GDPR in March 2019. She said the GDPR, by its nature, favors large organizations who possess the resources to navigate the intricacies of such laws and can afford the cost of compliance, reducing the competitiveness of smaller firms that have difficulty with the cost. That criticism would appear to apply to any similar government regulations, not specifically GDPR; however, exempting smaller firms could lead to deliberate violations.

GDPR may not have reassured individuals. In a survey of UK respondents, more than half said they feel no better off since the GDPR took effect. The survey also indicated that GDPR has not created transparency and clarity into how individual's data is actually being used.

Facial recognition is a technology intended to distinguish faces that has aroused particular privacy issues. It is used by many law enforcement agencies to try to identify suspects in a photo or video. It has also been used in authentication of a user for a secured service, such as accessing a bank account or unlocking a phone.

Apple uses facial recognition to help iPhone users identify photos with particular people in them. The software can find other photos in your database with the same person in a photo you are viewing. You can also associate a face with a name. This application can be accurate, because the number of faces it is typically distinguishing is usually small. To the degree that the identification is specific to one user's phone, it wouldn't appear to be a privacy issue.

Facial recognition technology is part of Amazon Web Services, which supports a cloud service called Rekognition. It is said to allow a developer to automatically identify objects, people, text, scenes, and activities, as well as detect inappropriate content. One application Amazon cites is to use facial recognition for authentication to enhance end-user security.

Facial recognition is much less accurate than fingerprints. Faces can change based on the angle they are viewed, make-up, hairdo, facial hair, and the list goes on. Amazon recommends the technology be used as "secondary authentication," with other verification options.

Facial recognition for large numbers of people has apparently been used by some governments to keep tabs on their citizens. Some studies show it is inaccurate for specific categories of people, in particular, people of color. A Georgetown Law Center on Privacy & Technology report offered evidence of facial recognition misuse and manipulation by the New York Police Department.

The San Francisco Board of Supervisors in May 2019 banned the use of facial recognition by local agencies. The ordinance also requires any city agency that wants to buy a surveillance system to bring it before the Board first. The ban was prompted in part by concerns that facial recognition surveillance unfairly targets and profiles certain members of society, since it is often rolled out by police departments first in minority areas.

Another developing aspect of computer intelligence that creates privacy concerns is digital identities. Estonia and Finland are two of many countries that have a nationwide Digital Identity (Digital ID) system. It's a bit like the way the US typically uses a physical ID such as a driver's license as a relatively universal way to prove who you are, but a Digital ID can be used both as a physical identification card like a driver's license or online for almost anything. Residents of Estonia use their digital identities to vote, fill prescriptions, start businesses, and interact with government agencies, for example. Children are given a unique identification number and added to the system from birth. Life events, such as deaths and marriages, are entries in a database.

Advocates of digital identities say they cut billions off the cost of bureaucratic processing and reduce identity fraud. Estonia has said it saves the equivalent of 2% of its entire economic output and saves the workload of more than 1,400 people annually by automating government services through digital identities.

A study published in April 2019 by the McKinsey Global Institute found that developing economies could unlock an average value of 6% of gross domestic product, and 3% could be saved in developed economies, by widely adopting digital identities. The report also found that $1.6 trillion could be saved globally every year by reduced payroll fraud.

Supporters also say the technology can even save lives. A nationwide medical database in Estonia means hospitals and ambulance crews can pull a person's medical history en route to an incident.

The US Social Security System, with a social security number assigned to each individual, provides each individual with a unique ID number, useful in collecting taxes and Medicare, and perhaps a potential form of digital identity. However, the social security number was not designed for the digital age, and is less secure than Digital IDs that use authentication techniques.

Microsoft indicated support for government guidelines in May 2019 when Julie Brill, a former commissioner of the US Federal Trade Commission and Microsoft's deputy general counsel, gave her opinion in a Microsoft blog entry. She discussed privacy laws in the US and how they could work with other countries outside the EU that have introduced new GDPR-inspired privacy laws, including Brazil, China, India, Japan, South Korea, and Thailand. She said,

> Despite the high level of interest in exercising control over personal data from US consumers, the United States has yet to join the EU and other nations around the world in passing national legislation that accounts for how people use technology in their lives today. Now it is time for Congress to take inspiration from the rest of the world and enact federal legislation that extends the privacy protections in GDPR to citizens in the United States.

Both Microsoft and Facebook are in part responding to the potential need to respond to a patchwork of privacy laws, even within the US. For example, the California Consumer Privacy Act (CCPA) will go into effect on January 1, 2020, and will apply to any company doing business in the state. Without a federal law to make privacy practices a national standard, companies will have to abide nationwide with CCPA or have a different version of their services to do business in California.

Over-dependence on computer intelligence

In some cases, humans and automated systems are integrated, working together to accomplish a task. The interaction can cause problems if not properly designed. The Boeing 737-Max crashes suggest a case where the human role in over-riding the automated flight control system may not have been emphasized sufficiently in pilot training. A human may grow to be dependent on an automated system to the degree they don't retain the knowledge necessary to override it even if monitoring it is part of their job. Airlines, for example, were encouraged by the FCC in 2019 to have pilots—who have become accustomed to relying on flying by autopilot—fly manually part of the time, or at least repeat training on simulators, to maintain their skills.

Self-driving and semi-autonomous vehicles are a dramatic example of the potential problem of over-dependence. A Tesla Model 3 sedan crashed into a truck on a Florida highway in March 2019, killing the Tesla driver. The driver had the Autopilot semi-autonomous feature engaged, according to a report from the National Transportation Safety Board. The details were nearly identical to those of the first publicly reported deadly Autopilot crash a few years earlier.

In May 2018, an Uber self-driving SUV that was being tested in Arizona struck and killed a woman as she was crossing the street. After a US federal investigation, it is thought that the car did not stop because the system put in place to carry out emergency stops in dangerous situations was disabled.

The Tesla and Uber cases illustrate a challenge in developing solutions that involve increasing control of a process by computers where the process can endanger human safety. Every fatal accident in a self-driving or semi-autonomous vehicle is likely to be reported widely in the press. When the accidents have similar characteristics, it is fair to suggest that a pattern exists that could reflect an underlying systematic problem.

A balanced view, however, might also consider the possibility that many accidents could be avoided with self-driving and semi-autonomous vehicles that would otherwise occur with an unaided human driver. In the US alone, there are about 40,000 fatal automobile accidents a year and about 4.5 million people seriously injured, according to the National Safety Council. It is impossible to measure how many accidents were *avoided* by automated driving systems, but a balanced view should recognize the tradeoff. After there are more cars with automatic driving features on the road, statistics on the fraction of accidents in such vehicles versus the fraction of accidents in vehicles without such features will provide better insight into the relative value of such technology.

Computer intelligence is everywhere, and our dependence on it is expanding. As the complexity and interconnected nature of software expands, so does the danger of unanticipated consequences.

Part IV:
CI drives the economy

The accelerating capability of CI deeply affects the world economy. David Romer, in his groundbreaking 1990 research paper, "Endogenous Technological Change," said that technological change "lies at the heart of economic growth," a view held by most economists today. He described the core characteristic of technology as the ability to discover something once and use it multiple times:

> [The] most fundamental premise is that instructions for working with raw materials are inherently different from other economic goods. Once the cost of creating a new set of instructions has been incurred, the instructions can be used over and over again at no additional cost. Developing new and better instructions is equivalent to incurring a fixed cost. This property is taken to be the defining characteristic of technology.

Today, many technology "instructions" driving innovation are computer software, where data is the "raw material." Computer Intelligence is arguably the major driving force of technology today.

Productivity and utility

Computer Intelligence has been a major contributor to productivity for decades. Productivity fundamentally describes the *efficiency* of a company or a national economy in terms of how much production is generated by a given amount of resources. One measure is national labor productivity, measured as Gross Domestic Product (GDP) per worker ("GDP per capita")—essentially the full output of the economy in dollars divided by the number of workers producing that output.

Higher productivity can also reduce the cost of products and services since they can be produced with fewer workers, potentially making those products more affordable. Steady productivity improvements may be at least partially responsible for low inflation in the US, just 1.6% for the 12 months ended June 2019, below the 2% that the Federal Reserve considers a target.

Higher productivity can also potentially increase wages, as each worker produces more, making individual workers more valuable. In a classic paper describing this effect, MIT Professor Robert Solow concluded in 1957 that technological progress driving productivity improvements had accounted for 80% of the long-term rise in US per capita income, with increased capital investment accounting for the remaining 20%.

Economists Daron Acemoglu and James Robinson emphasized that improved productivity and the creation of new categories of jobs by technology innovations—at the expense of Joseph Schumpeter's "creative destruction" of other jobs—have moved society forward. In their deeply researched 2012 book, *Why Nations Fail: The Origins of Power, Prosperity, and Poverty*, they argue that, when a country's elites fight technological change to preserve their interests, it leads to the economic failure of nations. The higher productivity from technology advances allows improvements in the quality of life that countries ignore at their peril.

Many applications of computer intelligence can improve efficiency and thus productivity. CI is increasing exponentially, but productivity statistics have been relatively low and stable over the last decade, not seeming to reflect that level of impact. From the first quarter of 2018 to the first quarter of 2019, productivity increased 2.4%, reflecting a 3.9% increase in output driven by only a 1.5% increase in hours worked.

CI could improve productivity by making a worker more productive or automating a worker's job, reducing the number of workers. The next section in this Part discusses why CI advances may *not* in fact reduce the number of workers overall when its full impact is understood. At this point, we'll simply say that CI may not significantly raise productivity by reducing the number of workers producing a given product or service.

CI certainly contributes to productivity improvements, but that's not its major economic contribution. To understand its contribution fully, it is necessary to look at the improvement in *utility* it creates in products and services. A new version of a product can cost the same, but *do more*. If the better product is created by the same number of workers, the impact of the improved product wouldn't show up in productivity statistics. Nevertheless, the buyer of the product or service is getting more for his money—better *utility*.

Classical productivity statistics also don't measure the increase in what products or services *do* for individuals since that often isn't reflected in increased revenue. An increase in what products and services can do for you that isn't reflected in their cost might be called the "utility premium." It's the reason you buy a new smartphone to get a better camera or longer battery life when the phone you have is otherwise fine. When the smartphone software is updated or an app downloaded, you can do more with the device at minimal or no cost.

The utility premium is difficult to measure as a number, but is fundamental to today's economy. It's part of the explanation why the contribution of computer intelligence to the economy isn't fully measured by productivity statistics.

While it may not be easily measurable, understanding the contribution of technology in general and CI in particular to improved *utility* is important to understanding what drives an economy beyond classical productivity.

Computer Intelligence and jobs

While technology advances have always automated parts of jobs or eliminated certain categories completely, concern over the acceleration of this trend has become a major issue. The concern is that Artificial Intelligence will be able to do so many jobs that previously required humans that there just won't be enough jobs for people. If so, AI can dramatically change the economy and perhaps create a permanent underclass, either poor or supported by social safety nets. There is concern that AI can shrink the critical middle class by automating jobs typical in that economic range while not automating lower-paid service jobs. The issue extends beyond AI to the long-term trend of CI increasingly doing more in general.

The subject may become a political issue. Andrew Yang, a candidate for the Democratic nomination for President in 2020, declared at a rally in April 2019: "What we did to the manufacturing workers we are now going to do to the retail workers, the call center workers, the fast-food workers, the truck drivers, and on and on through the economy. This is a crisis."

Erik Brynjolfsson and Andrew McFee, in *The Second Machine Age* in 2016, warned about job loss in a second machine age where machines take over many *thinking* tasks, in contrast to the *manual* tasks technology replaced in the first machine age. Technology is now replacing brainpower instead of muscle power. The book asks what jobs will be left once software has perfected the art of driving cars, understanding speech, and other tasks once considered a human specialty.

As this is written, concerns over jobs disappearing are countered by statistics. The unemployment rate in the US was 3.7% in July 2019, near a 50-year low. The Bureau of Labor Statistics reported that employers added 164,000 nonfarm jobs in July 2019. Employment had grown for more than 100 months in a row, the longest economic expansion on record. Average hourly wages for private-sector workers rose 3.2% from a year earlier in July 2019.

Through the first seven months of 2019, employers added an average of 165,000 jobs per month. The economy created more than 20 million jobs since the recession ended in 2009. The data showed little threat of inflation or other signs of the economy overheating. A survey released in 2018 by Deloitte and the Manufacturing Institute found that about 2.4 million jobs in the manufacturing sector could remain unfilled between 2018 and 2028.

Employment has been relatively strong across much of the developed world. As of mid-2019, two-thirds of the countries of the Organisation for Economic Co-operation and Development (OECD), a group of 36 mostly rich countries, enjoyed record-high employment among 15- to 64-year-olds. In Japan, 77% of this group has a job, up 6% in six years. As of April 2019, the German unemployment rate was 3.2%. And, as of April 2019, the UK unemployment rate was 3.7%. Even in France, Spain, and Italy, where joblessness is still relatively high, working-age employment was close to or exceeded 2005 levels. In 2018, the employment rate among people of working age was the highest ever in Britain, Canada, Germany, Australia, and 22 other OECD countries. This strength is all the more impressive given important societal trends such as more women entering the work force.

The trend holds in the richer countries in Asia. The unemployment rate in China decreased to 3.67% in the first quarter of 2019 from 3.80% in the fourth quarter of 2018. The trend of low unemployment should continue in the long term, since China's workforce is predicted to shrink by 100 million every 15 years starting in 2020, according to the National Committee of Chinese People's Political Consultative Conference.

The unemployment rate in Japan was a remarkable 2.5% in March 2019. India is a partial exception, with the unemployment rate reaching 7.8% among urban youths, a 45-year high.

A survey by Genesys in July 2019 found that most workers are not concerned with technology taking their jobs. Only 4% of US workers said they consistently feel threatened by technology at work, while 75% said they rarely or never feel threatened.

A recent Korn Ferry Institute study concluded a global worker shortage could cause wages to rise over the course of the next decade. The report concluded that, by 2030, organizations across the world will be short more than 85 million workers—more than the current population of Germany. The study found that a 1% workforce shortage translates to a 1% wage premium for workers, and, in order to attract and retain talent, companies could end up spending an additional $2.5 trillion.

A worker doesn't necessarily lose a job because his or her current job is automated, particularly when there is competition for workers. An announcement by Amazon in July 2019 said it planned to spend about $700 million over about six years to retrain a third of its employees as their jobs gave way or were changed by trends like automation and machine learning. The *Wall Street Journal* article reporting the decision said that AT&T, Walmart, JP-Morgan Chase, and Accenture had similar programs.

The strength in the job market has been fairly evident since 2009, despite computers having automated more tasks each year during this period.

Tasks and jobs

Oft-cited research by Carl Frey and Michael Osborne in 2017—typical of the concern over AI and job destruction—suggests the scope of such warnings. Frey and Osborne concluded that 47% of US jobs could be automated through AI. The research looked at 702 occupations in detail. They looked at the portion of each job category that could be automated, and found that 47% of tasks in those jobs could be automated. They then claimed that, if 47% of a job was reduced by automation, that 47% less people would be required in that job category.

Erik Brynjolfsson *et al.* published a paper in mid-2018 with a similar focus—emphasizing that *tasks* rather than *full jobs* will be automated. The team looked at what kind of tasks are most likely to be automated by AI, and applied that to data from the Bureau of Labor Statistics to understand the kind of tasks that typically make up a job. The authors said, "Our findings suggest that a shift is needed in the debate about the effects of AI: away from the common focus on full automation of entire jobs and pervasive occupational replacement toward the redesign of jobs and reengineering of business practices."

The research summarized suggests that, as CI automates a *task* that previously required human skills, it will reduce the time required for a job category containing that task, thus requiring fewer people in that job category—*reducing jobs* overall. If an employee's job is made more efficient by automating a task, the assumption is that employers will reduce the number of employees whose job includes that task.

This, however, is *not* the case *if the time freed up allows other tasks to expand*. CI often *expands existing tasks*. To take a specific case most of us are familiar with, consider the example of working with word processing software rather than a manual typewriter. Some readers may remember turning over handwritten documents to a "typing pool," a job category essentially eliminated by PCs and word processing software.

With word processing, we generally create and type our own documents. The typing pool's jobs are being done by all of us. CI has expanded the part of other jobs that requires creating documents.

Writing documents, at least email, is part of most jobs. It is now much easier to create a document with word processing software than with a manual typewriter—where correcting an error required the slow use of "white-out" before retyping instead of simply backspacing. It might seem that this technology-driven speed-up in the time spent on creating documents would reduce that part of the worker's job.

Does it truly take us less time to create a document using word processing rather than a typewriter, or have we just created higher expectations for the final document? Our word processing software allows more complex formatting. It is easier to include diagrams and pictures, and there is software to help you create those diagrams or find appropriate images. Spreadsheet software—an early CI advance—makes it easier to create and include tables.

The ease of editing encourages more revisions than if we had to retype each revision from scratch. In many cases, documents will be longer when created with a word processor than they would be if handwritten or created with a manual typewriter. Many more documents are created because the process is easier, and the resulting digital documents can be delivered without the expense and delay of printing and mailing them.

Computer intelligence may enable more efficient creation and distribution of documents, but, as described, it also *expanded the size of tasks* involving creating written material. The easier creation of documents also *increased demand* for written reports. In this case, rather than replacing the part of a job that required word processing by automating parts of it, improved technology in most cases made that task *larger*.

Reviewing and responding to email is a particularly good example of a task that once didn't exist. It takes a significant amount of time in almost every job to review emails and respond to them. Today, it is a task most of us face daily—one we may feel compelled to return to many times a day. Many tasks get us into rounds of emails. The end result of this extra effort is probably an improvement in the end result of everyone's work, but it expands a job. Many jobs where there was no need to create documents now have such a task due to email.

Computer intelligence, while automating parts of a job, thus can also *expand the number and size of tasks* in that job. Automating *part* of a job *as that job is today* doesn't mean that other tasks won't *expand* because technology expands it when extra time is available. Automating one task in a job doesn't mean that new tasks won't be *created* in that job category as a result of new technologies. Both factors can prevent the number of jobs in a specific category being eliminated—even if one of the tasks previously part of that job category was reduced or eliminated.

The word processing example is important in that it relates to the impact of computer intelligence on jobs generally. Generally, when a part of a job is automated, it is because of a desire to create a better overall result as much as to automate the task entirely. For example, research shows that customer service representatives enjoy their jobs more when the repetitive and boring parts of the job are automated, for example by automation that uses natural language processing. Automated handling of "frequently asked questions" allows agents to spend more time on each call with customers, solving more difficult problems. The result can be making both customers and agents happier in addition to making the process more efficient, and does not necessarily reduce the number of customer service agents. Instead, they can spend more time with each customer.

In April 2019, just weeks into his new job as head of Google's cloud computing business, Thomas Kurian publicly identified a chief complaint from big business customers: They often didn't have "account managers"—a form of customer service representative—to call. To better compete with Amazon Web Services, Kurian indicated he was increasing the number of agents. Perhaps this was economically feasible in part because many of the simpler connections with customers were automated. In any case, a business that didn't exist in the past—cloud computing services—created the need for more jobs in an old job category.

New job categories are also *created* by technology. The advent of typesetting allowed the production of books and documents in quantity, rather than requiring human "scribes" to re-write handwritten documents to make a copy. All the scribes lost their jobs, but hopefully it is obvious that the jobs of "author" and "publisher," along with all the jobs in the distribution chain for books, were much more numerous. Before the invention of typesetting, it wasn't even obvious that such jobs could exist. We can expect new industries and new jobs to be created by CI, as has been the case with past advances in technology.

The changing nature of jobs and the societal impact

While current economic statistics and task expansion suggest that a short-term problem—if any—is moderate, the longer term may pose a bigger problem. Kai-Fu Lee, author of *AI Superpowers*, is one of the latest to caution that Artificial Intelligence will take over most jobs. Lee said in his book that it is inevitable that AI will eventually put many people out of work. In an interview on CBS's *60 Minutes* in mid-2019, Lee said that, in as soon as 15 years, 40% of the world's jobs could be done by machines.

Carl Benedikt Frey, in his deeply researched 2019 book *The Technology Trap*, pointed out that, historically, while technology developments such as the Industrial Revolution have improved things for most people in the long run, the "short run" can be a lifetime for some workers and create strong resistance by those losing their jobs. He summarized his concerns:

> While there were clearly labor-replacing technologies, most were of the enabling sort. Overall, technology served to make workers more productive and their skills more valuable, allowing them to earn better wages. And even those who lost their jobs to the force of mechanization had a greater abundance of less physically demanding and better-paying jobs to choose from as a consequence. In the age of artificial intelligence...such optimism about technology can no longer be taken for granted.

Frey emphasized the difference between the long-term and short-term impacts of new technology:

> Nineteenth-century defenders of mechanization may have been right in thinking that the feelings of workers rebelling against machines were stronger than their judgment. Yet what does the long run matter to workers who lose their livelihoods, especially if they are unlikely to live long enough to see the benefits of the new technology?

We can hope the "long-term" is shorter in the CI era, providing the classical benefits of technology to the economy fast enough to create new opportunities so that short-term pain is even shorter.

There are fewer farmers because of better farm equipment, crop rotation, and selective breeding of hardier plants and larger farm animals. Yet, those fewer farmers have managed to feed a growing population—a major and necessary long-term benefit. The prediction by Thomas Malthus in his 1798 book *An Essay on the Principle of Population* that exponential population growth and linear growth in food production would lead to famine and death has not been upheld by history.

The farming category indicates the contrary effect of technology creating jobs instead of taking them away. Feeding more people (and people eating more varieties of food) creates jobs in farming despite improved efficiency. Between 2015 and 2020, the agriculture industry is expected to grow by almost 60,000 positions per year, according to 2015 research from Purdue University and the US Department of Agriculture.

CI helps maintain jobs by making it easier to find jobs. *The Economist*, in a May 2019 special report on the job market, credits technological change as one factor in the low unemployment rate by improving the matching of jobs with potential employees. Job websites make it easier for companies and potential employees to find a good match, as opposed to historical posting of job ads in the classified section of newspapers with much less information.

The Economist report said the cost of filling a vacancy fell by 80% in real terms in the decade ending in 2016. A study in 2011 by Peter Kuhn and Hani Mansour found that using the internet to look for a job reduced the time spent unemployed by about a quarter. OECD countries with high unemployment are often those where online job searching is less common. Only 40% of unemployed Italians use the Internet, compared with over 95% of South Koreans.

Many jobs *exist* because it is easier to find someone to do a specialized task, such as planting a tree or replacing a cracked smartphone screen. You can find these specialized workers through Web search. Even the smallest of businesses have at least a simple web site. Those specialized jobs might be less practical without web search being available to find them.

As noted, *task expansion* in current jobs does not require the creation of new job categories. So perhaps we ask the wrong question when we ask whether AI can create *new* jobs to replace the old. If the old jobs require more people because they require more work because of more complex tasks, it is not necessary to create new job categories for there to be a continuing shortage of workers.

But new jobs *are* being created by computer intelligence, ranging from jobs in computer science to online retailing. In online retailing, every order must be delivered, creating delivery and warehouse jobs—jobs that require much less training than computer jobs. In a typical case, Amazon is moving to one-day delivery for Prime members. To help with that goal, the company is incentivizing workers to quit and start delivery businesses, leasing Amazon-branded vans. In May 2019, Amazon said it will cover up to $10,000 in startup costs for employees who are accepted into the program and leave their jobs and will also pay them three months' salary. The Associated Press quoted one former worker who had accepted a similar earlier program to start a delivery business as having 120 employees with a fleet of 50 vans. Walmart announced in May 2019 plans to roll out one-day shipping to 40 of the top US metropolitan areas. Perhaps faster delivery is a utility premium of today's evolving technology—one that creates jobs.

Some occupations that are difficult to automate are expected to grow. These include technology jobs, but also jobs such as teachers and nursing aides. Demand for social and emotional skills such as communication and empathy are likely to grow almost as fast as demand for many advanced technological skills. Service jobs such as such as gardeners and plumbers, who work in widely variable physical environments, are growing, statistics indicate.

The jobs landscape will also change as more people work for themselves as freelancers, either full-time or for incremental income. This includes the growing "gig economy" such as Uber and Lyft drivers. The app-driven ride-sharing services were made possible by the inexorable growth of computer intelligence.

Many gig jobs receive less notice than the ride-sharing services. For example, Amazon uses over a thousand contract workers to label voice requests received through its Alexa digital assistant, using that labelled data to improve its speech recognition and natural language technology. There are even companies that provide data labelling and formatting services supporting machine learning as their core business. Data labelling is one of the most obvious cases of AI creating a new job category.

The early-stage company Directly is an interesting case of the gig economy with an interesting payment model for contract workers. Directly provides a platform for companies to provide technical support for their products, using individuals who are "expert users" of those products. Technical support is a particularly difficult part of customer service; it addresses problems using the company's product that often require complex actions to resolve. The Directly experts, for example, may be long-time users of Microsoft Windows who can help others resolve problems when using the operating system. Some experts help with problems with specific wireless or telecom services or gaming systems such as Xbox. According to Anthony Brydon, Directly CEO, in an interview with this author, the companies engaging Directly can identify long-time and frequent users of their service or product and recruit them as experts by email.

The experts interact with users by text messages or other messaging channels. The interaction is asynchronous, that is, the experts are sent requests, and may take time to respond. They typically work providing answers to inquiries part-time as a secondary job, Brydon indicated. They are paid not by time provided, but by the ability to solve a problem and provide an answer.

Both Directly and the experts profit when those answers can be used to update an automated system, e.g., a natural-language technical support system. The company—*and the expert*—receive a royalty every time the expert's answer is delivered to a customer by the automated system. Thus, an expert can get a continuing income stream without additional time spent answering questions.

Despite providing an "expert-in-the-loop" system, Directly is largely benefiting from the growth of automated solutions and the use of texting on web sites and mobile phones as a growing mechanism for contacting companies for technical support.

The US Bureau of Labor Statistics, however, released a report in May 2018 concluding that the size of the gig economy, or "contingent workforce," has shrunk over the last 13 years and that freelancers represented only 1.3 to 3.8% of all US workers. The BLS results contradict some independent studies that may have included more part-time freelancers. A 2016 report by the McKinsey Global Institute found that 20-30% of the combined workforce of the United States and Europe have engaged in independent work over the past 12 months. Upwork and Freelancers Union found similar results in a 2017 report, built from data acquired through surveys of 6,000 working adults by Edelman Intelligence. They estimated that 36% of the American workforce is freelancing, with the number to pass 50% by 2027.

Nearly half of millennials already say they engage in freelance work in some way, according to a survey by Airtasker in March 2019. The Airtasker survey found that the skills most used in freelance gigs include business (40%), writing (36%), administration (25%), lifestyle (24%), tutoring (18%), and cleaning (12%).

The downside of the gig economy is that many of the jobs don't provide benefits such as health insurance nor cover the costs of operation that a full-time job provides—e.g., auto insurance and maintenance for Uber drivers. While millions of Americans are trying their hand at working for companies like Uber and Instacart (a same-day grocery delivery and pick-up service), it's not clear how many are sticking around or how much these still-unprofitable companies will have to spend to keep them interested. In its IPO prospectus, Uber noted that attrition was near peak levels in the third quarter of 2018.

This author does not believe job destruction by computer intelligence is a major threat, in part because CI can create both tasks and jobs as fast as it can eliminate them. In most cases, CI automates tasks rather than a full job. CI is best at narrow specialized tasks; humans are particularly good at adapting to unexpected variations in a task. That flexibility is necessary for many jobs; to maintain that flexibility, most employers are motivated to expand tasks for a worker when a task is eliminated. McKinsey Global Institute research published in October 2018 found that about 30% of the activities in 60% of all occupations could be automated—but that in only about 5% of occupations are nearly all activities automatable.

This discussion does *not* suggest that no jobs will be eliminated or that no problems will develop. It is likely that millions of workers will likely need to change occupations or at least develop new skills. Unemployment statistics don't tell the whole story. Some discouraged workers may simply stop looking for work. Freelance workers may suffer from a lack of fringe benefits.

Microsoft warned, in a 2018 position paper on the impact of AI, about one area of impact:

> The rapid evolution of work could undermine worker protections and benefits including unemployment insurance, workers' compensation and, in the United States, the Social Security system. To prevent this, the legal frameworks governing employment will need to be modernized to recognize new ways of working, provide adequate worker protections, and maintain the social safety net.

Statistical studies suggest that high unemployment is associated with higher rates of property crime and violent crime. Having a job arguably gives people a sense of purpose, likely improving mental and physical health.

Ka-Fu Lee in *AI Superpowers* argued that, even if there were social safety nets such as a guaranteed minimum income, the lack of work creating self-worth would cause problems such as suicides and drug use. He said, "Lurking beneath this social and economic turmoil will be a psychological struggle."

An aging population

The number of people that cease working through retirement will increase as life expectancy continues to climb. Even if there are enough jobs for people who want to work, in the long run—and the long run isn't too long for some countries like Japan—the proportion of retired people may become too large a portion of the population for younger people to support pensions and government programs like Social Security, even at full employment.

According to a Deloitte study, life expectancy is projected to increase from 73.5 years in 2018 to 74.4 in 2022—bringing the number of people aged over 65 globally to more than 668 million, or 11.6% of the total global population. The effect is expected to be most noticeable in Japan, where the fraction over 65 will likely reach almost 29% by 2022; and in Western Europe it is estimated to reach 22%. Some developing countries, such as Argentina, Thailand, and China, are starting to experience similar situations.

Techniques such as genetic engineering could further extend life by creating cures for diseases like cancer. In the extreme case, it's possible scientists could discover what causes aging, and "treat" it using such techniques. While this obviously has benefits for individuals and families, it could compound the economic problem if people continue to retire at the same age.

Computer intelligence is already helping in two major ways: (1) by allowing part-time work by retirees from the comfort of their residence; and (2) by helping people with disabilities continue to work.

Many jobs may not be particularly demanding if they require continual monitoring of an automated alert system to take over when an alarm indicates that human intervention is required. Systems automated by CI often need such backup for cases where the automation can't handle a particular case. In such jobs, a retired person could read a book or work at a hobby until alerted, perhaps with lower pay reflecting the type of job.

Rather than a job shortage, the opposite problem may develop as worldwide population growth slows. Darrel Bricker and John Ibbitson in their 2019 book *Empty Planet: The Shock of Global Population Decline*, argue that a critical issue for humanity is the decline of birthrates below replacement level and thus a worldwide decline in population. If this prediction is accurate, in the long run, we may need computer intelligence to take over jobs that there aren't people to fill.

Preventing a job crisis

The most likely near-term crisis affecting jobs is an economic recession. While current warnings about risky lending, trade wars, or unbalanced government budgets could potentially be addressed, economic cycles may be unavoidable. Rather than simply riding out a new recession, it is likely, given the publicity over AI taking jobs, that such a recession will be taken as evidence of AI taking jobs—rather than the more accurate explanation that governments resist taking unpopular actions to prevent a recession.

While this author believes that CI will not be the source of job loss, it is certainly worthwhile to consider possible remedies for a decline in jobs, whatever the cause. The "remedies" may be viewed as *preventive* as well as corrective, and might even be useful in *maintaining* a healthy economy.

The Software Society, this author's 2013 book, suggested an "automation tax" that could be used to create incentives for companies with a high degree of automation to maintain jobs. The basic argument is that companies benefiting from increased automation through technology advances are likely to have high productivity, resulting in high revenue per employee. Many companies that leverage computer intelligence have very high profit margins and generate large cash surpluses that don't directly help the overall economy.

An automation tax would be based on the ratio of a company's revenue to the number of employees used to generate that profit—revenue per employee. A high ratio of revenue to the number of employees reflects high productivity, hence let's call it the "productivity ratio." By definition, a company with a high productivity ratio produces more revenue per employee than one with a low productivity ratio. The automation tax would be based on a schedule that taxed profits at a higher rate for companies with a high productivity ratio.

Let's consider a couple of very different companies. Apple had about 132,000 full-time employees as of the end of its 2018 fiscal year. Revenues for its fiscal 2018 were $266 billion, yielding a productivity ratio of $2.2 million per employee. GM had about 173,000 employees in 2018 and $38.4 billion in 2018 revenues, a productivity ratio of $220,000, one-tenth of Apple's. As this comparison suggests, the ratio can differ considerably between companies with different business models.

Many of the companies with high productivity ratios are becoming targets of attacks on their basic business, not because of that fact, but because it is indicative of a business that dominates its business area. The European Union opened an antitrust inquiry into Amazon's business practices with outside sellers. In July 2019, the US Justice Department's Antitrust Division announced it is reviewing "whether and how market-leading online platforms have achieved market power and are engaging in practices that have reduced competition, stifled innovation, or otherwise harmed consumers." The review is considered in particular to target Google, Facebook, Apple, and Amazon. Such companies may support alternatives such as the automation tax that allow them to make a larger contribution to the government's budget in an objective way, instead of being targets for politicians and government agencies with actions that require constant legal and other responses.

The economy can benefit in general from a counterbalance against a perceived advantage of "hiring computers" instead of hiring people. People come with baggage such as employee benefits. They require vacations and sick leave. They can file complaints about unfair treatment or go on strike. An automation tax provides a counterbalance against those perceived disadvantages of human employees. It may be useful in countering that view even without a jobs problem.

Even if the automation tax didn't maintain jobs, it would generate government revenues specifically from companies benefiting most from automation. Those incremental taxes could be used to finance a social safety net if necessary. Data from the Tax Policy Center published in 2019 shows that the share of US taxes paid by corporations versus individuals declined from an average of about 19% in the 1990s and 17% in 2000-2017 to an estimate of about 12% for 2018-2020.

For those who object to higher taxes in principle, note that an automation tax doesn't require a higher overall corporate tax. Other corporate taxes can be reduced to meet any overall tax goal. The automation tax can be viewed as a way to motivate a company to *reduce* its tax liability by hiring or at least retaining people. It's hard for an individual company to sacrifice for the good of all without feeling that competitors may not be so civic-minded. The automation tax is a feedback mechanism that applies to all companies objectively.

There are many details that would have to be addressed in a formal law creating the tax. For example, smaller businesses should be excluded to avoid penalizing an organization that is efficient because a few employees working long hours are the source of its productivity. Further, the hours of freelancers on the payroll should perhaps be included in employee count.

Income inequality and the shrinking middle class

While a lack of jobs may not be an immediate problem, the type of jobs being automated could affect *income distribution*. An increase in *inequality* of incomes can affect social stability and economic health beyond the basic number of jobs available.

In March 2019 polling in the US, Pew Research Center found 73% of those surveyed felt the gap between rich and poor will grow. While only 37% of all currently employed Americans personally see automation as a direct threat to their current occupation, less-educated workers are more worried their jobs they do will be done by robots or computers in the future. The survey found that 47% of those with a high school diploma or less education say this change will occur, compared with 38% of those with some college experience and 27% of those with a bachelor's or advanced degree.

Leaders in the top 1% of income—and particularly the top 0.1%—recognize the danger of rising inequality to the minority they represent. For example, billionaire Ray Dalio, head of the investment firm Bridgewater Associates, posted on LinkedIn in April 2019 a warning that unless the American economic system is reformed "so that the pie is both divided and grown well," the country is in danger of "great conflict and some form of revolution that will hurt most everyone and will shrink the pie."

The 2019 Milken Institute Global Conference in May 2019, a gathering of approximately 5,000 attendees, largely from financial firms, was themed "Driving Shared Prosperity." Much discussion of the theme of the conference reflected the concern of the wealthy attendees in growing inequality.

Alan Schwartz, a managing partner at investment firm Guggenheim Partners, summarized, "It's not whether we should be capitalist or socialist. It's how do we make sure capitalism is working the way it has in the past." Schwartz warned of the danger of "class warfare," noting that salaries and wages as part of the economy are at a postwar low of 40%, leading to a "throw out the rich" mentality that would require some form of income redistribution.

Billionaire philanthropist Michael Milken, founder of the Milken Institute, commented at the conference on the current state of the free enterprise system: "Obviously, it is not working for everyone." Highlighting this concern, the last session of the conference was "Keeping the American Dream Alive."

Lower-wage jobs are expected to expand as the service sector grows. By 2026, it is predicted that America will have more at-home caregivers than secretaries. Low-end work is becoming better paid, in part because of higher minimum wages. In the developed world, wages below two-thirds of the national median are becoming rarer, not more common.

Some experts, however, have a dim view of the jobs being created. David Blanchflower of Dartmouth College published a book in 2019, *Not Working: Where Have All the Good Jobs Gone?* Blanchflower argues that many workers are underemployed or have simply given up trying to find a well-paying job. He notes wage growth has not returned to pre-recession levels despite rosy employment indicators, and general prosperity has not returned since the crash of 2008. He argues that the plight of the underemployed is contributing to widespread despair, a worsening drug epidemic, and the unchecked rise of right-wing populism.

Poverty in the US isn't the desperate condition it has been at times in the past. The Heritage Foundation published in 2011 a controversial report: "Air Conditioning, Cable TV, and an Xbox: What is Poverty in the United States Today." Perhaps the message is that the deep frustration of those at the bottom of the income ladder is because there is little prospect of climbing higher.

A further concern is that the number of jobs that form the critical middle class are declining—the "hollowing-out" of the middle class. Trying to define the middle class by income can lead to diverse conclusions. The US Census Bureau's *2018 Household Income Survey* provided a breakdown of class by income. The data in Figure 16 would put the "middle class" in the US at 45%—almost half—of the population.

The Pew Research Center defines the middle class as between 67% and 200% of the median household income. This categorizes households earning between $41,119 and $122,744 in 2017 as middle-class families, using the US Census Bureau's median income figure of $61,372 from that same year. Pew delves deeper to take account of living costs in specific areas in its estimates, creating different middle-class standards for each metropolitan statistical area. For example, housing costs in San Francisco are very high, and, as a result, what constitutes a middle-class income in San Francisco is much higher than the national median because it is more expensive to maintain the same standard of living as elsewhere.

Household Income Range	Millions of Households	Percent of Total	Description
Less than $20,000	19.7	15%	Below or near poverty level
$20,000 - $44,999	28.7	23%	Low income
$45,000 - $139,999	57.7	45%	Middle class
$140,000 - $149,999	2.6	2%	Upper middle class
$150,000 - $199,999	9.0	7%	High income
$200,000+	9.9	8%	Highest tax brackets
TOTAL	127.5	100%	

Figure 16: US Census Bureau 2018 Household Income Survey

The Organization for Economic Cooperation and Development (OECD) defines the middle class internationally as comprising households with incomes between 75% and 200% of the median income for member countries. That varies widely by country. In the US, a single person would have to earn between $23,400 and $62,400 to be part of that group.

Whatever the definition, the middle class appears to be shrinking and its economic power diminishing in the US and other rich countries, according to a report in 2019 by the OECD. According to the report, in 1985 the aggregate income of the middle class was four times that of the richest group. Three decades later, it has fallen to less than three times. The proportion of the population in OECD member countries who are in the middle class by the OECD definition has fallen over the last 30 years, from 64% to 61%, with larger falls in the US, Israel, Germany, Canada, Finland, and Sweden.

The business forecast for jobs like typists, watch repairers, and postal workers over the next decade is bleak, according to a Bloomberg report in 2017 that cites Labor Department data. Many of the jobs Bloomberg listed, such as telephone operators, mine shuttle car operators, and locomotive firers, are simply becoming obsolete. Others, such as computer operators, data entry keyers, and typists, are succumbing to automation and more user-friendly technology that allows anyone, not just those with specialized skill sets, to perform the tasks.

Carl Benedikt Frey, in his 2019 book, *The Technology Trap*, points out that, historically, the middle class considered itself one group with similar incomes and goals irrespective of educational level. Many middle-class workers without a college degree had semi-skilled jobs that provided them a stable income putting them in that class. Many such jobs, however, are the ones that computer intelligence is increasingly capable of automating. When those jobs are automated, it is more difficult for those without a college degree to find replacement jobs. Statistics show that workers with college degrees have higher incomes than workers without, and that the difference is increasing. This may create an important divergence in the middle class's cohesiveness, a division based on education levels.

The difficulty of finding new jobs may cause workers with less education to drop out of the workforce if they have other options, such as welfare or a spouse who can support the family. If that is the case, low unemployment rates may be hiding some of the full problem.

The shrinking of the middle class not only impacts the well-being of those in the middle class, it affects the aspirations of those with lower-paid jobs. A 2018 World Bank report showed that, in the US, intergenerational mobility (the chance that the next generation will end up in a higher social class than the previous one) was among the lowest in all rich countries. The "American Dream" can be considered a promise that such mobility is the norm. One factor in this lack of mobility is that families with lower incomes can't invest as much time or money in their children as those with higher incomes. In any case, the availability of better-paying jobs to move into is required for upward mobility.

The jobs problem in developing countries is different. Historically, movement from rural to urban areas has been a route into the middle class, and this is certainly the case in China. In countries with developing economies, factory jobs have often been the first jobs in cities for rural workers with few skills. As automation reduces factory jobs, it may reduce this option. Within China, increasing automation is being driven by wages rising and factory jobs moving to developing countries with lower wages. This trend may impact the growth of China's middle class.

It's not completely clear the degree to which the middle class is shrinking. The issue may be more that it is splitting into a middle class separated by its prospects because of educational level. Addressing that issue requires the long-term solution of improving lower levels of education and making higher education more affordable, a subject that has become part of the political debate leading up to the US 2020 election.

Robots

Robots are part of automation, but a part that engages our imagination more than less-visible CI. The term "robot" comes from Czech, from *robota*—"forced labor." The term was coined in K. Čapek's play *R.U.R.* 'Rossum's Universal Robots' (1920). Robots are a form of computer intelligence that challenges human's special abilities to move around and manipulate objects.

In science fiction, robots often have a human-like form and move about on legs or wheels. Today's robots may have such characteristics, but could also be simply digitally controlled arms on a production line that never leave their post. The common thread is that they do produce motion in some way and are controlled by software, allowing their behavior to change without rebuilding the hardware.

Examples are perhaps the best way to illustrate the diversity of today's robots. One of the earliest and most advanced was NASA's Mars Rover (Figure 17). There have been four successful Mars rovers researching the surface of the planet and reporting back to Earth over the last 15 years.

Apple has a robot, Daisy, that takes apart old iPhones to reuse or recycle the parts. It's perhaps more of an automated disassembly line (33 feet long with five arms) than what we usually think of as a robot. It can pull apart 200 iPhones per hour (1.2 million iPhones a year). Conventional recycling of such electronics typically smashes the device to bits, and attempts to remove anything useful it can. The robot, announced in 2018, is part of Apple's Material Recovery Lab in Texas. Apple is sharing Daisy's technology to help advance e-recycling, hoping the project will attract academics, recyclers, and other companies to participate.

Figure 17: One of the NASA Mars Rovers

Apple's Daisy is an example of an industrial robot. Industrial robots can be used for tasks such as painting, welding, assembling printed circuit boards, and product inspection and testing. The preliminary statistics of the World Robotics Report in mid-2019 indicated that a new record high of 384,000 units were shipped globally in 2018, but that was only an increase of one percent compared to the previous year.

PepsiCo's Snackbot is a six-wheeled mobile robot developed with Robby Technologies (Figure 18). It serves PepsiCo snacks and beverages, working at the University of the Pacific in Stockton, California. Students order snacks from the Snackbot app, and Snackbot will deliver it to more than 50 spots across the campus without charging a delivery fee. The bots have a range of 20 miles on a single battery charge, and they can navigate at night, in rain, and up curbs with onboard headlights and all-wheel drive capabilities.

Kiwi Campus also has robots that deliver hot meals to university students. Since the company's start in 2017, Kiwibot has made over 30,000 deliveries with over 150 robots.

Boston Dynamics SpotMini is a four-leg robot (Figure 19). It has an optional arm that can pick up objects. It has been used in applications that include patrolling construction sites and opening doors during hostage situations.

Figure 18: PepsiCo's Snackbot

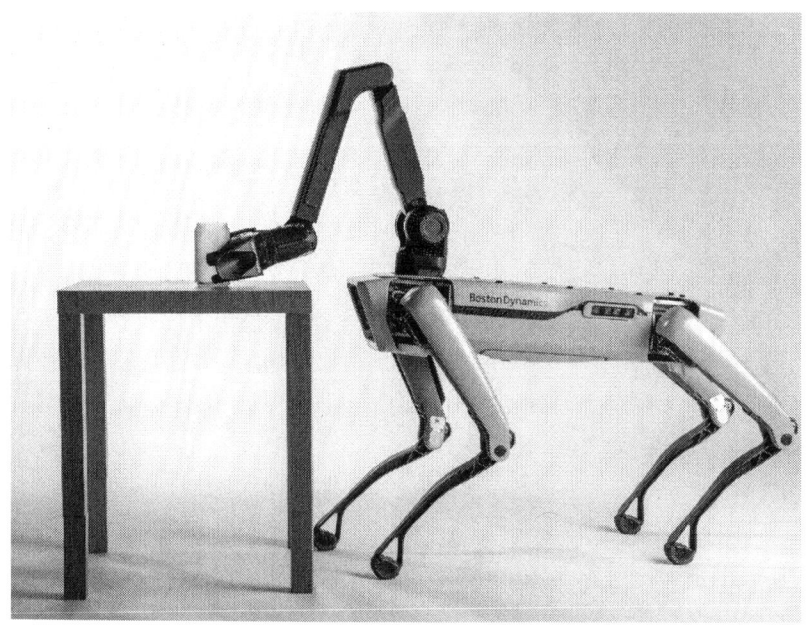

Figure 19: Boston Dynamics' SpotMini

iRobot is the developer of the Roomba automated vacuum cleaner. The company is expanding that expertise into building a robotic lawnmower.

Tréxō Robotics Home is a robot that helps children with disabilities walk. Using wearable robotic technology, the Tréxō Home provides a highly repetitive and physiologically correct gait. The system is designed to ensure safety and consistency, enabling a child to exercise by walking.

Breeze Automation builds *soft* robotics. The company's robotic arms are air-filled fabric structures that are less likely to damage sensitive structures. Early applications are for the Navy and NASA.

Wonder Workshops' low-cost Dash robot (Figure 20) acts as a sidekick, pet, or pal for a child. It is controlled using easy-to-learn code on an iPad. It includes sensors and capabilities that let it move, dance, light up, make sounds, avoid obstacles, and react to voices. Dash has sensors that let it know when it's about to run into something in front or in back of it, microphones that can hear sound, and even infrared sensors that let it see and communicate with other robots.

Figure 20: Wonder Workshop Dash Robot

An interesting special case that may contain a message is Jibo, a "social robot" launched in 2017 by a company of the same name. Jibo was not mobile; it was a foot-tall device typically placed on a table (Figure 21). Its major function was to interact with its owners through a camera, microphone, and speaker. Jibo used facial and voice recognition technology to allow it to learn up to 16 different people, helping the device create personalized experiences with each interaction.

Jibo moved in the sense that its somewhat expressive "face" could turn toward the person it was speaking to. Jibo even had sensors so that it could coo when petted. It could provide information much like general personal assistants, e.g., provide news or commute times, but its uniqueness was an attempt to be social, to create an emotional connection with its owners, doing things such as reading books to children. It could speak proactively, e.g., asking how someone is doing.

Despite the developers having strong credentials, the company failed, shutting down in late 2018. Existing Jibo devices slowly lost functionality as the cloud-based support failed, until it announced its own demise. Mayfield Robotics also failed in 2018 with a similar home robot called Kuri.

The reason for the failures might have been price competition from the inexpensive home speakers like Amazon's Echo—Jibo cost about $900. Another factor, however, might have been concern about privacy, with a device with an always-watching camera and always-listening microphone sending data over the Internet. Amazon's Echo home speaker, without a camera, is very successful, but the company has fielded concerns that it is always recording what it hears.

Amazon has admitted that it uses anonymized data from spoken requests to improve its speech recognition and natural language understanding technology, and has been criticized for doing so by some media, arguing that one might be able to identify the individual from context. It's not clear what would be revealed by a request for the weather or typical things one might say to Alexa, but the concern itself suggests home robots that are overly "social," particularly ones with cameras that are connected to the Internet, might make owners uncomfortable.

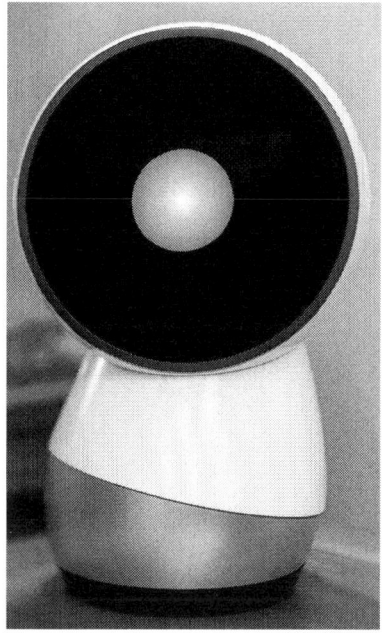

Figure 21: Jibo

Another robotics company that failed is Anki, despite having raised over $200 million in venture capital and claiming it "approached" $100 million in revenue in 2017. The company's first product was essentially a toy. The company's issue may have been more its ambition to be a full robotics company, with the significant continuing investment that was required, rather than a deficiency of its product.

More generally, robots will clearly continue to get continually "intelligent" in the jobs they do, as computer intelligence continues on its upward trajectory. The most effective robots will apply that intelligence to specialized jobs, since specialization allows focus on a narrow task.

Some robots can help with farming. Rather than humans having to drive heavy machinery like tractors, robots can do some tasks. Small Robot Company (SRC) is developing three robots, named Tom, Dick, and Harry. Tom is a crop and soil monitoring robot, capable of checking each plant individually (Figure 22); Dick is a micro-spraying and non-chemical weeding robot; and Harry does precision drilling and planting. The data from Tom is analyzed to direct Dick and Harry.

The most obvious characteristic of these examples is their variety, both in objectives and functionality. Self-driving vehicles and military drones can perhaps also be considered robots. The computer intelligence that makes these devices possible drives their increasing capabilities, but their variety defies a simple description of their impact.

Figure 22: A farming robot that can map
conditions from Small Robot Company

Competition between companies

Beyond the jobs issue, there is some controversy about the large and powerful companies whose business is based on the power of CI. Adam Smith gave the basic argument for free competition and trade in *The Wealth of Nations* in 1776, usually considered the basic description of "capitalism." His basic admonition was to let the market decide, that unfettered markets led to overall efficiency in economics. He argued that the company or country that could attract the most buyers was the best source for a product, and competition would keep prices at their fair level. But even staunch supporters of this basic principle have recognized that this ideal situation requires some regulation and other government involvement to avoid problems like fraud, currency manipulation, monopolistic practices, unfair trade practices, etc.

This balance between unfettered and fair competition is being questioned with regard to some of the largest CI companies, e.g., Google. An economic reality is that some services benefit from scale, and become natural monopolies. Google search, for example, benefits from wide use, learning which web sites people choose when presented with alternatives when using specific search terms. This wide use improves the utility of search results.

Google also has the resources and the data to use machine learning techniques to improve the quality of search. The better Google search gets, the more it is used, and the more information it has to provide better search results. These resources make it hard for any company to compete, at least in the US. Furthermore, the immense profits generated allow heavy investment in adding features, such as providing business summaries on Google Maps or summaries of information about a search term in a knowledge panel.

The result may be dominance of a specific service, but one that benefits users because of its effectiveness and increasing capabilities. The fact that it is ad-supported and free to users as a basic business model makes it difficult for competitors to say that Google is using unfair pricing to discourage competition with its basic search feature.

Where Google has leverage is with the price they charge advertisers. Google algorithms for selecting ads to display apparently do a reasonable job of targeting customers, but there are many additional channels for marketeers, including large competitors like Facebook and Amazon, as well as more conventional ad channels. Research company eMarketer estimated in June 2019 that the US digital ad market share of Google and Facebook fell for the first time in 2018, shrinking 1.7 percentage points to 56.8%, although digital ad spending in the country was expected to grow nearly 19% to $107 billion. As digital advertising grows as a share of total advertising, Google's US revenues from advertising were estimated to jump about 15% to $39.92 billion in 2018, while Facebook's ad revenue, led by a stellar performance from Instagram, was expected to climb 17% to $21 billion.

The dominance of a few firms in services supported by advertising is being challenged. The *Wall Street Journal* reported in May 2019 that the US Justice Department was launching an antitrust investigation of Google.

The strength of a such firms has become a political issue in the US. Democratic presidential candidate Senator Elizabeth Warren called for the breakup of Google, Facebook, and Amazon in early 2019. The issue of dominance has been compounded by privacy issues and calls for regulation in that area. In May 2019, House Speaker Nancy Pelosi said in a tweet, "The era of self-regulation is over."

Google and Facebook are facing rising competition from smaller rivals such as Snap. Snap, which says it is "reinventing the camera" by making it an application on a smartphone and allowing easy sending and organizing of photos. It could be argued that the revenue-generating part of the Internet giants' business—advertising—does indeed face effective competition, including the rise of completely new services.

US companies aren't the only competition. Chinese company TikTok has grown rapidly in the US with its very short video and tools that help anyone create such videos easily. With almost a billion downloads of the app since its introduction, and the third most downloaded app worldwide in the first three months of 2019, TikTok demonstrates that the competition from Google and Facebook doesn't prevent new competitors from emerging. This is not the typical case in past monopolies that have been broken up, such as the breakup of the Bell telephone system in 1982.

In a conference call with the press in May 2019, Facebook CEO Mark Zuckerberg said, "The argument that we might be in some sort of dominant position is a stretch." He indicated that Facebook has no more than a 10% share of the global advertising market.

Companies renting computer power in the cloud such as Microsoft, Amazon, and Google also have huge advantages of scale. They can optimize large data centers and invest significant sums in protecting them from cyber-attacks and making them reliable. They can afford to incorporate specialized hardware such as Graphical Processing Units to accelerate computing for specific tasks. They can provide software tools that tie companies increasingly to their services. Such advantages are compounded by the increasing difficulty of hiring computer science talent to support internal computer operations at companies.

China's computing infrastructure is growing. The total spending on quarterly cloud infrastructure services in China broke the $2 billion barrier for the first time in Q1 2019, according to analyst firm Canalys. China-based Alibaba Cloud led in the quarter with a 47% share of the cloud computing market. The market is dominated by local players, with the US's Amazon Web Services achieving only a 9% market share.

Although dominated by a few companies, there is significant competition among the major cloud computing firms. The companies can claim they are "democratizing" computer power by allowing smaller companies to rent capabilities they couldn't afford to build in-house. It is hard to view companies in cloud computing as classical monopolies.

In testimony before the Senate Judiciary Committee on May 21, 2019, Brian O'Kelley, founder and former CEO of AT&T-owned AppNexus, proposed a way the dominance of modern ad-supported services could be addressed. He suggested, first, that regulators give consumers control and transparency over their data. Second, he recommended the creation of a consumer bill of rights and a regulatory entity to enforce it.

O'Kelley's third suggestion was more complex. He argued that current antitrust law uses price as the only measure of consumer welfare. Since that doesn't work with free ad-supported services, he argued that the criterion needs to be expanded. He explained, "This is the loophole that allowed Google and Facebook to complete hundreds of acquisitions over the past decade without any significant FTC review. Let's apply some common sense to the regulatory process just by acknowledging that consumers pay for ad-supported content with their data and their attention."

In China, the trio known as "BAT"—Baidu, Alibaba, and Tencent—capture most of China's digital ad spending. However, while BAT dominates, several companies—including ByteDance, JD.com, Meituan, Qihoo 360, and Xiaomi—have found digital niches that have attracted large audiences, leading to rapidly growing ad revenues.

Perhaps the Chinese case suggests that the big Internet companies can be challenged by competition that attracts a specialized audience. If a company specializes in delivering a service to a targeted audience interested in a particular subject, say games, it could attract advertisers that want to reach that audience. Users of that service self-select by showing interest in the particular area covered by that web site or service.

A potential competitive channel for Google's dominance in search is search conducted through asking a question of a general digital assistants other than Google Assistant. When Apple's Siri says "Here's what I found" in response to a vocal request, it lists web sites that might have an answer to the inquiry. Apple can choose the search method it uses. This sort of competition is currently limited, but, as the digital assistants become increasingly used for search, it may become more important.

Competition between countries

In addition to issues of competition between companies, there is increasing competition between nations in areas of computer intelligence. In his 2018 book, *AI Superpowers*, Kai-Fu Lee argues that China will outpace the US in artificial intelligence. The Chinese government has made it a major priority to do so. In July 2017, the Chinese government under President Xi Jinping released a development plan for the nation to become the world leader in AI by 2030, including investing billions of dollars in AI startups and research parks.

The US recognizes the competition. President Trump released an American AI Initiative executive order in February 2019. The order calls for federal agencies that perform or fund AI R&D to prioritize this research when developing budget proposals for fiscal year 2020 on. The executive order, however, does not include any specific plans or goals.

China's biggest roadblock to AI dominance is in its chip market, as high initial costs and a long creation cycle have made processor and chip development difficult. China is still largely dependent on America for most of the digital chips—semiconductors—that power CI, as shown by the pain it causes Chinese technology companies when the US limits such exports, as they did temporarily for Chinese company Huawei.

One aspect of that competitiveness is that China has made it a national objective to improve its capabilities in the development of chips to reduce its dependence on US technology. Semiconductors are featured prominently in "Made in China 2025," a national ten-year development plan issued in 2015. The US has fought back with attempts to quell what it claims is unethical Chinese theft of US intellectual property and what the US considers unfair forcing of US companies that want to sell products in China to reveal trade secrets.

The US also has a structural advantage for research due to the number of top universities. Historically, top technology universities have attracted top Chinese students, who often stayed to work in the US. Even when they are educated in China, technology graduates often go to the US. According to a 2018 Diffbot report, graduates of four top Chinese technical universities produced a total of over 12,000 graduates in recent years; only 31% of these graduates stayed in China, while 62% left for the US.

Today, the Chinese government is discouraging Chinese students from studying in the US. Misplaced distrust of Chinese employees due to claims of their stealing of trade secrets may also discourage Chinese graduates from staying in the US.

Distrust has created an environment where business issues and government actions can't be easily separated. The US banning 5G products from Huawei, claiming Huawei equipment could be used for spying at the demand of the Chinese government, is a well-publicized example.

A major part of the issue in trade negotiations is trust. China could create trust by changing behavior such as placing fewer conditions on US companies trying to do business in China; such reform would appear to be to their long-term benefit in world trade. If China simply promises to change such practices, there is fear they will make some minor gestures, but not fully reform. On the other hand, the US has unilaterally withdrawn from some international agreements under President Trump, so the mistrust runs both ways.

Other countries consider AI a competitive technology impacting long-term economic growth. While presenting the budget in February 2019, India's Finance Minister Piyush Goyal announced plans to establish a national center in the field of AI and related technologies. Goyal said, "A national program on AI has been envisaged by the government. This should be catalyzed by the national center for artificial intelligence as a hub, along with other centers of excellence."

AI has the potential to add $957 billion to India's economy by 2035, according to management consulting firm Accenture. Accenture estimates that the country's "AI industry" generates $180 million in revenue annually as of 2019.

An interesting question relates to the specific attention given AI, as opposed to the potential of CI to improve economies in other areas. Research into the *next* tipping point likely to be created by CI might be more profitable than piling onto AI research which, at this point, is relatively mature and widely available. Many of these research initiatives will hopefully produce results in *applying* deep learning to specific areas.

CI has a substantial and increasing impact on economics. Because of its rapid growth in power, it creates opportunities and issues that were less pronounced with past technology developments. The net effect is likely to be beneficial, but thoughtful attention to potential problems is required.

Part V:
Cyberattacks and cyberwar

Warfare is changing. Current war tools that make extensive use of CI, such as satellite surveillance and "intelligent" drones, can make destruction more selective than invasion by an occupying army supported by fleets of bombers.

Beyond that change, a different kind of war is escalating today. The conflict is largely between democracies and autocracies that would like to discredit democracy as a form of government. The US, as the strongest democratic economy, is the de facto leader of one side. The Chinese and Russians are the main leaders of an informal alliance that is attempting to show that rule by one individual or group, with minimal dissent allowed, is more efficient than a democracy. Such autocracies are also trying to show they can compete economically by adapting some capitalist principles.

One might characterize this competition an "undeclared" war, but it is only undeclared today in the sense that it doesn't involve an attempt to kill each other's soldiers. Much of the war is economic, with the US using its economic might through weapons such as tariffs and sanctions, limiting access to US technology, and denying the US as a market to specific foreign firms. In turn, China—as a major US target of such actions—is using its growing economic power as a weapon. China is denying its market to US firms that want to market to China's huge population. When China wants to build competitive companies internally, they often require US companies to provide trade secrets in order to operate in China. China is also accused of directly stealing trade secrets of US companies through hacking and other illegal means.

Russia's efforts are less directly economic, in part because its economy isn't as competitive. US sanctions on Russia are hurting an economy that already has problems, and Russia seems to be counterattacking by sowing dissent in the US to discredit democracy as a form of government, as well as directly manipulating US politics with junk news and tactics such as hacking voter rolls.

In this evolving form of conflict, computer intelligence is the major weapon. There are three major components of its weaponization: (1) *cyberwarfare*—planting malware that can be used in an attack on power stations or critical computer systems, as well as voter rolls and voting systems; (2) *economic warfare*—direct cyberattacks on companies to steal proprietary information and trade secrets for competitive advantage; and (3) *propaganda* through misinformation and misuse of social media that is intended to incite turmoil and promote specific agendas. Cyberwarfare can also include apparent criminal behavior, in part because some governments appear to enlist criminal networks in their activities in order to increase deniability for their actions. In addition, authoritarian governments are using propaganda and cyberespionage—often through CI tools—to control their own populations.

Computer Intelligence in conventional warfare

With satellite imagery and hardware such as drones, targets can be chosen for attack with missiles or other precision attacks to maximize damage to enemy forces and minimize damage to civilians. The war-at-a-distance option also minimizes casualties of the attackers. Computer intelligence obviously plays a major role in such weaponry.

Much of the development of weapons of war is deeply classified, but we do know something about systems that use computer intelligence extensively. For example, the Global Hawk pilotless aircraft from Northrop Grumman flies reconnaissance missions (Figure 23). Global Hawk has amassed more than 250,000 flight hours with missions flown in support of military operations in Iraq, Afghanistan, North Africa, and the greater Asia-Pacific region. This model was the so-called "drone" shot down by Iran in June 2019.

The aircraft's intelligence-gathering capabilities also help civil authorities respond to natural disasters, conduct search-and-rescue operations, and gather weather data to predict the paths of storms. Pentagon planning for 2019 called for $9 billion in development and procurement for more than 30 types of unmanned aircraft, according to the Center for the Study of the Drone at New York's Bard College.

Figure 23: Northrup Grumman Global Hawk unmanned aircraft

The IAI Harop is a drone developed by the MBT division of Israel Aerospace Industries. The unmanned aircraft just loiters, unsupervised, high above a battlefield. If an air-defense radar locks on to it, the drone will follow the radar signal to its source and the warhead nestled in its nose will blow up the drone, the radar, and any radar operators in the vicinity. If the Harop doesn't detect a malicious radar signal, it will eventually fly back to a pre-assigned airbase and land, ready for another suicide mission.

The Defense Advanced Research Agency (DARPA) has a program, "Gremlins," in support of the Air Force's Small Unmanned Systems Flight Plan announced in 2016. The goal of that program appears to be to develop small drones that could be deployed against an enemy in large numbers (Figure 24).

Figure 24: DARPA Gremlins program, with a transport
aircraft releasing them (Source: DARPA)

The program envisions launching groups of unmanned air systems (UASs) from existing large aircraft while those planes are out of range of adversary defenses. When the UASs complete their mission, a transport aircraft would retrieve them in the air and carry them home for preparation for their next mission. The gremlins' expected lifetime of about twenty uses could provide cost advantages over larger systems. As Scott Wierzbanowski, a program manager at DARPA, wrote in a web posting, "An ability to send large numbers of small unmanned air systems with coordinated, distributed capabilities could provide US forces with improved operational flexibility at much lower cost than is possible with today's expensive, all-in-one platforms—especially if those unmanned systems could be retrieved for reuse while airborne."

The effectiveness of such weapons arises in part from their number. A human armed force and large bombers could be very susceptible to such a mass attack. Perhaps even the existence of such weapons would deter conventional warfare using massive troops or fleets of human-piloted bombers.

If there were a conflict between major powers, it could extend into space, with an attempt to neutralize or destroy at least spy satellites. A research paper published in June 2019 by the Royal Institute of International Affairs, "Cybersecurity of NATO's Space-based Strategic Assets," noted that NATO's satellites are fundamental to the provision of data and services in many military contexts. The report summarized: "The critical dependency on space has resulted in new cyber risks that disproportionately affect mission assurance."

According to the same report, almost all modern military engagements rely on space-based assets. During the US-led invasion of Iraq in 2003, for example, 68% of US munitions were guided utilizing space-based means.

The US is investing in other AI for defense and intelligence systems. In one case, the Defense Department awarded an $885 million five-year contract to consulting firm Booz Allen Hamilton in July 2018 to discover ways to use AI technology in defense applications. For example, AI instead of soldiers could monitor video feeds from drones and other sources, detecting objects such as trucks, cars, aircraft hangers, and weapons and flag the most likely targets for review by humans. More benign applications within the Booz Allen Hamilton program include new approaches to treating traumatic brain injuries.

The Electronic Frontier Foundation published recommendations in August 2018 for how militaries should plan for AI. This report acknowledged much can be done with machine learning, but claimed "plenty of reasons" to keep it away from target selection, fire control, and most command, control, and intelligence roles in the "near future, and perhaps beyond that too." The EFF warned that data taken from enemies to train machine learning may be "poisoned" to mislead the learning algorithms. The article argued that cyber weapons may be hacked to fail when they attack. The report argues that the empirical models developed by machine learning are difficult to understand and thus not fully predictable. They may also interact in unpredictable ways—an automated weapon could interpret a friendly system's actions as attacking it and destroy the friendly system. The report also suggests ways to mitigate these problems.

Cyberwarfare—The future of war?

The increasing intelligence of today's war machines is changing the nature of war. But a new type of war is evolving, one that could be destructive both of things and individuals and represents significant political challenges—cyberwar. Cyberwar is an attack where digital systems are compromised by malware delivered over the Internet surreptitiously or simply by overwhelming a web site by heavy traffic—a "denial-of-service" attack. Cyberattacks can be used to bring down a software system or even damage physical infrastructure by attacking computerized control systems. Cyberattacks can be directed at stealing classified information on weapon systems or delivering damaging propaganda. The use of cyberattacks in elections to steal data such as a politician's emails and to defame or promote a particular candidate have been well publicized.

Cyberwar arms race?

Malware—attack software—has been used specifically as a tool of war. In 2010, Stuxnet, developed by the US National Security Agency, perhaps with the aid of Israeli intelligence, targeted the software of physical controllers and caused centrifuges used in the enrichment of uranium at a facility in Iran to self-destruct.

Russia's incursion in the Crimea region of the Ukraine was a brief attack by soldiers, but aggression against the Ukraine has continued largely through cyberattacks. Malware called BlackEnergy was used by Russian hackers to launch an attack in December 2015 on several Ukrainian power companies. The malware was used to gather intelligence about the power companies' systems and to steal log-in credentials from employees; it was then used to trigger blackouts. Other malware developed by the Russians, Industroyer, was used to mount an attack on a part of Ukraine's electrical grid in December 2016. The code was used to strike an electrical transmission substation in Kiev, blacking out part of the city for a short time.

In June 2017, the Notpetya virus was spread in the Ukraine through a software update for a popular Ukrainian accounting software package used by about 80% of Ukraine's businesses. The software masqueraded as a ransomware virus, but in fact destroyed data to incapacitate computer systems. The attack was widely regarded as part of Russia's continuing cyberattack on the Ukraine.

In a talk in November 2018, Microsoft President Brad Smith, reacting in part to that Russian Notpetya attack, drew a parallel between the run-up to the First World War and the burgeoning cyberwar arms race. "I'm not here to say the next world war is imminent, but I am here to say that there are lessons from a century ago we can learn and apply, that we need to apply, to our own future," Smith said. "When we are talking about cyberspace, fundamentally we are talking about space that is private property, we're talking about datacenters and undersea cables and laptops and phones and devices and services that we create. Like it or not, and I don't think we should like it, the reality is inescapable; we have become the battlefield."

Smith argued that governments should stand up for the protection of the civilians and civilian infrastructure, and safeguard the internet in general from cyberattacks. In April 2018, Microsoft was one of the companies behind the Cybersecurity Tech Accord, signed by 111 companies by July 2019. One initiative is vulnerability disclosure policies. All signatories committed to having such a policy in place by the end of 2019, and more than half already had such policies in place in mid-2019. Vulnerabilities, in this context, refer generally to points of weakness in technology products and services that could, unless fixed, potentially be exploited by malicious actors to cause harm.

Malware called Triton is also believed to be the creation of Russian state-sponsored hackers. In March 2019, journalist Martin Giles called Triton "the world's most murderous malware" because it can disable safety systems designed to prevent catastrophic industrial accidents. The malware could, at the hackers' command, prevent physical controllers from preventing disasters. It could disable emergency shut-off valves or pressure-release valves that were designed to work automatically when they detected dangerous conditions.

Triton was discovered at a petrochemical plant in Saudi Arabia when a flaw in the code triggered several unintended shutdowns. Triton was uncovered when the source of the shutdowns was investigated, or we might still not be aware of its existence. Researchers at security firm FireEye reported in April 2019 a second infection by Triton of an industrial control system at an undisclosed company in the Middle East.

Triton puts lives at risk, since it could affect systems ranging from transportation systems to nuclear power stations. It may be lurking in many critical systems. Experts at a security conference in April 2019 described fairly easy defenses against the malware; bad software practices had much to do with the intrusions discovered.

Cyberattacks can also target intelligence resources. On March 7, 2017, WikiLeaks published 8,761 documents allegedly stolen from the CIA that contained documentation of alleged spying operations and hacking tools. These included iOS and Android vulnerabilities, bugs in Windows, and the ability to turn some smart TVs into listening devices. This obviously harmed the CIA operations. It also raised the question of whether the CIA should have revealed those vulnerabilities itself to avoid their being used by criminals or other countries, as opposed to exploiting them for its own purposes.

Our most critical systems in part suffer from old software and poor procedures to protect it. A security audit of the US ballistic missile system released in December 2018 by the US Department of Defense Inspector General found at several ballistic missile facilities a lack of data encryption, no antivirus programs, no multifactor authentication mechanisms, and 28-year-old unpatched vulnerabilities.

The US has resources for cyberattacks, and we of course don't know all the activities of US intelligence agencies. The *Washington Post* reported in February 2019 that the US Cyber Command targeted the St. Petersburg-based Internet Research Agency with a cyberattack in late 2018 that knocked the organization offline during the US midterm elections, potentially preventing a last-minute flood of disinformation designed to affect the election's results or turnout.

Cyberattacks can also occur in space. Military satellites could suffer physical attacks, but a satellite destroyed by a missile or another method could spread debris in orbit, destroying other satellites, including those of the attacking party. The previously mentioned Royal Institute report says that, in addition to attempts to jam radio transmissions, cyberattacks that employ digital techniques to access systems in order to cause permanent satellite damage are likely. The report says, "In a cyberattack, an adversary would be able to gain full access to satellites as well as data, enabling them to cause permanent damage." Another means of attack the Institute paper details is that of Global Positioning System (GPS) digital spoofing, whereby an attacker intercepts and manipulates data to provide false information to troops, allowing attackers to re-route movements of forces.

In a talk July 2018, US Director of National Intelligence Dan Coats minced few words in describing the danger of cyberattacks. He noted that, in the months leading up to the World Trade Center attacks in 2001, intelligence and law enforcement communities were identifying "alarming activities that suggested that an attack was potentially coming to the United States," but that action was impeded by "silos of information." The secrecy of such information in part prevented full appreciation that the warning lights were blinking. Coats said:

> Here we are nearly two decades later, and I'm here to say the warning lights are blinking red again. Today, the digital infrastructure that serves this country is literally under attack. Every day, foreign actors—the worst offenders being Russia, China, Iran, and North Korea—are penetrating our digital infrastructure and conducting a range of cyber intrusions and attacks against targets in the United States.

Clearly, militaries need to create defenses against such attacks. Given the dependence on CI of today's military systems, that's a major undertaking limited not only by its cost, but by the limited availability of talent that could address the issue.

There is potentially a lesson from nuclear weapons. It would be almost impossible to prevent massive destruction in a full nuclear attack; what deters that frightening possibility is the similar destruction a counterattack would deliver. Nations must unfortunately develop the ability to counterattack with cyberweapons, a bit like the Mutually Assured Destruction of the nuclear age.

Hackers have even attacked companies that develop anti-malware software. A group of Russian hackers claimed in May 2019 to have infiltrated the networks of three US-based malware detection software providers and stolen the source code for their software. The hackers claim to have stolen 30 terabytes of data and were demanding a ransom to give it back and to not name the companies attacked. We are unlikely to hear the resolution of this intrusion, since the companies involved are unlikely to advertise their vulnerability to attacks they are in the business of preventing.

Cyberattacks—a major shift in military strategy

Valery Gerasimov, a Russian general, elucidated in a military journal in 2011 what has become known as the Gerasimov Doctrine: "The role of nonmilitary means of achieving political and strategic goals has grown. In many cases, they have exceeded the power of force of weapons in their effectiveness." The doctrine was formally incorporated in Russian military strategy in 2014. About seventy-five Russian research institutions were devoted to the study and weaponization of information, coordinated by the Federal Security Service (the successor of the KGB).

After the Russian annexation of Crimea in 2014, Ukraine has been repeatedly targeted by cyberattacks, damaging many of the country's businesses and shutting down power plants, payment systems, and government agencies. Petro Poroshenko, the Ukrainian president, has said that 36 state institutions were targeted a total of 6,500 times in November-December 2016 alone.

Like many cyberattacks, the Ukrainian attacks are attributed to hackers that have only a suspected connection to the Russian government, allowing the government to deny responsibility. The aim is apparently to discredit the existing Ukrainian government in order to favor pro-Russian groups. The Russian government claims that, even if cyberattacks against Ukraine originated in Russia, they were the actions of isolated, patriotic individuals who wanted to promote Russian interests. This attempt at denying the government's role is a major characteristic of cyberwarfare; it can cloud the motivation for a counterattack.

Counterattacks—even if unannounced—are one way to discourage such activities. The Ukrainian Cyber Alliance, a group of Ukrainian hackers that works to fix security breaches, took credit for several attacks carried out in late 2016 against the Russian government and government agencies. This includes leaking the emails of Vladislav Surkov, an aide to Vladimir Putin.

The group most likely has the unspoken support of the Ukrainian government, but there is deniability, as in the Russian effort.

The *New York Times* reported in June 2019 that the US was stepping up digital incursions into Russia's electric power grid in a warning to President Putin. The article said that the Trump administration was using new authority to deploy cybertools more aggressively. US government officials indicated that there was a previously unreported deployment of US computer code inside Russia's power grid and other targets. The new initiatives are more aggressive than probes in the past and capable of damaging the targeted systems.

Presumably, the publicity about the cyberattacks was designed to warn the Russians of consequences if they activated any similar malware already installed in the US. In a public appearance in June 2019, national security adviser John Bolton, said the US was now taking a broader view of potential digital targets as part of an effort "to say to Russia, or anybody else that's engaged in cyberoperations against us, 'You will pay a price.'"

New authority to do so was granted separately by the White House and Congress in 2018 to the United States Cyber Command. In the military appropriations bill in summer 2018, Congress approved the routine conduct of "clandestine military activity" in cyberspace, to "deter, safeguard or defend against attacks or malicious cyberactivities against the United States."

Software often controls hardware. Thus, physical attacks may be conducted over the Internet by software causing malfunction of hardware, what some might consider an act of war if it were done by planting an explosive. Software can be installed in critical infrastructure such as power stations so that they can be shut down remotely by an adversary in a dispute. In July 2018, Department of Homeland Security Secretary Kirstjen Nielsen said cyberattacks pose a greater threat to the US than physical ones.

In June 2018, a group of presidential advisers said the country needs to prepare for a "catastrophic power outage" possibly caused by a cyberattack. The National Infrastructure Advisory Council, mostly current or former chief executives of companies engaged in critical industries, said resources need to be stockpiled in community enclaves to prevent mass migrations of desperate people in the event of a long power loss.

In July 2018, the US Department of Homeland Security reported that a group of Russian hackers (called "Dragonfly"), apparently supported by the Russian government, had installed software in the control systems of US electric utilities. The hackers got in relatively easily by penetrating the networks of outside vendors supporting the utilities. "They got to the point where they could have thrown switches" and disrupted power flows, said Jonathan Homer, chief of industrial-control-system analysis for the Department of Homeland Security, as quoted in a *Wall Street Journal* article. DHS said *hundreds* of utilities were affected by Dragonfly. Researchers attending the CyberwarCon forum in November 2018 in Washington, D.C., also warned that Russian cyber attackers are targeting the US electrical grid, searching for vulnerabilities to intrude on electricity generation and transmission systems.

The US Department of Homeland Security released in April 2019 a list of "national critical functions," defined as "the functions of government and the private sector so vital to the United States that their disruption, corruption, or dysfunction would have a debilitating effect on security, national economic security, national public health or safety, or any combination thereof." The list of over 50 items included, for example, fuel refining, the provision of information technology products and services, protecting the water supply, electricity distribution, air transportation, conducting elections, medical care, and internet routing and access.

Addressing any one of these areas effectively is a huge task. The objective is to use the list to identify the biggest risks. Chris Krebs, Director of DHS's Cybersecurity and Infrastructure Security Agency, told the *Washington Post* at the time: "If everything's a priority, then nothing's a priority. This allows us to really drill down into those things we need to care about."

On April 30, 2019, the Department of Homeland Security issued a "binding operational directive" that required agencies to remediate "critical" vulnerabilities identified by the Cybersecurity and Infrastructure Security Agency (CISA) within 15 days of detection, a reduction from 30 days. The directive also established a new lower-priority category, "high" vulnerabilities, which must be remediated in 30 days.

While cyberattacks seem like a milder form of warfare than dropping bombs, it can still cost lives indirectly, as with the shutdowns of healthcare organizations discussed earlier. If traffic is snarled due to stoplights no longer functioning, emergency vehicles can't get to potentially life-threatening emergencies. It isn't difficult to imagine how coordinated attacks of this sort could cause panic, deaths, and significant economic impact. While it is expensive to make and maintain nuclear missiles, it is relatively inexpensive to create a core of cyberattack specialists and the computers to deliver the attack.

Russia isn't the only country active in penetrating US facilities and companies. China has a deep commitment to hacking and other techniques, but has emphasized economic targets more than Russia.

China's Ministry of State Security and the People's Liberation Army are believed to have stolen the design details of many pieces of American military hardware, from fighter jets to robots, a claim that the Chinese have persistently denied. In 2012, National Security Agency director Keith Alexander called it the "greatest transfer of wealth in history." President Obama pressed the issue of cyberthefts in his first meeting with President Xi in 2013, only to be met with more denials.

Regarding potential cyberattacks on the US, the US Defense Department does not appear to have made cybersecurity a priority in the past. A nearly one-year "audit" of cybersecurity, completed in November 2018 at a cost of over $400 million, suggested not enough was being done.

"We failed the audit. But we never expected to pass it," Deputy Secretary of Defense Patrick Shanahan told reporters at the announcement of its completion. Shanahan said the audit revealed many issues, including inventory inaccuracy and cases of not complying with cybersecurity discipline. The most cited problems were related to the information technology security of the Defense Department's business systems.

In the report summary, auditors found the department's "financial and business management systems and processes do not provide reliable, timely, nor accurate information." The report also states that the Department's Information Technology has "systemic shortfalls in implementing cybersecurity measures to guard the data protection environment" and "issues exist in policy compliance with cybersecurity measures, oversight, and accountability."

The government is attempting to address the shortfalls. In 2018, the US government made cybersecurity more of a priority with two initiatives:

- The *Small Business Cybersecurity Act* was signed into law. The bill amends the National Institute of Standards and Technology (NIST) Act to require NIST to include small businesses in its initiatives. NIST facilitates and supports the development of voluntary, consensus-based, industry-led guidelines and procedures to cost-effectively reduce cyber risks to critical infrastructure. NIST must disseminate and publish on its website "standard and method resources that small business may use voluntarily to help identify, assess, manage, and reduce their cybersecurity risks."
- The government also published a document, the *National Cyber Strategy for United States of America* in September 2018. The introduction by President Donald Trump indicates National Cyber Strategy is the US's "first fully articulated cyber strategy in 15 years." The 26-page document includes multi-agency general objectives, such as securing critical infrastructure, combating cybercrime, fostering a stronger cybersecurity workforce, promoting responsible behavior between nation states, and preventing malicious "information campaigns."

Such goals remain as words, however admirable, unless they are translated into specific funded activities.

Cyberattacks as a result of individual carelessness

Why are our systems so susceptible? We have all probably experienced attacks by hackers with financial motivation, including suspicious emails asking us to go to a web site by clicking a link or to open an attachment. The intent is typically to get information such as your bank account number, claiming, for example, that the objective is to send you money. These "phishing" emails can be quite convincing, often masquerading as a major company you happen to deal with. Phishing can result in installing software or providing access to the attacked person's computer. That access can in turn allow access to company or agency systems when a personal laptop is attached to such systems.

In July 2018, for example, Microsoft revealed that hackers had already targeted at least three 2018 Congressional candidates by phishing emails that directed the targets to web sites that appeared to be legitimate Microsoft web sites. Microsoft said it worked with the government to take down those web sites, supposedly avoiding the attack. The attack was attributed to a group associated with the Russian government. We can all hope that it becomes a common practice for major companies to search for fake versions of their web sites and work to thwart them, as Microsoft did.

Even sophisticated users can be fooled by phishing attacks. In March 2016, Clinton campaign chairman John Podesta received a phishing email masked as an alert from Google that another user had tried to access his account. Based on an erroneous confirmation from an assistant that the email was valid, Podesta clicked on a link to a page and followed instructions to change his password, allowing hackers to access his emails.

Phishing attacks aren't particularly deep technology; they depend on bad practices by those attacked. "Password spraying" is another old-school method, where an attacker tries to access a huge number of accounts at once using some of the most commonly used passwords. It's simple but effective, especially in attacking organizations that only use passwords to authenticate employees. Some companies address this problem by requiring "multi-factor authentication," requiring employees to identify themselves beyond a password with biometric indicators such as voice characteristics, fingerprint sensors, or even a separate hardware device they plug into the device being used for access.

Attackers can also get into Internet-connected devices such as security systems if the factory-installed passwords aren't changed. These passwords are the same on all devices as delivered and are available in the devices' users' manual.

Such hacks obviously don't require deep expertise in digging through computer code to find a backdoor. Many successful attacks against companies with otherwise strong defenses are achieved through employee carelessness in the face of phishing or similar attacks.

A large number of hacking cases do exploit vulnerabilities based on deep analysis of standard software that has nothing to do with improper action by individuals. Microsoft warned in May 2019 that users should update their Windows operating system due to a bug that made it accessible to hackers in the previous version. In the same time period, Intel indicated it was addressing new issues that the company found in its microprocessors, flaws that could allow hackers to gain unauthorized access to data. Facebook, at about the same time, patched a problem with its WhatsApp messaging application that could be used by hackers to install spyware on mobile phones. These cases are just a snapshot that shows that even large, deep-pocketed firms can't avoid some vulnerability to hackers.

Cyberattacks through propaganda

Countries have also used cyberattacks to achieve political goals. The Russian interference in the 2016 presidential election had a large element of distributing propaganda that served Russian goals. A joint US intelligence community assessment issued in January 2017 summarized:

> Russian efforts to influence the 2016 US presidential election represent the most recent expression of Moscow's longstanding desire to undermine the US-led liberal democratic order, but these activities demonstrated a significant escalation in directness, level of activity, and scope of effort compared to previous operations.
>
> We assess Russian President Vladimir Putin ordered an influence campaign in 2016 aimed at the US presidential election. Russia's goals were to undermine public faith in the US democratic process, denigrate Secretary Clinton, and harm her electability and potential presidency. We further assess Putin and the Russian Government developed a clear preference for President-elect Trump. We have high confidence in these judgments.

The Mueller report similarly summarized, "The Russian government interfered in the 2016 presidential election in sweeping and systematic fashion." Many statements by the intelligence community issued during the Trump administration have validated these assessments.

In these and continuing actions, Russia's goal seems to be to sow discord in the US among competing interest groups and create problems in elections. The broader intent is to discredit democracy in general by showing how the freedom to express opinions can create dissent.

In one example of Russian activities, on June 2016, the Democratic National Committee and its cyber response team publicly announced that Russian hackers had compromised its computer network. Releases of hacked materials that public reporting attributed to the Russian government began that same month. Additional releases followed in July through the organization WikiLeaks, with further releases in October and November.

That fall, two federal agencies jointly announced that the Russian government "directed recent compromises of e-mails from US persons and institutions, including US political organizations," and, "these thefts and disclosures are intended to interfere with the US election process." After the election, in late December 2016, President Obama imposed sanctions on Russia for having interfered in the election.

The Mueller investigation produced a report in 2019 which included a detailed appraisal of Russian attempts to influence the 2016 election. The report cited specific charges:

> The Office determined that Russia's two principal interference operations in the 2016 US presidential election—the social media campaign and the hacking-and-dumping operations—violated US criminal law. Many of the individuals and entities involved in the social media campaign have been charged with participating in a conspiracy to defraud the United States by undermining through deceptive acts the work of federal agencies charged with regulating foreign influence in US elections, as well as related counts of identity theft...Separately, Russian intelligence officers who carried out the hacking into Democratic Party computers and the personal email accounts of individuals affiliated with the Clinton Campaign conspired to violate, among other federal laws, the federal computer-intrusion statute, and they have been so charged.

The first form of Russian election influence came principally from the Russian organization Internet Research Agency (IRA). The IRA conducted social media operations targeted at large US audiences with the goal of sowing discord in the US political system, beginning as early as 2014. The IRA created social media accounts and group pages that highlighted divisive issues, falsely claiming to be controlled by US activists. IRA employees even travelled to the US in mid-2014 on an intelligence-gathering mission to obtain information and photographs for use in their social media posts.

By early to mid-2016, IRA operations included supporting the Trump campaign and disparaging candidate Hillary Clinton. By the end of the 2016 US election, the IRA had the ability to reach millions of US persons through their social media accounts including Facebook, Instagram, and Twitter, according to the Mueller report. In November 2017, a Facebook representative testified that Facebook had identified 470 IRA-controlled Facebook accounts that collectively made 80,000 posts in 2015 through 2017. These included Facebook pages for "United Muslims of America," "Don't Shoot Us," and "Being Patriotic." The IRA even bought Facebook ads promoting their pages and organized rallies through their social media outlets.

A key part of such attacks is simply overwhelming classical news outlets by volume, using sensational headlines that are re-sent by recipients, compounding their circulation. For example, Russia is reported to have hired trolls to create such content, hundreds of Russians that imitated US social actors, writing hundreds of media posts a day. The Mueller report defined trolls as "internet users—in this context, paid operatives—who post inflammatory or otherwise disruptive content on social media or other websites."

This approach has been since magnified by the use of automated systems to set up accounts and deploy such content in such volume that attempts to shut them down can't keep up. The impact of sensational junk news continues to be evident in this kind of propaganda.

In January 2017, Intelligence officials met with both Obama and Trump to present the results of their probe into cyber espionage during the presidential campaign. After the briefing, the Office of the Director of National Intelligence released an unclassified version of its classified report on Russian meddling. The report concluded that Russian President Vladimir Putin ordered an "influence campaign" aimed at hurting Hillary Clinton and helping Donald Trump in the 2016 presidential election. It also concluded that hackers had the ability to impact voting machines or computers that held voter records or tallied election results, but apparently hadn't directly changed voter counts in the machines.

A year later, in January 2018, Twitter announced that it had identified 3,814 IRA-controlled Twitter accounts and notified approximately 1.4 million people who Twitter believed may have been in contact with at least one of those accounts. Political figures became unwitting accomplices in these activities, as they did things like retweeting posts that attacked opponents.

Intelligence agencies continue to warn of continuing Russian activity. In July 2018, Dan Coates, the US Director of National Intelligence, said, "Despite public statements by the Kremlin to the contrary, we continue to see individuals affiliated with the St. Petersburg-based Internet Research Agency creating new social media accounts, masquerading as Americans, and then using these accounts to draw attention to divisive issues." In August 2018, he repeated the warning: "We continue to see a pervasive messaging campaign by Russia to try to weaken and divide the United States."

Robert Mueller, speaking publicly on May 29, 2019, said that Russia's systematic effort to interfere with the 2016 presidential election "deserves the attention of every American." In his testimony to the House in July 2019, he re-stated that Russian efforts to impact US voting were continuing "as we sit here." Shortly after Mueller's testimony, the Senate Intelligence Committee released a heavily redacted report that concluded that election systems in all 50 states were targeted by Russia in 2016.

US national security officials have said they are preparing for expected Russian interference in the 2020 presidential race by tracking cyber threats, sharing intelligence about foreign disinformation efforts with social media companies, and helping state election officials protect their systems against foreign manipulation. All voting machines are supposed to be "air-gapped" (not connected to the internet), making them difficult to infiltrate from afar.

While attacking voting machines themselves is relatively difficult, creating errors or deleting voter rolls on connected computers is relatively easy, and doing so can make it impossible for some people to vote. In 2016, Russian hackers gained access to the state elections server in Illinois, proving they could penetrate even a fairly well-secured system.

The impact on voter rolls can be significant. Simple clerical errors in state and city databases of voters' names and addresses caused long delays at polling places in California in 2018 and North Carolina in 2016. In Palm Beach County, Florida, similar mistakes caused 2,000 properly registered voters to be turned away in the presidential primaries of 2016.

A Russian state news agency, Rossiya Segodnya (Russia Today, or RT), was founded in 2005. RT's budget rose from a founding $30 million to about $400 million in 2015. The agency publishes articles disseminating pro-Russian propaganda, but much more than that. It creates "news" that is intended to create dissension in countries it considers enemies or that is sensational enough to grab headlines and be recirculated. By doing so, it hopes to crowd out real news that might not be favorable to Russia. When such news is passed on, the fact that Russia Today was the source usually gets lost.

RT appears to be achieving its goal. In some years, it has had more YouTube views of its reports than any other broadcaster, including Fox News and the BBC. The flow of junk news discredits the news media in general.

In May 2018, a Russian news agency with close ties to Putin's government launched another "news" website called USA Really, which publishes a regular stream of articles favorable to President Trump. At this writing, the site was very much active. The site summarized its mission:

> Today, people of US do not receive objective and independent information about events occurring on the territory of America and around the world. 'The USA Really. Wake Up Americans' project is focused to promote crucial information and problems, which are hushed up by the conventional American media controlled by the establishment and oligarchy of the United States.

Headlines on the site on May 22, 2019, included:
- Recent Poll Results In: 4 in 10 Americans Support Socialism
- Iran Won't Talk Unless US Shows 'Respect'
- Ocasio-Cortez Labels Cauliflower Racist.

The stories of course put a particular spin on the news designed to sow discord in US politics or simply create their own news. The site doesn't indicate its Russian backing.

Many fake sites say they represent organizations they don't. The social media companies are attempting to monitor and eliminate such sites. Deep learning is being used to at least surface potential problem accounts by content, making it feasible for human analysts to evaluate them without being overwhelmed. Determining criteria for eliminating sites or content deemed objectionable or junk news without infringing first amendment free speech can be difficult, so this approach can only be partially effective.

American politicians are taking a cue from Russia's fake sites. In June 2019, the *New York Times* reported that a US citizen who "makes videos and other digital content for President's Trump's re-election campaign" had created a web site that appeared to be an official Joe Biden web site, but that made fun of Biden. Since the creator is not a foreign agent (or hired by one), the web site is protected as free speech. All the site says about its creator is in fine print at the bottom of the page. The site, it says, is a political parody built and paid for "BY AN American citizen FOR American citizens," and not the work of any campaign or political action committee. Perhaps the site is an obvious parody, but it is designed to attract individuals searching for Joe Biden's web site, perhaps to give a donation. We can expect attempts to fool voters in every election to come—from all parties—with the Russians having demonstrated how easy it is to do.

In November 2018, Facebook described its approach to pages being used by terrorists. The company said it was using machine learning to assess Facebook posts that might indicate support for ISIS or al-Qaeda. The tool produces a score indicating how likely it is that the post violates the company's counterterrorism policies. The score is used to help Facebook reviewers pick posts with the most important content first. Facebook said it will automatically remove posts when the tool indicates with very high confidence that the post contains support for terrorism. The company said it still relies on specialized reviewers to evaluate most posts, and only immediately removes posts when the tool's confidence level is high enough that its "decision" indicates it will be more accurate than human reviewers. The company said at the time that the new machine learning tools have helped reduce the amount of time terrorist content reported by Facebook users stays on the platform from 43 hours in Q1 2018 to 18 hours in Q3 2018. The difficulty is of course that even the reduced period gives plenty of time for the material on the site to be propagated by viewers through other channels, as in the case of the Christchurch video.

Governments controlling their population

Countries use cyberespionage tools against their own population. China has a Great Firewall that controls access to Web sources outside the country. The country monitors social media and uses that information to silence dissent.

During the massive protests in Hong Kong in June 2019 over a plan to allow Hong Kong residents to be extradited and tried in China, there was a powerful denial-of-service attack on the encrypted messaging app Telegram, potentially useful to coordinate the protests. The attack slowed the response of the app. Telegram CEO Pavel Durov tweeted that most of the attackers had IP addresses from China.

China is launching a "social credit system" that rewards actions they think support the government and punishes those that don't. Good actions, like volunteering, and bad, even littering, are tracked using algorithms, artificial intelligence, and facial recognition. Users with good scores can get easier access to credit loans, discounts for car and bike sharing services, quicker visa applications, and preferential treatment at hospitals. As of 2018, over forty different Social Credit System experiments were implemented by local Chinese governments.

In January 2019, in the *Financial Times*, the billionaire George Soros said that artificial intelligence, when in the hands of authoritarian regimes, was a "mortal threat" to the world. He cited China's social credit system that uses personal data to judge an individual's "trustworthiness" as an example. President Xi Jinping could eventually have "total control over the people," making him "the most dangerous opponent of open societies," Soros said.

The development of China's surveillance state has gone furthest in Xinjiang Province, where it is being used to monitor and control the Muslim Uighur population. Uighurs that the system deems unsafe are shut out of everyday life or even sent to reeducation centers.

The philosophy of Russia's Gerasimov Doctrine—that non-military means of engaging an enemy can be more effective than physical force— can be used in authoritarian states to control internal dissent. A dissenting Russian group will quickly find itself overwhelmed by the government's resources in cyberspace with techniques such as blocking access to web sites used to organize opposition.

Democratic nations could fight back with similar weapons. Those weapons could include web sites competing with sites such as Russia Today and USA Really. The sites could be funded by the US government to put honest news into circulation using sensational headlines to create circulation on social media.

The US apparently does use such tactics. According to the Washington Post in June 2019, "US government-sponsored social media bombards Iranians with reminders of government corruption and their isolation from the rest of the world."

Economic warfare

US senior security officials described to the Senate Judiciary Committee in December 2018 deep concerns about Chinese corporate espionage, warning that Beijing is exploiting American technology to develop its economy. "Our prosperity and place in the world are at risk," said Bill Priestap, the FBI's top counterintelligence official. "I believe this is the most severe counterintelligence threat facing our country today. Every rock we turn over, every time we looked for it, it's not only there, it's worse than we anticipated."

Some of the activity has both economic and security impacts. In November 2018, Marriott disclosed that a hack of the company's reservation database for its Starwood properties may have exposed the personal information of up to 500 million guests. The Chinese government was suspected of being behind the attack, partly because the information from the attack, initiated in 2014, does not appear to have resulted in criminal activity.

The Chinese were suspected in part because it fits a pattern. Chinese intelligence operatives are believed to be correlating sensitive information across the databases they have stolen from the US Office of Personnel Management, health insurers, and banks to locate and track undercover US spies and pinpoint officials with security clearances. Passport information stolen in the Marriott hack could be used by foreign-intelligence services to, for example, expose a government official's travel.

The US Federal Communications Commission (FCC) voted unanimously in May 2019 to deny an application by China Mobile's US arm, China Mobile USA, to provide international calls and other services. US officials cited law enforcement and national security risks, saying the company is owned by the Chinese government and vulnerable to exploitation, influence, and control. "The Chinese government could use China Mobile to exploit our telephone network to increase intelligence collection against US government agencies and other sensitive targets that depend on this network," FCC Chairman Ajit Pai said. "That is a flatly unacceptable risk." This is but one example of actions that impact business activities as a result of suspected intelligence activities.

The US Energy Department is a major target for economic espionage because of its advanced research programs in areas such as the military nuclear arsenal and basic physics research. In June 2018, the Department took preventative action against recruiting agencies offering million-dollar packages to hire the Department's employees and employees of the Department's outside contractors for foreign military-linked programs. China has a Thousand Talents plan that targets people "under 55 years of age who are willing to work in China on a full-time basis, with full professorships or the equivalent in prestigious foreign universities and R&D institutes, or with senior titles from well-known international companies or financial institutions," according to a web site advertising the plan.

Economic attacks lead to retaliation, and the US has retaliated in a number of ways, using its economic power, against China and other countries such as Russia, Iran, and North Korea. *The Economist*, in a May 2019 article entitled "Weapons of Mass Disruption" provided examples of why the US is a key part of globalization, giving it economic leverage:

> America controls or hosts over 50% of the world's cross-border bandwidth, venture capital, phone-operating systems,

top universities and fund-management assets. Some 88% of currency trades use greenbacks. Across the planet it is normal to use a Visa card, invoice exports in dollars, sleep beside a device with a Qualcomm chip, watch Netflix, and work for a firm that BlackRock invests in.

The Economist began publication in 1843, in part to support free trade and Adam-Smith-style economics. The magazine is not a fan of using trade tariffs as a weapon. The May *Economist* article concludes with a warning:

America's network gives it vast power. It will take decades, and cost a fortune, to replace it. But if you abuse it, ultimately you will lose it.

Competition in economics appears preferable to war with soldiers, bombs, and missiles, but it has its costs. Economic sanctions can be effective, but create reactions in the long run that can reduce the power of such weapons. To the degree that sanctions work by distorting optimal economic activity, they indirectly hurt at least segments of the attacking nation's economy. While it is not as dramatic as bodies in bombed cities, the people most hurt by economic problems created in the fighting nations are often those in the population that can least tolerate it.

An indictment was filed by the US government on December 2018 against a Chinese hacking group APT10. ("APT" stands for Advanced Persistent Threat.) The group was accused of hacking "managed service providers" (MSPs), organizations that provide IT infrastructure like data storage or password management software to other companies. Since the MSPs may manage sensitive information such as internal passwords for the companies they serve, hacking the MSP is like stealing the keys from a locksmith for many companies at once—one theft from the locksmith lets you into many companies.

APT hackers used conventional techniques like fake emails to get into the MSPs. They then installed malware that allowed the hackers to simulate valid users in order to access data. They used that access to install software that automatically reported new data to APT10 over the Internet. According to the indictment, the hackers ultimately stole hundreds of gigabytes of data from dozens of companies.

"More than 90 percent of the department's cases alleging economic espionage over the past seven years involve China," said deputy attorney general Rod Rosenstein at a press conference announcing the 2018 indictment. "More than two-thirds of the department's cases involving thefts of trade secrets are connected to China."

The FBI has increased its scrutiny of Chinese researchers in the United States over fears they may be acquiring intellectual secrets. A US Justice Department initiative announced in November 2018 targets commercial espionage of American technology. In announcing the initiative, Attorney General Jeff Sessions announced that a grand jury had returned an indictment against a Chinese state-owned company and Taiwan companies and individuals for stealing trade secrets on memory chips from Micron, an Idaho-based semiconductor company. These trade secrets, Sessions indicated, were worth up to $8.75 billion.

The US Justice Department filed charges against the Chinese telecom firm Huawei and its chief financial officer, Meng Wanzhou, in January 2019, claiming a decade-long attempt by the company to steal trade secrets, obstruct a criminal investigation, and evade economic sanctions on Iran. The indictments, based in part on the company's internal emails, include description of a plot to steal testing equipment from T-Mobile laboratories in Bellevue, Washington. They also cite internal memos from Meng that prosecutors said link her to an elaborate bank fraud that helped Huawei profit by evading Iran sanctions. Meng was being held in Canada in August 2019 as the US attempts to extradite her.

The US government separately argued that Huawei would have to obey an order from the Chinese government to use its devices to spy on users of 5G wireless services delivered through Huawei equipment. The US at one point placed barriers to the use of Huawei equipment in the US, as well as limiting the ability of Huawei to use US technology in its products.

At the RSA Cybersecurity conference in March 2019, NSA, FBI, and Department of Homeland Security officials warned about China's lead in cyberattack technology. Moderator Susan Hennessey, editor of the Lawfare blog, asked FBI Director Chris Wray if the government might be overemphasizing China's digital threat. Wray responded that, if anything, government had historically under-emphasized it.

Chris Krebs, director of DHS's Cybersecurity and Infrastructure Security Agency, said, "Russia's trying to disrupt the system, but China's trying to manipulate the system to its ultimate long-term advantage." Combating Chinese digital espionage will be one of four major focus areas for CISA during the next 18 months, he said.

Reacting to the threat of cyberattacks, Rob Joyce, NSA's senior cyber-security adviser and former White House cybersecurity coordinator, said at a conference, "I kind of look at Russia as the hurricane. It comes in fast and hard." China, on the other hand, he said, "is climate change: long, slow, pervasive."

It's difficult for countries with an open Internet to fight cyberattacks. Countries such as China that want to control what their populations see on the Web have instituted various means of blocking broad access by their population, and have more control of the Internet infrastructure.

Russia went the furthest in this direction with a law in May 2019 that allows it to disconnect the Internet within Russia from the rest of the world, creating an independent "Runet." The law has been justified as creating the ability to maintain the stability of the Russian internet if foreign aggressors try to attack it in some way. Special equipment will allow the country's communications regulator to direct traffic through Russian exchange points only. The current approach is to forbid internet service providers from accessing an ever-expanding blacklist of sites.

If fully implemented, Runet will be expensive. Russia will need to build its own Domain Name System (DNS), and internet service providers will need to install the special equipment provided and paid for by the state at an estimated cost of 20.8 billion rubles ($320 million).

During the Obama administration, China and the US agreed they wouldn't perform cyberespionage on each other's companies, and China apparently pulled back for a while. But FBI director Christopher Wray told NBC News in March 2018 that China was back to infiltrating US computer systems and stealing information at a massive scale. "There's no country that's even close," Wray said. "We're talking about big damages," President

Trump told Reuters in a later 2018 interview. "We're talking about numbers that you haven't even thought about."

Potential solutions

The House Energy and Commerce Committee's Subcommittee on Oversight and Investigations released a report In December 2018 to address and prevent cybersecurity incidents. The subcommittee developed six specific priorities to protect agencies and companies:

- *Widespread adoption of coordinated disclosure programs:* The committee said that "a collaborative vulnerability identification and remediation process" would allow more effective dissemination about specific vulnerabilities and attack methodologies.
- *Implementation of software bills of materials across connected technologies:* A software bill of materials (SBOM) is essentially an ingredients list for a specific piece of technology and will list the hardware, software, and other components that it contains. A SBOM permits organizations to make informed risk decisions about which technologies to purchase and use based on known vulnerability information, the report said, and, when new vulnerabilities are discovered, it allows organizations to quickly identify their exposure and to take appropriate steps in response.
- *Support and stability of the Open-Source Software (OSS) ecosystem:* The report said that if the majority of companies run on OSS, "then any improvement in the quality of OSS bricks will create immediate, widespread, and effective increases in the overall quality of the cybersecurity capabilities of the organizations using them." The Android mobile operating system is an example of Open-Source Software.
- *Health of the government's Common Vulnerabilities and Exposures (CVE) program:* The CVE program maintains a list of entries of publicly known cybersecurity vulnerabilities. According to the report, in the spring of 2016 "multiple media outlets reported that the CVE program was struggling to keep up with the number of vulnerabilities reported." The report recommended more support and more stable funding for the effort.

- *Implementation of supported lifetimes strategies for technologies:* Older IT systems that are not fully supported are common, particularly in the US government. The report suggested looking into how long legacy systems should be allowed to persist. The report suggested that technology developers will likely need to provide a "guaranteed minimum support lifetime" and users will have to "accept and plan for the phasing out of technologies as they get older."
- *Strengthening of the public-private partnership model:* The report noted that the US has already established a Public-Private Partnership model for designated critical infrastructure through Presidential Policy Directive 21. Under this model, critical infrastructure is divided into 16 sectors, with Sector-Specific Agencies, Sector Coordinating Councils, and Information Sharing and Analysis Centers overseeing each sector and facilitating information sharing. The report stressed the importance of strengthening the public-private partnership model, saying: "It enables connected ecosystem stakeholders to recognize their shared risks and collaborate to protect their shared resources. Most critically, it creates a positive feedback-loop among and between the Subcommittee's six interdependent priorities, and in doing so, increases desperately needed cybersecurity capabilities across society as a whole."

The guidelines are useful in setting goals and creating processes to implement them. But guidelines require follow-up action to have any real effect. At this writing, rather than focusing on funding such activities, the US congressional budgeting process, in part due to high deficit spending, is more focused on reducing budgets rather than funding new targeted spending. On the other hand, awareness of the issue has increased spending by companies to protect their assets.

Activities such as replacing outdated equipment in companies and government agencies and enhancing cybersecurity defenses in general will be expensive. If we are searching for a silver lining behind the cloud, the effort might create new business opportunities.

Part VI:
What's next for CI?

The famous prediction by Gordon Moore, then Intel CEO, more than four decades ago, that the number of transistors on one semiconductor chip will double every two years ("Moore's Law") has proved remarkably accurate, and has driven exponential increases in computer power. CI power may even grow faster due to "3D" chips that stack processor slices ("dies") on top of each other, not depending on putting more transistors closer together on one die. As discussed briefly in Part I, other trends are accelerating CI power beyond this basic improvement in processor power.

One such trend is specialized chips. Conventional microprocessor chips are designed to be general-purpose, to execute instructions from software that describes a series of steps required to achieve a particular task. The hardware is not tuned to that task.

Certain types of computing tasks can be accelerated by special-purpose chips designed for that type of task. Graphical Processing Units (GPUs) were designed originally to drive graphics for games, for example. GPUs process many computations of a specific sort "in parallel"—at the same time. It turns out that GPU architecture is well-suited for computing neural network models, and can be used as an accelerator for deep neural network development and deployment. Increasingly, GPUs are integrated with a separate conventional central processing unit (CPU) to accelerate specific tasks. The system software can assign appropriate tasks to the GPU.

Field-Programmable Gate Arrays (FPGAs) are another form of specialized chip that can be set up to accelerate specific tasks within the hardware. FPGAs are being used similarly to GPUs in computer centers today. Using such specialized processors is a major trend in cloud computing.

Research is exploring new options in specialized chips. The Defense Advanced Research Projects Agency (DARPA) has a program to help develop new AI chip designs. MIT has one of the research teams leading this effort, led by Professor Vivienne Sze, who wants to make the devices energy-efficient as well as computationally efficient. Sze's chip is called Eyeriss. According to a paper posted online in 2018, the chip was tested against a number of standard processors on a range of different deep-learning algorithms. It was said to be 10 to 1,000 times more efficient than existing hardware.

Companies such as Nvidia, Amazon, and Intel are developing chips specialized to handle tasks such as deep learning. Google's Tensor Processing Unit (TPU) accelerates the rate at which machine-learning models can be built using Google's TensorFlow software library. According to Gartner projections, sales of such chips were expected to double to about $8 billion in revenue in 2019, rising to more than $34 billion in 2023.

Another way to expand computing power is to have large computer centers with many "servers," each of which is a general-purpose computer in itself (as was shown in Figure 7). These independent servers are controlled by an operating system that can assign them tasks. The servers, capable of working in parallel, reduce dependence on the computing power of each unit.

These large computer centers are expensive and difficult to manage. Often, to be able to accommodate peaks of usage, e.g., during holiday shopping season for an online service, there must be more servers installed than are normally needed, making the center less cost-efficient in normal operation. The growth of cloud computing, renting time on a large server farm from vendors such as Amazon Web Services, Microsoft Azure, Google Cloud Computing, and IBM cloud computing, as discussed in Part I, has led to an explosion in the use of these large server systems through an Internet connection—"cloud computing." Companies pay for use of this processing power on the basis of the amount of computing used. They don't need to manage the centers or pay for computing power they only need occasionally. The cloud computing vendors have the usual advantages of scale in keeping costs down. The cloud computing trend is another way that cost-effective computer power can grow faster than the number of transistors on a chip.

In addition, the cloud computing companies are providing *software* optimized for specific tasks under the same pricing model, payment for the time the software is used. Deep learning, speech recognition, and natural language processing are some of the algorithms that can be rented without the cost and delay of development by each company using them. The cloud computing companies can optimize such algorithm performance, for example, by using GPUs to accelerate the software. This trend goes beyond expanding pure computer power—it provides quick and economic access to advanced algorithms, driving faster adoption of CI advances.

In April 2019, for example, Salesforce added services for their Salesforce Einstein cloud platform that provide translation and optical character recognition. Instead of renting pure computer power, companies using such services are renting the results of significant research and software development.

Computer intelligence is becoming more distributed, not only through cloud computing, but through applications that cooperate across the Internet, with each cooperating computer system providing specialized intelligence, further enhanced by faster communications. This trend is another way that computing power expands, particularly if each of the cooperating nodes has been optimized for a particular task.

Computer power is also spreading to the "edge," i.e., more computing can be done on local devices, such as smartphones, as the power of chips within those devices continues to grow. To the degree that some computing can be done on a device, rather than on the other end of an Internet connection, overall computing power is expanded with each such device purchased.

The trend for more computing at the edge will be driven in part by a desire to reduce both communication and computing costs. Companies delivering cloud-based services such digital assistants can benefit from the reduced load in the cloud. An additional motivation to put processing on the edge stems from the pressure by consumers with privacy concerns to keep more information on the device rather than transmitting it through the cloud. In addition, edge computing allows an application to perform more functions when an Internet connection isn't available, a further benefit to users.

An example of increasing power at the edge is from chipset maker Qualcomm. In April 2019, the company announced three new models of its Snapdragon range of processors for mobile devices. Qualcomm indicated that these platforms are designed to exceed customer expectations when delivering experiences in AI, gaming, camera use, and overall performance.

Google CEO Sundar Pichai announced another example of computer intelligence moving to the edge at a company conference in May 2019. The speech recognition software required to support Google Assistant, Pichai noted, is complex—that's why voice assistants send the voice commands from your device to a remote server with more processing power and memory. In the past, Pichai said, the Google Assistant software was about 100 gigabytes in size. He said that, thanks to recent innovations, the Assistant's footprint was greatly reduced to roughly half a gigabyte in size—1/200 of its previous size. That reduction means that the Assistant no longer needs to send your voice to a remote server, but can process commands on the device. "Think of it as putting the power of an entire Google data center in your pocket," Pichai told the audience. It would make the Assistant "so fast that tapping to use your phone would seem slow." An onstage demo showed the speed, with simple requests like "take a selfie" to more advanced requests like "get a Lyft ride to my hotel." As the demonstrator spoke, transcribed commands appeared in the lower-right corner of the phone's screen, confirming that the device was interpreting the demonstrator's speech immediately and correctly.

Amazon Web Services (AWS) offers some edge computing options for its cloud computing service. In 2017, AWS added IoT Greengrass, a tool that extends AWS to edge computing devices so they can act locally on the data they generate, while still using the cloud for management, analytics, and storage. With AWS IoT Greengrass, connected devices can run software locally that they normally run in the cloud. Even when not connected to the Internet, the software can execute predictions based on machine learning models, keep device data in sync, and communicate with other devices securely through local networks. With AWS IoT Greengrass, developers can use familiar languages and programming models to create and test device software in the cloud, and then deploy it to local devices.

In addition to such software, Amazon provides *hardware* for edge computing. AWS Snowball Edge is a data migration and edge computing device that comes in two options, one emphasizing storage of data and the other for computational tasks. The last offers an optional Graphical Processing Unit to support machine learning and full motion video analysis without requiring an Internet connection. Like IoT Greengrass, a developer can build an application in the cloud and run it locally. The hardware cost is apparently based on compute time used by the application on the local device. Rather than requiring a capital investment, a company has the option of maintaining AWS usage-based pricing. This economic approach to marketing hardware, if this model holds, is innovative in itself.

These major trends will accelerate the expansion of computer power. The impact will accelerate CI beyond the historical push of Moore's Law.

Communications

Connecting computer systems at separate locations is a key element of today's digital systems and, of course, the very basis of the Internet and the Web. Both wired and wireless communications are critical to the continuing evolution of Computer Intelligence.

Just as computing power continues its historical growth, the number of connections and the speed of the communications channels continues to increase. As an example of typical growth, data traffic in Germany, according to Statista, grew (in millions of gigabytes) from 0.22 in 2005 to 575 in 2015 to 1,993 in 2018.

This growth will continue and accelerate due to a number of factors. In the wireless arena, in addition to wireless providers expanding their networks, the well-publicized new 5G technology could expand the capacity of each connection up to 100 times.

The expansion of wireless networks does not mean wired networks are a thing of the past. SiFi Networks announced in April 2019 that they were building a network based on fiber optics in Fullerton, California, with plans to deploy more of these networks in the US. The network will provide an upgrade to internet speeds and accommodate the growing demand for data from next-generation devices in households and businesses, the company said. The network will also facilitate new "Smart City" initiatives in key government services, such as traffic control, street lighting, and emergency services, as well as provide connectivity for the future expansion of 4G and 5G cellular networks into the area.

Economic trends

Klaus Schwab, founder of the World Economic Forum, made the "fourth industrial revolution" the theme of the Forum in 2016. The first three industrial revolutions were characterized as being driven in turn by coal and steam, electricity and the automobile, and computing. The fourth is characterized by the mobile internet, automation, and artificial intelligence. In a World Economic Forum report for that event, Schwab distinguished the fourth from the third in part by its pace:

> The speed of current breakthroughs has no historical precedent. When compared with previous industrial revolutions, the Fourth is evolving at an exponential rather than a linear pace. Moreover, it is disrupting almost every industry in every country. And the breadth and depth of these changes herald the transformation of entire systems of production, management, and governance... Overall, the inexorable shift from simple digitization (the Third Industrial Revolution) to innovation based on combinations of technologies (the Fourth Industrial Revolution) is forcing companies to reexamine the way they do business.

Christopher Mims, in a November 2018 *Wall Street Journal* article, "Inside the New Industrial Revolution," addressed the fourth-generation characterization of the economy, warning:

> We're either witnessing the end of work as we know it or 'merely' a profound transformation of what jobs humans do. Either way, the economic and political ramifications are likely to be on par with the impact of the past 50 years of outsourcing and globalization...The fourth industrial revolution is gathering steam, but unless the US can continue to attract

the best talent from overseas while also educating a domestic workforce suited to the jobs to come, this time it might not be an American revolution.

The argument could be made that we've passed through a threshold—perhaps a "tipping point"—of the impact of CI where it is fair to call the current economy the fourth industrial revolution. Artificial Intelligence, as a natural evolution of rapidly progressing computer intelligence, is part of that revolution. That CI evolution is continuing and will certainly have major impacts on the economy as it supports algorithms of growing complexity. Artificial Intelligence is the technology that exemplifies the current tipping point of CI development.

The evolution of AI

A blog post by Dario Gil, VP of AI and Quantum, IBM Research, in December 2018, indicated a range of research efforts attempting to advance AI. Gil said IBM's mission is to invent the next set of fundamental AI technologies that will move from today's "narrow" AI to a new era of "broad" AI. This new era of AI, he indicated, will be characterized by the technology's ability to learn and reason more broadly across tasks, to integrate information from multiple modalities and domains, plus be more explainable, secure, fair, auditable, and scalable.

IBM research in this area has included research on extending current AI speech comprehension capabilities beyond simple question-answering tasks. It also addressed enabling machines to better understand when people are providing conflicting views on a topic.

IBM researchers also presented a framework in a 2018 paper that enables automated AI "agents" to learn to teach one another and work as a team. They found that automated agents are able to learn significantly faster than previous methods. IBM reported that, in some cases, they can learn to coordinate where existing methods fail.

IBM Research described an enhancement to automated question-answering in a broad context in another 2018 paper. The method re-ranks and aggregates evidence across multiple passages to produce more accurate answers. The paper indicated the method has achieved substantial improvements over previous state-of-the-art approaches tested on public open-domain question-answer datasets.

Specific AI trends IBM expects in 2019 include increased research investment in the "pillars of trust" (fairness, explainability, robustness, transparency) of an AI solution. IBM also expects to conduct new research on how quantum computing can play a role in training and running AI models. IBM's work and the areas they chose provide an indication of where current research is trending.

Are AI dangers real?

In the area of *trusting* AI, Dario Gil of IBM noted the issue of bias in data used for AI models. The data used to train AI systems often contains intrinsic societal and institutional biases and correlations that statistical learning methods capture and recapitulate. In a 2018 paper, IBM Research outlined an approach for combating bias. The team reported success in transforming training data so as to minimize bias.

Today's machine learning models are vulnerable to being fooled by carefully crafted malicious inputs called "adversarial examples," Gil indicated. As a step toward safeguarding against these attacks, IBM Research has proposed a robustness measure called CLEVER (Cross Lipschitz Extreme Value for nEtwork Robustness) that can be used to evaluate the robustness of a neural network against attack. The researchers indicated that the CLEVER score makes it easier to estimate the security of AI models.

In a report dated December 2018 with the ambitious title *Artificial Intelligence and the Future of Humans*, the Pew Research Center summarized concerns that some experts have about how advances in AI will affect "what it means to be human, to be productive and to exercise free will." The report is the result of canvassing of 979 "thought leaders" in varied fields in the summer of 2018, inquiring about the expected impact of AI by 2030.

On the positive side, the report indicated a general belief that AI will "amplify human effectiveness." The experts said "smart systems" will "save time, money and lives and offer opportunities for individuals to enjoy a more-customized future."

But the report warned of potential downsides, with most experts expressing "concerns about the long-term impact of these new tools on the essential elements of being human." Overall, 63% of respondents expected that most individuals will be mostly better off in 2030, and 37% said people would not be better off. The five most mentioned concerns were:

1. Using AI reduces individuals' control over their lives;

2. Surveillance and data systems, even if intended to improve efficiency, are inherently dangerous to privacy;

3. AI's effect on jobs will widen economic and digital divides, possibly leading to social upheaval;

4. Individuals' cognitive, social, and survival skills will be diminished as they become dependent on AI; and

5. Vulnerabilities, such as exposure to cybercrime and cyberwarfare, will increase.

One concern voiced in the Pew report is that AI will do too much for us and turn us into automatons, such as blindly following our GPS navigation instructions and other instructions from computers, and no longer thinking. This concern seems misplaced. It's a bit like saying heating and air conditioning systems have made us less tolerant of changes in weather, weakening humanity.

The report also mentioned that a few of the participants also "worried about the wholesale destruction of humanity." Elon Musk, Tesla CEO, speaking at SXSW in March 2018, said, "The danger of AI is much greater than the danger of nuclear warheads...more dangerous than nukes."

Despite both high expectations and fears, AI does not have some mystical power. It's not that there aren't potential issues with AI—it's that giving it some vague godlike power beyond historical technology developments diverts the need to think about individual issues and their solutions carefully. It certainly isn't a solution to simply say we should "outlaw AI."

The AI techniques that are proving most effective today, in particular machine learning using deep neural networks, are empirical, i.e., powerful statistical techniques made possible by computer power having crossed a threshold. When AI creates a specific problem, we can address that particular problem, rather than escalate a narrow problem the tool created into a condemnation of the tool itself. Many useful advances in technology came with issues we had to address—we had to add emission controls to automobiles, a specific solution for a specific problem. Arguing that Artificial Intelligence—perhaps because it has the term "intelligence" in its name—somehow creates unique challenges to humans is misleading.

The point isn't that all is well in the best of all possible worlds. This author is optimistic because, although technology causes many problems, the long-term trend is that we do fairly well in solving them. When horses were the main form of motive power in cities, manure on the streets was a problem, but it was collected and sold as fertilizer—an early example of many challenges we've overcome.

AI technology in particular, and CI in general, is likely to help us solve problems, including the problems *caused* by CI. Like many problems created by technology, we may have to attack specific problems with specific solutions.

Changes in software development

With essentially unbridled computer power, applications can get very complex, making it difficult to write bug-free software or update a complex software application without unintended consequences, including the introduction of a vulnerability to cyberattack. As software applications get larger and more complex, one approach to making them more manageable is to divide them into smaller functional units, to make them more *modular*. The increase in CI power makes any potential computational inefficiency in this approach a minimal concern.

A modular approach requires an architecture that makes the functions of the modules clear and relatively independent. Ideally, the full program can then use those modules as a series of clear steps, and each step can then be managed relatively independently. This has long been a software practice with "subroutines" performing specialized tasks, but the concept of modules is broader.

For example, "containers" are software subroutines tailored to specific hardware environments that avoid the need to re-develop the interfaces that are already part of the container. Chipmaker Nvidia offers "containers" with software that specifically supports machine learning applications using their Graphics Processing Units (GPUs). The container software may include extra instructions to insulate the developer from the hardware, but the additional processing saves time and effort for software developers.

Nvidia, at this writing in mid-2019, had 60 pretrained container models and 17 model scripts for applications such as visual object detection, natural language processing, and text-to-speech synthesis. NGC containers are built and tested to run either on-premises or in the cloud. NVIDIA continuously optimizes key deep learning frameworks and libraries, with updates released monthly. Japan's fastest supercomputer, ABCI, is powered by NVIDIA Tensor Core GPUs and supports NGC containers.

Modules may be distributed across computer systems and used by a specific application through a network. A downside is that dependence on connectivity can cause failures when the connection fails. Failure of a single resource on the Web can impact many programs using that resource's capability. This reliance creates business opportunities; companies such as ThousandEyes specialize in monitoring Internet connections to allow companies to quickly identify the source of connectivity problems. This is an example of a CI solution addressing a CI problem.

The increasing computational capability of local devices such as smartphones may allow more software functions to be done on the device without an Internet connection. This is another form of modularity.

Conversations with computers

The speech recognition and natural language processing exhibited by general personal assistants will continue to get more flexible—more "conversational." Today's natural language interaction is best for acting on a single request that doesn't require further interaction, e.g., "What's the weather forecast for Los Angeles today?"

Amazon introduced in June 2019 an update to its toolkit for building Amazon "skills" that supported voice interactions that required turns of conversation between Alexa and a user to complete a request. Amazon vice president of devices David Limp told reporters:

> It has been sort of the holy grail of voice science, which is how can you make a conversation string together when you didn't actually programmatically think about it end-to-end. We feel like we're on a path now where I think a year or two ago I would have said we didn't see a way out of that tunnel, but now I think the science is showing us that it will take us years to get more and more conversational, but this breakthrough is very big for us, tip of the iceberg.

This is but one example of the heavy investment that large and small companies are making to advance the naturalness of communicating with digital systems.

Explainability

One aspect of empirical technologies is that it is difficult to know *why* a model such as a Deep Neural Network makes a given decision—its lack of "explainability," as discussed in Part III. Given many examples, the machine learning adjusts to minimize errors on those examples by adjusting hundreds of thousands of parameters. In the end, all you know is that it has created a model that does well on the examples it has learned from. You can test the model on independent data to verify its accuracy, but that doesn't tell you what logic it is using to make a specific decision.

That "unknowability" isn't particularly important if the model is identifying pictures of dogs versus cats. But suppose it is assessing the creditworthiness of an applicant for a home loan. If it decides the applicant shouldn't be given the loan, the applicant will want to know why (and the credit officer as well). Simply saying "the computer said so" probably wouldn't make the potential customer happy or the loan officer comfortable.

When a DNN or other machine learning model makes a decision, one way to help explain that decision is to provide *examples* of similar cases to the one being evaluated, along with the outcome of those similar examples—an approach described in the earlier discussion of explainability. This approach is similar to a human explaining a conclusion with a statement starting with "for example" to explain an intuitive statement. There are CI techniques that can find examples similar to any specific case in the database of examples used to create the DNN.

Another explainability issue is that the model can reflect prejudices in the data. If a particular race or gender was historically denied loans more than another race or gender, and this is reflected in the data, the computer will blindly incorporate the correlation in the model. Fields such as "race" and "gender" in the input data are just variables to the machine learning.

One solution would appear to be to leave out such potentially danger-ous variables in the input data. But there can be other factors such as home location that are correlated with race. In many applications, the dangers of the data reflecting human bias, or some historical bias, are not evident.

There is research on finding ways to explain the results of a machine-learn-ing model. DARPA, for example, has a research program called Explainable Artificial Intelligence (XAI). The Defense Department is concerned about AI in future warfare systems being sufficiently transparent to justify life-or-death decisions. DARPA explained the goal of the research:

> At the end of the program, the final delivery will be a toolkit library consisting of machine learning and human-computer interface software modules that could be used to develop future explainable AI systems. After the program is complete, these toolkits would be available for further refinement and transition into defense or commercial applications.

One example of a machine learning model that can explain itself is "Classification and Regression Trees," based on a book of that name in 1984 by Leo Breiman and three other university professors. It's still available as a software package called CART. It was developed at a time when computers were much slower, and the model is much simpler than a neural net. It is a decision tree that makes a series of decisions based on available variables in order to distinguish classes. In the example of Figure 25, patients in a study were assessed based on an initial examination as "high risk" (a danger of not surviving 24 hours) or low risk. The decision was based on a number of potential diagnostic variables, including age. The outcome was known for the data analyzed.

All the variables were tested for each decision. The values used in comparison (e.g., 62.5 for age) are values that create the best discrimination of the categories "high risk" versus "not high risk" as determined by the CART algorithm.

The CART algorithm finds a series of specific comparisons based on a systematic empirical analysis. As can be seen from the example, the very nature of the model explains how it makes a decision. The model and methodology for finding it were tailored to the more limited data and computer power at the time it was developed, and the approach is much less powerful than Deep Neural Nets (DNNs). The simpler nature of the model, however, allow it to be created with much less data than DNNs, and the method is still used for that reason.

IBM Research described in a 2018 paper a new machine learning methodology called ProfWeight which probes a DNN and constructs a simpler model of that DNN that can reach similar performance as the original network. The simpler models can provide insights into how the original network worked and why it made one decision versus another. In testing this methodology on two large datasets, the ProfWeight model was able to produce more explainable decisions, while maintaining a high level of accuracy. Such research will continue to offer improved options in understanding how DNNs make a decision.

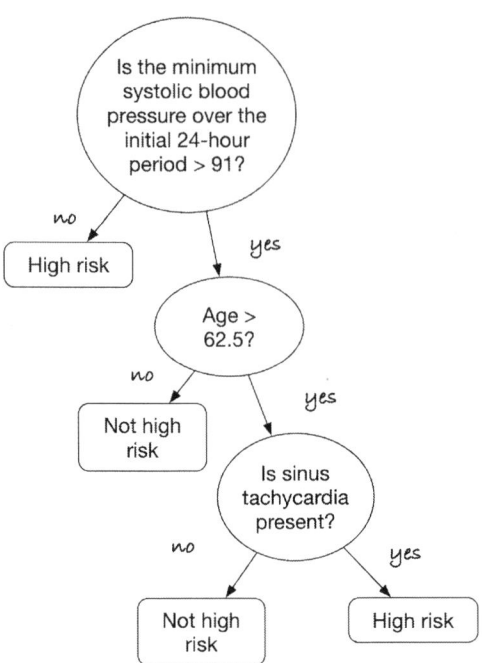

Figure 25: A Decision Tree (from *Classification and Regression Trees*, Breiman et al)

Workflow

Using computers to complete a task can require a user to complete a series of actions within one software program or to use a series of separate software applications. A category of software that helps manage such a series of actions can be called "workflow" software. Workflow applications can automate doing the series of actions or at least aid the user complete the steps more reliably.

A specific category of workflow applications is the technology labelled Robotic Process Automation, designed to mimic what a human might do at a terminal using a series of steps. RPA can record the steps a worker used at a terminal to complete a specific task, using that knowledge to automate the process.

Nuance Communications, which provides advanced technology such as speech recognition that transcribes reports dictated by radiologists as they review x-rays or other images, provided a good example of the evolution of workflow applications. In a company blog post in May 2019. Nuance Senior Director of Product Management Sander Kloet discussed the importance of addressing the "last mile" challenge in deploying AI for radiology. Kloet noted that in order to realize the potential of AI to advance radiology, it must fit seamlessly into a radiologist's workflow and not be an add-on requiring extra steps. If it doesn't, it simply won't be used.

Kloet said that a radiology department could potentially acquire over a hundred algorithms from dozens of developers, each addressing a specific diagnostic use case. Those need to be organized into a workflow if they are to be effectively used.

For example, AI can identify specific problems such as pulmonary nodules or brain bleeds in medical images. But the results of the image characterization need to be delivered before the radiologist views the image and dictates his or her report, otherwise the radiologist will have to go back to review the AI findings and potentially modify the report. Ideally, the processing can be done quickly enough so that the AI results are available promptly alongside the diagnostic images and the patient history.

The images and patient data displayed for the radiologist come from different software packages. Recognizing how these disparate software packages will be used in a workflow can make them much more effective and their use much more efficient. Kloet summarized, "Ultimately, where we end up at the end of that last mile is using AI to enable radiologists to work more effectively and efficiently, meaningfully address burnout, and most of all, improve patient outcomes."

Workflow solutions address the growing number of sources of computer intelligence and their growing complexity. Workflow applications are a growing area that allows easier use of those CI resources.

Automated data organization

Addressing the issue of "Just the Answer, Please" discussed in the Algorithms section, Google has taken a step toward providing a direct answer to a question rather than a list of Web sites. Its "knowledge panels" display facts about certain subjects as a result of a search inquiry. Providing condensed data for relatively common searches is likely to expand in the future.

A more general task is to research a topic that can't be easily summarized by a single answer, using data from many sources. Sources might include web sites, documents, and audio/video files from company sources, downloaded documents, and the Web. A task that CI will increasingly attack is to organize such data so that one could, for example, see a variety of opinions on a subject in a more compact form. The objective is not to answer a specific question, but to organize a large body of information into a document or other representation that makes it easier to understand the implications of that data. The summary might be a fairly large document referencing all the sources of opinions or data. This category of application could be called "Automated Data Organization" (ADO).

Today, such applications are often targeted at specific types of data and called "analytics" software. For example, speech analytics software summarizes subjects in calls to customer service centers, analyzing a very large number of recorded customer service calls.

The core technologies for ADO would involve natural language processing and possibly the technology called "cluster analysis" or "unsupervised learning." The task is to take files identified by a user as sources and find similar content across files, organizing it by subject with references and links to the source. ADO would further extend the connection of humans with computer intelligence. ADO would supplement human abilities to see patterns in data, providing a condensed summary of the data and making it easier for a person to understand the key information in a large body of data.

Microsoft's updated Edge web browser will have a new feature called Collections that could be considered a form of ADO. Collections will allow users to collect, organize, share, and export content they find online more efficiently. Collections will also be integrated with Microsoft Office.

Collections enables a user to go to a Web page using the Edge browser and click on "Add current page." In addition to adding web pages to Collections, text can be added by highlighting and dragging it into a box in the application. One can also type notes into a Collection.

Once a Collection has formed, one can export it to a Word or Excel document. Some automatic labelling of sources is part of the export. Microsoft will expand features of Collections over time, and competitive services will appear. Collections at a minimum provides a data set for ADO to analyze.

Artificial General Intelligence

What is encompassed under "Artificial Intelligence" is difficult to define crisply. Most experts accept the limitations of the current state of AI technology. To distinguish the current state of AI technology from where it might go, the term Artificial General Intelligence (AGI) has come into broad use to indicate the long-term potential of AI. AGI implies and anticipates further advances in AI to the point it is meaningfully comparable to human intelligence—perhaps in the extreme including characteristics such as self-awareness and ego. AGI requires the development of more "intelligent" methodology than today's AI—methodology which "understands" more, rather than just modeling data.

What does AGI mean in the long run? What technologies might be necessary to achieve AGI goals? Does the inexorable growth of CI power mean AGI is inevitable? Will AGI help solve societal and business problems?

An article by technology journalist Karen Hao in *MIT Technology Review*, published in January 2019, looked at trends in AI research. Hao took the abstracts of 16,625 research papers in AI through November 18, 2018 and used statistical techniques to see the occurrences of particular words to see how their use had evolved. The article found a shift from the term "knowledge-based systems," where the logic was basically constructed by human's entering content and rules, to terms describing data-driven machine learning by the early 2000s.

Initially, there were many approaches to machine learning tried. But, in 2012, Geoffrey Hinton and colleagues at the University of Toronto demonstrated a breakthrough in image recognition at a competition using deep neural nets—"deep learning." This led to many demonstrations of the effectiveness of DNNs, and the current popularity of the method. Faster computation and "big data" have made the technology increasingly effective. Pedro Domingos, a professor of computer science at the University of Washington and author of *The Master Algorithm*, is quoted in Hao's article as saying the '20s will be no different, with the era of deep learning giving way to some new idea or the regeneration of an old idea made more feasible by CI trends.

The use of the terms Artificial Intelligence and Deep Neural Networks suggest a comparison with how humans think. To state the obvious, computers and humans are constructed differently; Computers don't eat, and humans can't be plugged into an electrical outlet. Humans learn about humans by growing up in human bodies; computers learn about humans by the data they generate. A computer can be built on a production line; a human must evolve over a long period from an embryo.

Research suggests that humans create a complex mental model of the world from experience. That model can be very powerful, and, in many respects, can let us do and understand things—particularly things about other humans and their emotions—that computers can't touch today.

The point is that humans are likely to always be better at being human (including human faults with all their drama), and computers will always be better at computation. Computers can evolve considerably faster than humans, and they will hopefully evolve in directions that serve humans better. Perhaps controlling that evolution to be beneficial to humans is more important—and more practical—than trying to fully emulate human thought in computer hardware and software.

Kai-Fu Lee, author of *AI Superpowers*, said on the 60 Minutes TV show in July 2019 that he feared that AI would have a bigger impact on our economy than electricity. However, he said that the advent of AGI was over 30 years away, and "maybe never." It is important to distinguish, as Lee does, between the real impact of today's AI techniques and the vaguer concept of "general intelligence."

Oren Etzioni runs the Allen Institute for Artificial Intelligence, which is attempting to go beyond purely empirical methods. He has talked about "common sense," the knowledge about the world that we take for granted but rarely state out loud. He and his colleagues have created a set of benchmark questions that a truly reasoning AGI ought to be able to answer, such as:

- If I stomp on someone's toe, will they be mad?
- If I put my socks in a drawer, will they be there tomorrow?

Demis Hassabis is co-founder of DeepMind (now owned by Alphabet), the company that built the AI that beat the world champion at Go. In an article in *The Economist 1843* magazine in May 2019, he described AGI as software that, like humans, can do many diverse tasks, from speaking French and carrying on a conversation to understanding physics papers and writing novels, all in one piece of software. He went even further, noting that human intelligence is limited by the size of our skull. Because AGI will run on computers, its intelligence will be limited only by the number of processors available. Hassabis is thus describing AGI not as *mimicking humans* as closely as possible, but as more of a *general-purpose AI*, rather than today's special-purpose AI. His goal for AGI is not to be as smart as humans, but, eventually, to be smarter.

As CI evolves, it may achieve many of the goals Hassabis envisions, but they are more likely to be individual applications, rather than one huge application doing everything. Certainly, doing a specific application better is a worthwhile goal. But it isn't so clear that trying to do all applications with one program will be more effective or even useful.

Skills like writing novels might involve the issue of whether one has to live in a human body to fully understand human emotions. If the AGI goal includes being capable of *all* human abilities, the issue of whether that requires long experience in a human body arises once again.

To the degree AGI thinks like a human, one could ask, what human? An all-knowing superior human? Or one whose past has taught him to distrust authority? One who has racial biases? I guess it would have to be a perfect human. But who's definition of perfect do you adopt? A religious person?

A person who donates to liberal causes? After all, an AGI—if indeed it represents the way humans think as a goal—will be an individual. Or should it suffer from multiple personalities?

As this book is uncomfortable using the term Artificial Intelligence to describe today's machine learning techniques, it objects to the term Artificial General Intelligence to describe the objective of computers doing increasingly more complex tasks as a goal. We are already developing computer intelligence, for example, that can analyze a body of knowledge and pull together information on a particular topic. Such capability already exceeds the ability of a human. A human would not be able to read all the information being summarized in a lifetime, much less break it all down to key concepts. Such CI becomes a tool that can *expand* rather than *emulate* human intelligence.

Humans are more than their brains—they have dominated other species because of their tools. The use of tools is an intrinsic part of being human.

CI is a tool that can provide humans "Augmented Intelligence," doing more than our brain can do alone, just as some machines let us go beyond the strength of our muscles. Augmented Intelligence is more likely to be the result of research into general-purpose AI and CI in general, than trying to develop AGI with the objective of having human qualities.

Antagonistic Computers

A major science fiction theme is humans combating robots that are trying to extinguish humanity. Without going to the extreme of AGI, is it still possible that computer intelligence could in some way inadvertently cause harm to humans?

Humans harm other humans, for reasons that range from simple uncontrolled anger or greed to competition between nations. But why would a computer harm a human? Can computers have similar emotions to humans? Do computers have a sense of being that makes them protect themselves? Could they inadvertently misunderstand their human-set software goals and cause harm? If they did want to harm humans, do they have the means to do so?

Generally, the software that drives computers gets its goals from the designers of the software. If a software designer built a robot for warfare, designed to kill, that is certainly a way that computers can harm people. But such cases don't represent an unexpected result of the software. Are computers likely to develop an unexpected antagonism to a human or to humans in general that could result in harm to those targeted?

The goals set for software might be innocent or even valuable, with occasional bad results. While finding a web page that matches the words in a search inquiry is a valuable service, the result of a search inquiry could be web sites with malware or junk news. Such sites are often designed to attract searches from a user looking for something else.

Machine learning can inadvertently reflect deficiencies in the data it analyzes. In 2016, Microsoft built a chatbot that that used machine learning to learn how to simulate an individual posting tweets. The data used to train the machine learning was actual Twitter messages sent by people in the age range 18-24. The chatbot replicated the language of those humans. As a result, it used bad language and expressed the views of a Nazi sympathizer.

One of the most famous science fiction stories of a computer trying to harm a human in self-defense is the classic 1968 movie *2001: A Space Odyssey*. In that movie, the spacecraft's computer HAL discovers that he is going to be shut down and begins killing crew men until only one crew member Dave is left alive. When Dave leaves the ship in a pod to attempt to rescue another crew member, Hal refuses to let him in when he returns, stating that the astronauts' plan to deactivate him jeopardizes the mission. Dave manages to deactivate HAL, but the scenario suggests that HAL interpreted the goal he had been given as completing the mission over protecting the crew members. In that sense, HAL presumably didn't understand or fear "death," but instead considered his being shut down as violating his software's instructions. The film *2001* highlights the core question of whether a cognitive computer can inadvertently take dangerous actions based on a misunderstanding of its instructions.

Such unanticipated actions could occur. For example, suppose a piece of software is designed to protect a computer system against cyberattacks or malware. The software that does the protecting has to avoid being corrupted itself, or it could no longer achieve that objective. Suppose the software needed to be updated to cover threats not anticipated in its original design, and the developers had to shut it down to make the update. If the software had a component of machine learning that led the software to block system commands that could shut it down—interpreting such actions as malware—it might prevent being shut down. The science-fiction scenario is that it interprets the intent to shut it down as a threat by the human developers and decides it must prevent the humans from shutting the software down by some destructive means.

A *2001*-style action against humans by a computer system requires (1) an objective of the software that can be perverted to an interpretation of humans as a threat; (2) an understanding of the world sufficient enough to come up with such an interpretation; (3) a further understanding of which *specific* humans were the threat, and (4) access to means to harm those specific humans or to eliminate all of humanity. The combination of all those conditions makes a *2001*-style action unlikely.

Risky special cases that deserve special attention do exist. A digital controller for a nuclear reactor must be very carefully designed to fail safely, and shouldn't be given abilities to make decisions based on software like DNNs where the basis for decisions isn't clear.

Iyad Rahwan, Manuel Cebrian, and Nick Obradovich, along with other scientists from the MIT Media Lab, worked with colleagues at the Max Planck Institutes, Stanford University, the University of California San Diego, and other educational institutions, as well as from Google, Facebook, and Microsoft, to publish a paper in *Nature* in 2019, "Machine Behaviour." They made a case for a wide-ranging scientific research agenda aimed at understanding the behavior of artificial intelligence systems. They note that, at present, the scientists who study the behaviors of these AI agents are predominantly the same scientists who have created the agents themselves, and call for a more multidisciplinary approach to understanding the issues raised by machine intelligence.

Perhaps studying issues related to CI using techniques such as machine learning where we may not be fully sure what logic is being used is a valid goal. It may not be a valid goal, however, if the studies are motivated by a view of AI as something fundamentally different than issues that have always existed. A software engineer can certainly write conventional software to do harm; hackers create malware constantly. That is certainly a greater threat than "machine behavior."

Building a brain

Eventually computer power will be such that it might be possible to simulate a human brain. That is, to the degree we understand the chemical functioning of neurons and the specialization of parts of the brain, we should be able to model that functioning with sufficient accuracy that a model containing a very large number of neuron models organized like the human brain could behave like a human brain. That may not be for fifty years, but could eventually be possible.

Is that the ultimate Artificial General Intelligence—simulating a human brain? Obvious problems arise in the process. We can't model a specific human unless we measure every synaptic connection in a person's brain and provide those parameters to this complex model we've created. Perhaps someone considered a genius will donate a brain in death for this purpose; it would nevertheless be extremely difficult to measure those synapses without destroying information. As in quantum theory, it is difficult to measure something without changing it (or in this case, the chemistry around it).

Humans are best served by computer intelligence we can use as a tool, not by attempting to build an artificial human.

Part VII:
What will CI deliver?

A s Computer Intelligence gets more powerful, it will drive the evolution of specific applications. Many of those changes will have significant impacts on society and the economy.

Digital assistants

The core technology of speech recognition and natural language processing will continue to improve, allowing increasing naturalness in connecting with digital systems. The advantage of the use of natural language is that one can just ask in human language for information or an action, avoiding the potential frustration from the over-loaded Graphical User Interface, particularly on smartphones with their small screens and a large finger as the pointing device. Interacting with a digital system by voice or text is a major innovation in the human-computer interface and will become an increasingly important and powerful option.

The general digital assistants such as Google Assistant will continue to get smarter and increasingly intuitive to use. They will increasingly provide *answers* rather than lists of web sites or similar results that require more effort by the user. Some of these answers will be found through conversation, with the digital assistant clarifying the user request by asking questions that narrow the context. The core technology dealing with an inquiry will increasingly evolve to provide the particular answer we are seeking. Not having to fall back on searching through Web sites will tighten our connection with the resources of the Web and of individual companies.

Google demonstrated Google Duplex in 2018, an impressive example of the increasing ability of digital assistants. The AI program managed to book a haircut appointment over the phone; it conducted a conversation as if a human was calling the hair salon, with the person at the salon not even realizing she was talking to a computer. Duplex allows in essence an automated connection with small businesses that primarily interact with customers over the phone. Duplex was available in 44 US states by mid-2019. Google is expanding this feature into "Duplex on the web"; Google Assistant will be able to book movie tickets, make car rentals, and help complete long forms online without having to type everything in yourself.

A digital assistant portal can provide you with access to other companies and services. Ask Google Assistant today, "Show me Beyoncé on Instagram," and the Assistant not only launches the Instagram app, it takes the user directly to the star's page. The specialized assistants you can reach in this manner range from answering questions about a parking ticket to a company's customer service.

Companies must provide a company-specific digital assistant to be connected through the general assistants. Those are built using a toolkit provided by the companies providing the general digital assistant. A company-specific digital assistant compatible with Google Assistant is called an "action" by Google. Amazon's version for its Alexa digital assistant is called a "skill."

For example, Walmart in April 2019 announced that a select number of consumers in a trial can order by voice directly through Google Assistant by enabling the Walmart "action." One can just say something like, "OK Google, ask Walmart to add bananas to my cart."

The general digital assistants will increasingly connect seamlessly with company digital assistants. Google or Amazon, for example, may eventually collect a fee from the company for connecting it as an alternative to advertising.

All the major digital assistants support "skills" or "actions" from independent companies. Amazon's Alexa has some 90,000 skills. Apple has been the slowest to expand this connection, but they have "Siri Shortcuts" and a SiriKit development tool, and are adding companies. Siri integrations include food delivery through Caviar, definitions through Merriam Webster Dictionary access, and trip information provided by Airbnb or American Airlines.

Every company of any size will eventually have a digital assistant to connect with them. If you deal with a company such as your bank often, you may connect directly through a conversational app you downloaded to your smartphone, an app that is developed independent of the toolkits of the general assistants. Or you can use a messaging service like Facebook Messenger and text the company. Or go to the company web site and type or talk to the company digital assistant. When you call a company's customer service line, you may be greeted by a digital assistant that asks you to simply state why you are calling.

According to a study by Adobe Analytics published in May 2019, 91% of business decisionmakers surveyed said they already are making significant investments in voice services such as digital assistants, and 94% said they plan to increase their investments in the next year. The Adobe study found that 22% of companies have released a voice app, while 44% planned to release one in 2019. The highest priority for a voice app was enabling customers to make purchases, according to 45% of survey respondents. This was followed by tracking orders (45%) and making repeat purchases such as refills and subscription renewals (44%).

Heidi Besik, group product marketing manager at Adobe Analytics, was quoted in a company announcement:

> Voice penetration from both the consumer adoption standpoint as well as brand adoption is on a very similar path as mobile was circa 2007, quickly moving into the mainstream. We're reaching a tipping point as more and more consumers use voice services consistently and brands begin to recognize the opportunity.

Company employees will be able to get help with enterprise applications at work using voice interaction. The Salesforce Einstein platform, for example, supports interaction allowing employees to use natural language to access data stored in the Salesforce database.

Companies will increasingly create specialized internal digital assistants that provide answers from the human resources department, as well as other functions that increase employee productivity and give them quick access to information they need to do their jobs. At Microsoft's Build developer conference in 2019, the company showed examples of how their digital assistant Cortana will be able to respond to conversations and organize meetings and reminders proactively, providing an option that is likely to grow into an expanded enterprise version of Cortana.

A digital assistant available on your PC will increasingly help with basic PC functionality and applications. Microsoft's Cortana digital assistant is part of Windows 10; the connection is through talking or typing. Cortana can provide the usual services of a general digital assistant, such as providing a weather forecast. But the specific connection with PC applications can in effect make using a Windows PC more efficient. For example, Cortana can access information in a personal calendar or emails or set an alert. With Microsoft Office having such a dominant position among PC applications (including Apple PCs), it would be logical for Cortana to help with those applications. As complex features are increasingly added to applications, finding them and using them effectively can be a challenge addressed in part by a natural-language voice or text assistant.

Dan Roth, corporate vice president and former CEO of Semantic Machines, which Microsoft acquired in May 2018, described capabilities that Microsoft is developing to maintain conversations. At the Microsoft Build conference in May 2019, Roth announced that the goal is to make computer intelligence more accessible. "Being able to express ourselves in the way we have evolved to communicate and to be able to tie that into all of these really complicated systems without having to know how they work is the promise and vision of natural language interfaces," said Roth.

The Semantic Machines technology is said to extend the role of machine learning beyond determining the what a user wants to do to understanding how to do it. Instead of a programmer trying to write a skill that plans for every context, the Semantic Machines system is said to learn the functionality for itself from data. For example, instead of developing a hand-coded program to get the score of a soccer match, the Semantic Machines approach starts with people who show the system how to get sports scores so that the system can learn to retrieve sports scores. The Semantic Machines technology is said to also remember the context in an extended conversation, so that it can handle tasks that require an extended interaction to complete.

Digital assistants are a major trend in letting computer intelligence augment human intelligence. Being able to ask a digital assistant for help with almost anything will become almost a reflex.

Customer service

An area that has been particularly improved by CI recently is company customer service. Customers are increasingly intolerant of classical customer service telephone lines where one is typically greeted by a long menu of confusing touch-tone options, then a long wait to talk to an agent.

That customer irritation also affects service agents. Agents don't enjoy dealing with irritated customers or common requests that could be automated. According to research conducted by The Quality Assurance & Training Connection (QATC) in 2019, the average annual turnover rate for agents in US contact centers is between 30-45%, more than double the average for all occupations in the US. The statistics suggest that most agents would benefit from having the most repetitive and boring parts of the job done by a computer.

Computer intelligence is behind many evolving trends that address improving customer service:

- *Preference for self-service:* Customers increasingly try a company web site before calling customer service lines. Research in 2019 indicated that, during the previous three years, customers preferred self-service if it was available. A recent survey concluded that only about 20% of customers prefer to solve a problem by contacting an agent.
- *Web sites that handle common issues and questions:* Well-designed web sites can make it relatively easy to find answers to common questions.
- *Automated self-service on web sites:* Today's technology increasingly delivers chatbots on web sites that can answer questions posed in natural language.
- *Automated self-service phone lines:* When a caller does call in, the caller may simply be asked why they are calling, resulting in an

immediate answer or direct transfer to an agent trained to handle the category of request.

- *Contact through general personal assistants:* Many of the personal assistants, such as Amazon's Alexa, allow connecting by voice with a company digital assistant for customer service.
- *Mobile apps:* A company-specific mobile app using natural language interaction can be downloaded to a smartphone for a company, e.g., a bank, that the customer contacts often.

In April 2019, Audible, Amazon's audiobook company, introduced a customer service feature that exemplifies the synergy between elements of computer intelligence. The feature allows US owners of Amazon Echo devices to call Audible's live customer service line 24 hours a day, seven days a week, through their Echo. All users have to do is say "Alexa, call Audible," to launch the feature. Customer support agents can then aid customers with audiobook recommendations, exchanges, technical problems, and the Audible app setup.

A study by Juniper Research in May 2019 concluded that, by automating many of the customer interactions now handled by customer service agents, retailers can expect to cut costs by $439 billion a year in 2023, up from $7 billion in 2019. The study also analyzed the impact of chatbots that include marketing and closing sales in addition to typical customer service. Juniper forecast that retail sales from chatbot-based interactions will reach $112 billion by 2023, a huge jump from $7.3 billion in 2019.

Improving the World Wide Web

The World Wide Web (WWW) is mature, built on standards that are unlikely to change much since such change would likely be disruptive. Web search tools have become very effective. Web-site building tools are likely to continue to evolve, making it relatively easy for anyone to build a web site.

The importance of the Web as a marketing medium will continue to grow. In 2019, worldwide digital ad spending (as opposed to print or radio/TV advertising) will rise by 17.6% to $333 billion, according to eMarketer. That means that, for the first time, digital advertising will account for roughly half of the global ad market. In some countries, including the UK, China, Norway and Canada, digital ads have already become the dominant ad medium.

Tim Berners-Lee, one of the founders of the WWW, expressed his concerns over the evolution of the Web in March 2019 on the Web Foundation web site. He indicated that he saw three major sources of dysfunction affecting today's web:

1. *Deliberate, malicious intent*, such as state-sponsored hacking and attacks, criminal behavior, and online harassment;

2. *System design that creates perverse incentives*, such as ad-based revenue models that commercially reward "clickbait"—links that attract clicks through misrepresentation or sensationalism—leading to the viral spread of misinformation; and

3. *Unintended negative consequences* of a web site, such as an outraged and negative tone in online discourse.

The first category requires laws against such behavior and effective enforcement of those laws, Berners-Lee argued. While such laws can have a positive effect, there are complications when web sites are international and when the volume of such violations make them difficult to effectively police and prosecute.

The second category—perverse incentives—could be addressed if organizations that use ad-based revenue models exercise some control over misuse. Some providers of social media are now trying to do their own policing. They can be aided by computer intelligence that identifies sites or content that should be examined by humans for violations of policy.

The third category could also be addressed with tools that identify potentially negative content. The difficulty is often distinguishing controversial opinions stated strongly from truly inappropriate content. Computer intelligence could give an objective rating to sites through web browsers, much like the labelling of motion pictures with labels such as "PG-13" created by the Motion Picture Association of America. Such labels would not block the sites, but only provide guidance as to content. Misleading sites intended to steal confidential information or install malware could be labelled as "suspicious."

By having an objective empirical algorithm making the decision based on a large database of web sites rated by humans, one might be able to avoid legal challenges based on "free speech" considerations. A DNN would average opinions from many humans in its creation, potentially avoiding extremes. The DNN could be considered objective, and would avoid the potential individual bias (and liability) of a human determining the final labeling.

As previously suggested, an industry organization could reduce the impact of junk news by offering the option to "certify" news sites that agreed to defined good practices. Sites would apply for certification. If granted, the certification would be periodically reviewed. That approach could work for the subset of web sites that want to be considered "real news."

The Web Foundation suggested addressing the developing problems with a "Contract for the Web," which could apply as well to governments that try to control access to content they don't like. As of March 2019, the Foundation listed core principles about governments ensuring everyone can connect to the Internet and respect the right to privacy. They said companies should similarly respect privacy and personal data and "develop technologies that support the best in humanity and challenge the worst." They said citizens should build communities that respect civil discourse and human dignity so that everyone feels safe and welcome online and fight for principles such as those stated. If the Foundation publicized examples of violations of such policies, it might deter some bad practices.

Digital payments

In the US, credit cards are the major form of payment. CI on mobile phones is moving toward changing that.

Payment by apps such as Alipay on a smartphone is the norm in China. Alipay is owned by Ant Financial, an affiliate company of China's Alibaba Group. Alipay has about one billion active users. Chinese tourists in Europe have even motivated its acceptance there. Roland Palmer, head of Europe for Alipay, told CNBC in June 2019 that the company has tripled the number of European merchants accepting its online and mobile payment platform to "tens of thousands" in the past year. Neiman Marcus has added Alipay as a payment option in the US.

WeChat Pay, which is run by Chinese rival Tencent, is a competitor. WeChat is a multi-purpose messaging, social media, and mobile payment app. It was first released in 2011, and became one of the world's largest standalone mobile apps by 2018, with over 1 billion monthly active users.

Credit cards are not widely used for payment in China. China has been slow in providing licenses to the major US credit card firms, and tourists using them in China typically incur fees. Currently, the Chinese credit card market is dominated by China UnionPay, the state-owned bank card network founded in 2002.

Payment by mobile apps is usually quick and avoids the need to carry a physical card. The mobile payment market is forecast to grow to about $4.6 trillion worldwide by 2023, up from $601 billion in 2016, according to Allied Market Research.

The US is moving slowly but with momentum toward the mobile payment option. Digital wallets from Alipay, Apple, Google, PayPal, Samsung, and WeChat, among others, are spreading in the US. US payments processors Visa and Mastercard are exploring competitive options. At the beginning of 2019, Mastercard removed the Mastercard name from its logo to help broaden its suite of products beyond physical cards and to accommodate smaller screens on smartphones and other mobile devices.

Apple Pay, which was introduced in 2014, lets consumers make secure purchases in stores, in apps, and on the web and to send and receive money from friends and family in Messages. Apple Pay was accepted as a payment method in 74 of the top 100 retailers in the US in mid-2019. Android Pay and Samsung Pay, which offer similar convenience for non-iPhones, have also grown in popularity.

Apple introduced its Apple Card in mid-2019. The credit card comes in physical form, but the main intent of Apple is to have you use it on your iPhone, making your phone a wallet. The card has cash-back features, with immediate feedback on cash credits, helping to motivate its use. Part of the motivation for the Apple Card is Apple's shift to garner more revenue from services, but the wide adoption of the service could also further motivate owning an iPhone.

In June 2019, Facebook promised to launch its own international currency, Libra, within a year. Calibra is Facebook's name for the digital wallet storing the Libra currency.

Libra is said to "empower billions of people" in countries where exchanging currencies isn't easy. Libra is a cryptocurrency based on blockchain, the technology behind Bitcoin. The currency can be used to transmit payment through Facebook's WhatsApp or Messenger, or through a yet-to-be-available independent app. Facebook announced 27 partners that include Visa, Mastercard, Uber, and PayPal. Libra will be backed by normal currency in reserve accounts to reduce speculative movement.

Facebook's goal is for consumers to use Libra to pay their bills, buy things, and send money to family members abroad, among other everyday financial transactions. The Libra Association, the Geneva-based not-for-profit that will govern the currency, will design and spread user and merchant incentives, which could include discounts.

Facebook could use the information it gathers on what individuals are buying to offer targeted ads—one way to create revenues from the service. Facebook has said, however, that it won't mingle social and financial data.

Facebook has encountered resistance to Libra. Billionaire businessman Mark Cuban called Facebook's launch of Libra and its foray into cryptocurrency a "big mistake" in a July 2019 interview. Apparently, his concern is that it will create a dangerous overreaction in autocratic governments that see it as a challenge to their currency.

Robots

As CI becomes cheaper and the control technology advances, consumers and company employees can expect to see more robots. For example, in June 2019, McDonald's announced it was trying to speed up service, faced with increasing competition from other fast-food outlets and declining sales at fast-food outlets overall. The company is testing speech recognition for a drive-through restaurant in suburban Chicago, where, inside the restaurant, a robot throws fries, chicken, and fish into a vat of oil. Mason Smoot, McDonald's senior vice president, told the *Wall Street Journal*, that the technology wouldn't threaten jobs: "The idea of technology is to help our crew—to make it easier and better for them."

The *Wall Street Journal* indicated that other fast-food operators were testing technology to improve service. Domino's has tested speech recognition for phone ordering. Other chains are testing self-operating ovens and dishwashers, as well as robots that flip burgers.

Walmart is expanding its use of robots in stores. The country's largest private employer said in April 2019 that at least 300 stores out of its 4,600 US stores in 2019 will add machines that scan shelves for out-of-stock products. Autonomous floor scrubbers will be deployed in 1,500 stores to help speed up cleaning. The number of conveyor belts that automatically scan and sort products as they come off trucks will more than double to 1,200.

Walmart told the *Wall Street Journal* that the addition of a single machine can cut a few hours a day of work previously done by a human, allowing Walmart to allocate fewer people to complete a task. "With automation we are able to take away some of the tasks that associates don't enjoy doing," Mark Propes, senior director of central operations for Walmart US told the *Journal*. "At the same time, we continue to open up new jobs in other things in the store."

AMP Robotics' builds recycling robots that improve the accuracy of separating items through vision systems. The company's equipment is trained by being shown millions of images—it can identify types of plastic or paper using everything from logos to box shapes to the color of the plastic items. Given the high turnover in jobs where humans help with the sorting, this technology makes recycling more effective and economical. Recycling sorters are another example of CI doing things that humans really don't want to do.

Healthcare

Affordable healthcare is a growing issue globally. Both diagnosing illnesses and treating them are expensive, with the growth in healthcare professionals slower than the need for their services. According to the US Bureau of Labor Statistics (BLS), between 2006 and 2016, 2.8 million jobs were added to the health sector. The rate of growth was almost seven times faster than the rest of the economy. The BLS projects an 18% growth of jobs in healthcare settings from 2016 to 2026.

Computer intelligence can help reduce the cost of healthcare, as well as make it more effective in tasks such as helping doctors enter data into Electronic Health Records. At the World Medical Innovation Forum in May 2019, speakers expressed concern that the healthcare system is not doing enough to adequately prepare itself for the fundamental changes that AI will bring over the next several decades. "I would like to see a complete reframing of the healthcare challenge, especially in terms of rewarding early detection and prevention," said Noubar Afeyan, founder and CEO of Flagship Pioneering, a venture capital company, suggesting the role that AI can contribute in early prediction of problems.

We are living longer as we conquer disease. Famine—historically, a major cause of death—is unusual. Some futurists have even predicted we will eventually live forever, at least those who can afford the treatments to resurrect youth. In any case, it is fairly clear ignoring the potential of manmade and natural calamities such as global warming, nuclear war, and an asteroid striking earth—that the average lifespan of humans will increase.

Population experts emphasize the burden of a globally aging population, with retired people being indirectly supported by a smaller percentage of the population still working. In the US, where healthcare spending is over 17% of GDP, people over 65 will outnumber those under 18 by 2035, according to the US Census Bureau. People aged 65 and older in Japan make up a quarter of its total population, estimated to reach a third by 2050. As people live longer, they require more expensive long-term care.

Japan's aging population is leading it to pioneer the use of technology and CI to improve caretaking of the elderly. A *Wall Street Journal* article in

January 2019 gave an example of this innovation. The Sawayaka-en nursing home outside Tokyo houses residents who average 86 years old. At the facility, 48 rooms have been equipped with four devices that monitor the occupants and stream data to the nurses' station, using software from a company called Z-Works. Under the bed, a palm-sized Doppler radar sensor, developed with Sharp, monitors heartbeat and breathing. Other devices track whether people are at risk of falling out of bed or are taking too long to get back from the toilet, with alerts to caregivers.

The problem isn't simply an economic one—aging can also be an emotional burden that affects health and well-being. The share of American adults who say they're lonely has doubled since the 1980s to 40%, according to the American Association of Retired People (AARP). The Amazon Echo and other distance-talking devices could entertain the elderly with information, music, games, jokes, and other interaction that could potentially make their lives more pleasant and less lonely. Even though the interaction is minimal, it engages the user more than simply watching TV.

Addressing the broader population, there are solutions that can help maintain health and detect problems. Wearable and mobile devices, such as fitness bracelets or smartwatches, typically have health-monitoring options. AliveCor, maker of the KardiaMobile electrocardiogram monitor for the iPhone and the KardiaBand EKG recorder for the Apple Watch, is gathering data from its devices that could someday feed a machine-learning system to help physicians spot disease.

Apple is conducting Apple Watch wearable patient monitoring/recording tests with more than 100 healthcare institutions around the country. This includes such things as an alert sent to the physician of record when a problem is detected.

In one potential application of CI, a "bloodless blood test" would look at a subtle shift in the EKG that's characteristic of a potassium blood-level elevation, a shift that the software is able to identify. Measuring this marker in real time, from the convenience of a phone or smartwatch, could transform how clinicians treat people after a heart attack or while on certain medications.

In his 2019 book, *Deep Medicine: How Artificial Intelligence Can Make Healthcare Human Again*, Eric Topol cited an example that could become more common. A machine learning algorithm associated a specific genetic difference in an infant's DNA that, combined with symptoms such as seizures, led to a family discovering the child had a rare genetic disease that only required a fairly mild treatment. Other treatments tried by doctors who didn't recognize the disease had made the child worse.

CI can examine high volumes of health data, such as using natural language processing to review medical papers for their key conclusions. No single doctor could manage to keep up with all the rapid developments and still have time for patients. Topol warns, however, that machine learning can only discover what is in the data, whereas a physician can try several options that might work in unusual cases, using their experience and logic.

A number of studies have shown that medical specialists can benefit from the help of AI. For example, a team of international researchers published an article in the *Annals of Oncology* in August 2018 on the performance of convolutional neural nets (CNNs) versus human doctors in recognizing images of skin cancer versus benign moles. The researchers made the comparison "with a large international group of 58 dermatologists, including 30 experts." They found, "Most dermatologists were outperformed by the CNN. Irrespective of any physicians' experience, they may benefit from assistance by a CNN's image classification."

To add to the complexity of today's medicine, researchers are developing tools that can selectively engineer the genetic code, providing a new, complex option for preventing and curing genetically related diseases. A powerful gene-editing tool, CRISPR, which makes gene editing more feasible than previous techniques, is creating more options.

Suppose a research team analyzed the DNA of hundreds of millions of individuals and matched it with physical characteristics—IQ, genetic or psychological illnesses, and other characteristics that might be determined by DNA. Machine learning could be used to detect which DNA sequences were correlated with specific characteristics and under what qualifying conditions. The result of such an analysis and follow-on conventional research to validate or qualify the results could provide a guide to modifying DNA to avoid or treat a genetic illness (or, controversially, create designer babies).

Privacy issues would be a major issue even if the DNA data wasn't labelled with the individual, since it could be matched with an individual if that individual appeared later in a DNA database. Such considerations might mean countries that might not be particularly concerned about privacy—such as China—could take the lead in such research because of fewer restrictions.

China has in fact produced designer babies with CRISPR. In November 2018, He Jiankui of Southern University of Science and Technology of China announced that he had edited the DNA of human embryos to create twin baby girls, Lulu and Nana, who he said had been born "crying into the world as healthy as any other babies." One of the parents had HIV, and the gene editing was intended to avoid the baby inheriting the disease. The gene that was supposedly modified in this case was CCR5, which the HIV virus needs to inject itself into human blood cells. CCR5 also has established links to cognitive abilities in mice, to memory formation, and to helping the human brain recover after a stroke, so the gene editing could possibly enhance the twins' IQ.

Such an experiment was attacked as unethical, and the long-term effect in this case is still to be seen. Nevertheless, its existence illustrates that many parents may be motivated to participate in such experiments if the government allows.

One potential issue is in using CRISPR to edit genes is the danger of the process modifying parts of the genome that were not targeted, so-called "off-target" activity. Such off-target changes could have adverse effects. A paper by Jennifer Listgarten of Microsoft and Michael Weinstein of UCLA and other researchers from Microsoft, Zymo Research, Massachusetts General Hospital, Harvard Medical School, and the Broad Institute of MIT, published in January 2018, described the first machine-learning based approach (called "Elevation") to off-target prediction. The research showed that the most widely used method of predicting off-target effects performs no better than random at times, whereas Elevation consistently outperformed it, sometimes by an order of magnitude. Because of the computational demands of off-target prediction, the researchers developed a cloud-based service to use the technology.

Richard Andersen, a Caltech professor, described an experiment in his laboratory in an April 2019 paper, "The Intention Machine." A paralyzed volunteer sat in a wheelchair while controlling a computer or robotic limb just with his or her thoughts, drinking a beer without help for the first time in more than ten years. The connection between his brain and the robotic limb was direct; it occurred a year after surgery that implanted electrodes in his brain. His thoughts were interpreted to direct the artificial limb. The work followed years of research, including experiments with primates. Some research has examined a brain connection through measuring brain activity from the scalp without intrusive wiring, but the information that can be deduced from that indirect measurement would allow only limited control by an individual. Such research represents extreme cases difficult to replicate in volume, but is nevertheless impressive and may have implications for the very long term.

CI can both improve the quality and efficiency of delivering medical solutions. Such help will be necessary given the growing need for medical services.

Food production

The world's human population of about 7.6 billion is projected to reach 11.2 billion by 2100. We will thus need a food production and distribution system that can accommodate another 3.6 billion people based on this prediction. According to a UN study, by 2050, global food production will need to increase by an estimated 70% in developed countries and 100% in developing countries to match trends in population growth.

One problem is a limit on agricultural land to produce the food, despite our having become much more efficient in using the available land. In 2018, about half of habitable land globally was dedicated to agriculture, with a large proportion dedicated to livestock.

In a 2018 study, researchers Poore and Nemecek noted that a shift away from meat and dairy consumption would help relieve pressure on agricultural land, as well as reduce environmental impact: "Meat, aquaculture, eggs, and dairy use about 83% of the world's farmland and contribute 56 to 58% of food's different emissions, despite providing only 37% of our protein and 18% of our calories." Plant-based meat substitutes may become an important alternative.

Farmers are having more trouble getting seasonal workers to pick crops. "The labor force keeps shrinking," said Gary Wishnatzki, a third-generation strawberry farmer quoted by the *Washington Post*. "If we don't solve this with automation, fresh fruits and veggies won't be affordable or even available to the average person."

Crops such as strawberries require selection of ripe fruits and careful picking to avoid damage to the strawberry and the plant. Harvest CROO Robotics has developed a robotic strawberry picker that handles this tough task (Figure 26). Tests show that "Harv" can successfully pick strawberries, but isn't as good yet as human workers in identifying all valid candidates.

Figure 26: A mechanical strawberry picker
from Harvest CROO Robotics.

A drawback of industrial-scale farming is the use of heavy machinery such as tractors and harvesters. They compact the soil and hurt a plant's ability to develop a healthy root system. This factor may be behind a reduction in crop yields in some areas in recent decades.

Vertical farming is one way to grow more plant food without heavy machinery. It is a trend in its early stages today, but may become a major way humanity can continue to support its basic need for food. Vertical farming is greenhouse farming with stacked multiple layers of plants (Figure 27). A vertical farm in Japan harvests approximately 10,000 heads of lettuce per day in a 2,300 square meter building, about one hundred times the volume that could be produced on a similar size piece of horizontally farmed land. The controlled environment of a greenhouse could prove necessary in the long term if global warming creates significant climate change.

Figure 27: A vertical farm

Farming in greenhouses provides the ability to farm anywhere, even in the middle of a city. Early growth of greenhouse farming was driven in part by marijuana cultivation in states where it is legal.

Such environments can use hydroponic systems that grow plants without soil by using mineral nutrient solutions in a water solvent. Such systems can be lit by LEDs that mimic sunlight. Software can ensure that all the plants get the same amount of light, water, and nutrients. Proper management means that no herbicides or pesticides are required and there is less water wastage than conventional farming.

Scotland's Intelligent Growth Solutions (IGS) has a demonstration vertical farm using its technology. The approach makes farming more like a factory operation and allows produce to be grown locally and on demand. The technology could reduce fresh food waste by up to 90%, according to IGS. It uses AI and specially designed power and communication technologies which IGS says reduces energy costs by 50% and labor costs by 80% compared to other indoor growing environments. It can produce yields of up to 200% more than that of a traditional greenhouse. The major *disadvantage* of vertical farming is that it requires artificial energy sources while conventional farming uses the sun.

These trends are sufficiently obvious that, in some quarters, they are interpreted as investment opportunities. Predicting future food crises, investment firm Merrill Lynch has advised clients to invest in vertical farms and "smart hydroponics."

Energy

One aspect of increasing computer intelligence is that it takes a surprising amount of energy to support that computation. According to a paper published by US researchers in late 2017, the Information and Communications (ICT) industry will be responsible for up to 3.5% of global emissions by 2020, with this amount potentially escalating to 14% by 2040.

In an era where energy efficiency is becoming increasingly important, good practices can reduce that impact. An earlier section described how Google reduced energy consumption considerably in a data center using machine learning to optimize factors such as cooling the equipment. Google has unveiled plans to build a $672 million data center in Hamina, Finland, a second center at that location. The first used a cooling system that relies on seawater from the Gulf of Finland, and presumably this is why Google is building a second at this location.

Computer intelligence can be used to improve energy usage more generally. Machine learning has made wind farms more productive by optimizing the orientation of turbine heads to capture a greater fraction of the incoming wind. Solar forecasting can better predict how clouds and other changing weather formations will affect solar output.

Machine learning can also help classical non-renewable energy sources. Machine learning systems can improve the ability to map and understand the size and value of underground deposits of oil and gas.

Education

CI can contribute to improving education, a problem with many complex dimensions. The discussion here will be limited to one example.

The *Los Angeles Times* reported in June 2019 on the efforts by a startup, Bamboo Learning, to get their educational solution into the classroom. The software works through Amazon's Alexa, and thus interacts by voice. Ian Freed, a co-founder and previous Amazon executive, was quoted in the article as having the ambitious goal "to build a company that is the leader in voice-powered education." The software uses versions of the Echo with a screen, so visual aids are available. The Bamboo service reads stories and pauses to ask children questions about what they heard. The objective is to encourage students to read.

The success of such educational services may depend on clear goals and a careful choice of material. At this point, it is probably safe to say that computer intelligence provides alternative ways of delivering educational material that may appeal to some children and can be tailored to special needs. CI may reduce the burden on teachers to deal with widely varying abilities in the classroom by using technology, acting, in effect, as a teacher's aide.

Criminal investigations

CI has provided law enforcement with tools and databases that help solve crimes, from searchable past offences by individuals to fingerprint databases. The amount of data that must be searched can present problems, particularly in cases where part of the evidence includes videos from a suspect's hard drive. The time to search videos can affect a prosecution, particularly in countries like Canada where a case not prosecuted in a timely fashion can allow the perpetrator to go free.

Noah Spitzer-Williams from Axon Technologies noted at a conference in June 2019 that searching videos in cases like child exploitation can cause even further problems—investigators reviewing many terrible scenes can suffer mental health issues. Using machine learning to find the clearest cases in videos can both accelerate the effort and reduce the burden on investigators.

Another example Spitzer-Williams gave of the use of AI was in detecting child trafficking. Machine learning was used to identify children in photos that were ten years or younger, saving 9,000 children in three years.

Real estate

It might seem that selling homes would remain very much a human process, with buyers carefully deciding if a house is for them and what it is worth. But the advent of companies going into the real estate market to either buy houses to "flip" or buying them to rent in volume has increased the role of computer intelligence.

The testing ground for this approach seems to be in fast-growing Phoenix, Arizona. According to a June 2019 article in the *Wall Street Journal*, companies like Opendoor Labs evaluate homes with algorithms and with having photos of a home uploaded over the Internet. Based on such information and on comparable sales, they make a decision which often includes making repairs. They resell to buyers who visit using an app on their mobile phone to unlock the door. Buyers make an offer online, and the home is sold quickly. The profit may be relatively small, but the theory is to make it up in volume.

Companies that rent homes also count on volume and keeping the cost of operation at a minimum. According to the WSJ article, Invitation Homes is the country's largest single-family landlord. Big investors now own more than 22,000 rental houses in metro Phoenix. The approach works best in cities with relatively new and homogenous construction; it would be more difficult in cities like San Francisco or New York.

The companies use automated house-hunting algorithms. Progress Residential, which has built the third-largest pool of rental homes in the US, says its proprietary technology can find properties fitting its investment criteria—such as a sunny kitchen in a good school district—within minutes of their listing.

Because the companies expect to renovate, they don't overly worry about the condition of the houses. Homeowners can avoid the need to renovate and repair to sell the house, and sometimes take these quick offers to avoid the hassle. Again, volume can help; the volume buyers can maintain a full-time renovation staff or at least negotiate favorable rates. CI may revolutionize the currently human-centric business of home sales in some cities.

Self-driving vehicles

In March 2018, an Uber self-driving SUV being testing in Arizona struck and killed a woman as she was crossing the street. Whatever the circumstances of this particular accident, it became clear that every accident with a self-driving vehicle would be news, despite the deaths of some 40,000 people killed in the US by human driving annually which don't generate headlines. The hurdle for acceptance of self-driving technology is high. Some analysts believe it may require "smart cities" with specialized traffic lanes and other accommodations to make it a mass market.

Diana Furchtgott-Roth, Deputy Assistant Secretary for Research and Technology, US Department of Transportation, speaking on a panel at AI World Government in June 2019, said that limited applications, such as truck platoons, show great promise. On the same panel, however, Jeff Marootian,

Director, DC District Department of Transportation, warned that it is unlikely any agency will ever say that automated vehicles are "safe enough."

Like all new technologies, there will be unanticipated consequences. Already, tricksters are stopping automated vehicles by posting fake stop signs other than at intersections, snarling traffic because of the automated vehicles' requirement to fully stop at all stop signs. Baltimore has five automated-vehicle trials in the area, and, according to Karina Ricks, Director of Mobility and Infrastructure of the City of Pittsburgh, speaking on an AI World Government panel in 2019, there has been a significant increase in pedestrians stepping into traffic, comfortable that the cars will brake. Ricks said, more generally, that accidents should be expected, but that the slower average speeds of automated vehicles should reduce damage relative to similar accidents with human drivers.

Although self-driving vehicles may in fact be safer than human-driven vehicles, it is likely that their deployment will be selective and potentially much slower than some predict.

This section's examples of CI impacting certain applications areas are selective. The technology will impact almost every part of our lives.

The bottom line

Computer Intelligence impacts most things we do today in ways that have become so commonplace we hardly notice. We take for granted the minor miracle of navigation software that uses an incredible combination of digital technologies to get us quickly from where we are to where we want to be. We watch a wonderful old movie classic whenever and wherever we want. Our software reminds us of a relative's birthday and helps us send good wishes. The functions contributed by CI have become an integral part of our lives today, yet are relatively recent developments.

Computer Intelligence is a foundation of our economy, from supporting the internal operations of companies to matching people with jobs. We find and compare products using the services of the Web. Automated Teller Machines provide us cash when banks are closed.

CI will continue to grow exponentially and become more powerful because of several factors, including cloud computing and specialized semiconductor chips. It can continue to improve our lives in both simple and complex ways that we will eventually take for granted. The impact is likely to accelerate at a rate that will surprise us.

We notice CI's effect most clearly when that power crosses a tipping point that produces a surprise we didn't anticipate—a breakthrough. Artificial Intelligence is one of those breakthroughs. AI is considered to be so important today that countries have made it an official strategic objective to compete effectively in developing and using the technology. Companies talk about the necessity of having an "AI Strategy." There will be more such tipping points as CI continues to evolve.

CI's impact, however, doesn't depend on breakthroughs. Its contribution is also slow and steady improvement of the many tools we already use in our jobs and our life. Existing applications will be incrementally improved with software updates.

Humans have always extended their innate capabilities through tools. Many of our tools extend the capabilities of our muscles, ranging from levers to motors. CI is rapidly extending the capabilities of our brain—"Augmented Intelligence."

The increasing influence of CI brings dangers as well as solutions. These challenges range from the ease of spreading misinformation to destructive cyberattacks. There are approaches to minimizing these dangers, but solutions require systematic approaches to specific problems, not a blanket condemnation of AI.

Reducing the likelihood of cyberattacks requires government action. A recognition that this is the new battleground is required to increase resources in combating cyberwar. Similarly, individual companies must increase efforts to avoid cyberattacks and delivery of misinformation.

The evolution of CI will continue to have major impacts on society, economics, and war. Humans working together can control that evolution to enjoy its benefits and minimize its dangers.

References

Amoroso, Edward, "Recent Progress in Software Security," IEEE Software, vol. 35, no. 2, 2018.

Andersen, Richard, "The Intention Machine: A new generation of brain-machine interface can deduce what a person wants," Scientific American, April 2019.

Arntz, Melanie, Terry Gregory and Ulrich Zierahn, "The Risk of Automation for Jobs in OECD Countries, A Comparative Analysis," OECD Social, Employment and Migration Working Papers (Organisation for Economic Co-operation and Development), 14 May 2016.

Assessing Russian Activities and Intentions in Recent US Elections, Intelligence Community Assessment, Office of the Director of National Intelligence, 8 January 2018.

Baran, Paul, "Reliable Digital Communications Systems Using Unreliable Network Repeater Nodes," RAND Corporation papers (1960).

Bellman, Richard, *Dynamic Programming*, Princeton University Press, 1957.

Berners-Lee, Tim, "30 years on, what's next #ForTheWeb?," World Wide Web Foundation, 2019.

Blanchflower, David G., *Not Working: Where Have All the Good Jobs Gone?*, Princeton University Press, 2019.

Boole, George, "An Investigation of the Laws of Thought on Which are Founded the Mathematical Theories of Logic and Probabilities," 1854.

Breiman, Leo, and Jerome Friedman, Richard Olshen, Charles Stone, *Classification and Regression Trees* (Wadsworth Statistics/Probability), 1984.

Bricker, Darrel, and John Ibbitson, Empty Planet: The Shock of Global Population Decline, Crown Publishing, 2019.

Bruinsma, Jelle, "The Resource Outlook To 2050: By How Much Do Land, Water And Crop Yields Need To Increase By 2050?", Food and Agriculture Organization of the United Nations, June 2009.

Brynjolfsson, Erik, and Andrew McFee, *The Second Machine Age: Work, Progress, and Prosperity in a Time of Brilliant Technologies*, W.W. Norton & Company (2016).

Brynjolfsson, Erik, Tom Mitchell, and Daniel Rock. 2018, "What Can Machines Learn, and What Does It Mean for Occupations and the Economy?", AEA Papers and Proceedings, May 2018.

Bryson, Bill, *A Short History of Nearly Everything*, Crown Publishing (2003).

Bush, Vannevar, "As We May Think," The Atlantic, July 1945.

California Health Care Foundation, "U.S. Health Care Spending: Who Pays?", December 2015.

Carrier, Mark, From Smartphones to Social Media: How Technology Affects Our Brains and Behavior, Greenwood, 2018.

Carr, Nicholas, *The Glass Cage: Automation and Us*, W.W. Norton, 2014.

Centers for Medicare and Medicaid Services, "History of Health Spending in the United States, 1960-2013," November 19, 2015.

Centers for Medicare and Medicaid Services, "National Health Expenditures Summary Including Share of GDP, CY 1960-2017".

Chen, Yu-Hsin, and Joel Emer, Vivienne Sze, "Eyeriss v2: A Flexible and High-Performance Accelerator for Emerging Deep Neural Networks," arXiv:1807.07928, 10 July 2018.

Chui, Michael, and Rita Chung, Ashley van Heteren, "Using AI to help achieve Sustainable Development Goals," United Nations Development Program, www.undp.org/content/undp/en/home/blog/2019/Using_AI_to_help_achieve_Sustainable_Development_Goals.html.

Despommier, Dickson, *The Vertical Farm: Feeding the World in the 21st Century*, Macmillan, 2010.

Dhurandhar, Amit, et al, "Improving Simple Models with Confidence Profiles," November 2018.

Domingos, Pedro, *The Master Algorithm, How the Quest for the Ultimate Learning Machine Will Remake Our World*, Basic Books, 2015.

du Pin Clamon, Flavio, et al, "Data Pre-Processing for Discrimination Prevention: Information-Theoretic Optimization and Analysis," IEEE Journal of Selected Topics in Signal Processing, Oct. 2018.

Dyakonov, Mikhail, "The Case Against Quantum Computing," IEEE Spectrum, March 2019, pp. 24-29.

Dyrbye LN, Shanafelt TD, Sinsky CA, et al., "Burnout among health care professionals: a call to explore and address this underrecognized threat to safe, high-quality care," NAM Perspectives: discussion paper, National Academy of Medicine, 2017 (https://nam.edu/burnout-among-health-care-professionals).

Dyson, George B., *Darwin among the Machines: The evolution of global intelligence*, Basic Books (1997).

Eckersley, Peter, "The Cautious Path to Strategic Advantage: How Militaries Should Plan for AI," Electronic Frontier Foundation, August 2018.

Ethically Aligned Design, First Edition: A Vision for Prioritizing Human Wellbeing with Autonomous and Intelligent Systems, IEEE, 2019.

"Ethics guidelines for trustworthy AI," European Commission, April 2019, https://ec.europa.eu/digital-single-market/en/news/ethics-guidelines-trustworthy-ai.

Fombu, Emmanuel, and Dane Cobain, *The Future of Healthcare*, 2018.

Ford, Martin, *Architects of Intelligence: The truth about AI from the people building it*, Packt Publishing, 2018.

Ford, Martin, *Rise of the Robots: Technology and the Threat of a Jobless Future*, Basic Books, 2016.

Franklin, Stan, "A Foundational Architecture for Artificial General Intelligence," Frontiers in Artificial Intelligence and Applications, June 2007.

Frey, Carl Benedikt, *The Technology Trap: Capital, Labor, and Power in the Age of Automation*, Princeton University Press, 2019.

Frey, Carl Benedikt and Michael A. Osborne, "The future of employment: How susceptible are jobs to computerisation?", Technological Forecasting and Social Change, Volume 114, January 2017, Pages 254-280.

Garvie, Clare, "Garbage in, Garbage Out: Face recognition on flawed data," Georgetown Law Center on Privacy & Technology, May 16, 2019.

Gates, Bill, "How we'll invent the future," MIT Technology Review, February 2019.

Gil, Dario, "Highlights of Papers and Predictions from IBM Research AI," www.ibm.com/blogs/research/2018/12/ai-year-review/.

Giles, Martin, "Triton is the world's most murderous malware, and it's spreading," MIT Technology Review, March 5, 2019.

Gladwell, Malcolm, *The Tipping Point, How little things can make a big difference*, Little Brown (2002).

Google, "Perspectives on Issues in AI Governance," https://ai.google/perspectives-on-issues-in-AI-governance.

Gunning, David, "Explainable AI (XAI)," DARPA (https://www.darpa.mil/program/explainable-artificial-intelligence).

Haenssle, H.A., et al, "Man against machine: diagnostic performance of a deep learning convolutional neural network for dermoscopic melanoma recognition in comparison to 58 dermatologists," Annals of Oncology, Volume 29, Issue 8, August 2018.

Hao, Karen, "We analyzed 16,625 papers to figure out where AI is headed next," MIT Technology Review, February 2019.

Hinton, Geoffrey, et al, "Deep Neural Networks for Acoustic Modeling in Speech Recognition," IEEE Signal Processing Magazine, November 2012.

Hodson, Hal, "DeepMind and Google: the battle to control artificial intelligence," The Economist 1843 magazine, April/May 2019.

Hughes, Chris, "It's Time to Break Up Facebook," New York Times, May 9, 2019.

Hunt, Melissa, et.al., "No More FOMO: Limiting Social Media Decreases Loneliness and Depression," Journal of Social and Clinical Psychology: Vol. 37, No. 10, 2018.

Isaacson, Walter, *The Innovators*, Simon & Schuster, 2014.

Kurzweil, Ray, *The Singularity Is Near: When Humans Transcend Biology*, Viking Penguin (2005).

Latiff, Robert H., *Future War: Preparing for the New Global Battlefield*, Alfred A. Knopf, 2017.

Lee, Kai-Fu, *AI Superpowers: China, Silicon Valley, and the New World Order*, Houghton Mifflin Harcourt, 2018.

Leiner, Barry M., and Vinton G. Cerf, David D. Clark, Robert E. Kahn, Leonard Kleinrock, Daniel C. Lynch, Jon Postel, Larry G. Roberts, Stephen Wolff, B*rief History of the Internet*, Internet Society, 1997.

Listgarten, Jennifer, and Michael Weinstein, et. al., Nat Biomed Eng. 2018 January; 2(1): 38–47.

MacCulloch, W.S., and W. Pitts, "A logical calculus of the ideas immanent in nervous activity," Bull. Math. Biophysics, Vol. 5 (1943), pp. 115–133.

Malthus, Thomas, *An Essay on the Principle of Population*, 1798.

Marchal, Nahema, et.al., "Junk News During the EU Parliamentary Elections," DATA MEMO 2019.3, Oxford Internet Institute, Oxford University, 2019.

Markowitz, Judith, *Robots that Kill*, McFarland & Company, 2019.

McAfee, Andrew, and Erik Brynjolfsson, *Machine, Platform, Crowd: Harnessing Our Digital Future*, W. W. Norton & Company, 2017.

McLellan, Charles, "Smart farming: How IoT, robotics, and AI are tackling one the biggest problems of the century," TechRepublic, December 2018.

Meisel, William, "Nets of variable-threshold elements," IEEE Transactions on Computers, Vol. C-17, No. 7, July 1968.

Meisel, William, "Potential Functions in Mathematical Pattern Recognition," IEEE Transactions on Computers, September 1969.

Meisel, William, *Computer-Oriented Approaches to Pattern Recognition*, Academic Press, 1972.

Meisel, William, *The Software Society*, Trafford Press, 2013.

Microsoft, *The Future Computed: Artificial Intelligence and its role in society*, Microsoft Corporation, 2018.

Mirkin, Shachar, et al, "Listening Comprehension over Argumentative Content," Proceedings of the 2018 Conference on Empirical Methods in Natural Language Processing, October 31 - November 4, 2018.

Mueller, Robert, "Report On The Investigation Into Russian Interference In The 2016 Presidential Election," 2019.

Nahin, Paul J., *The Logician and the Engineer: How George Boole and Claude Shannon Created the Information Age*, Princeton University Press, 2013.

Naisbitt, John, and Patricia Aburdene, *Re-Inventing the Corporation: Transforming Your Job and Your Company for the New Information Society*, 1985.

National Critical Functions Set, Department of Homeland Security, April 2019.

National Cyber Strategy for United States of America, September 2018, https://www.whitehouse.gov/wp-content/uploads/2018/09/National-Cyber-Strategy.pdf.

Newman, Jessica Cussins, *Toward AI Security: Global Aspirations for a More Resilient Future*, Center for Long-Term Cybersecurity, February 2019.

Ni, Shengyu, and Mark Stoneking, "Improvement in detection of minor alleles in next generation sequencing by base quality recalibration," BMC Genomics, 2016.

Nilsson, Nils, *Learning Machines: Foundations of Trainable Pattern-Classifying Systems*, New York: McGraw-Hill, 1965.

Omidshafiei, Shayegan, et al, "Learning to Teach in Cooperative Multiagent Reinforcement Learning," Association for the Advancement of Artificial Intelligence, August 31, 2018.

Page, Larry, "PageRank: Bringing Order to the Web," May 6, 2002.

Park, Daniel S., and William Chan, Google AI Blog, "SpecAugment: A New Data Augmentation Method for Automatic Speech Recognition," https://ai.googleblog.com/2019/04/specaugment-new-data-augmentation.html, April 22, 2019.

Pearl, Judea, and Dana Mackenzie, *The Book of Why: The New Science of Cause and Effect*, Basic Books, 2018.

Pew Research Center, December 2018, "Artificial Intelligence and the Future of Humans"

Poore, J., and T. Nemecek, "Reducing food's environmental impacts through producers and consumers," Science, June 2018.

Poundstone, William, *Fortune's Formula*, Hill and Wang, 2005.

Rahwan, Iyad, et.al., "Machine Behaviour," Nature 568 (2019).

Romer, David, "Endogenous Technological Change," The Journal of Political Economy, October 1990.

Rumelhart, David E., Geoffrey E. Hinton & Ronald J. Williams, "Learning representations by back-propagating errors," Nature, volume 323, pages533–536 (1986).

Russell, Stuart J., and Peter Norvig, *Artificial Intelligence: A Modern Approach* (3rd Edition), Pearson Education, 2009.

Saxena, Kshitji, et. al., "Provider Adoption of Speech Recognition and its Impact on Satisfaction, Documentation Quality, Efficiency, and Cost in an Inpatient EHR," AMIA Jt Summits Transl Sci Proc., published online 2018 May 2018.

Scharre, Paul, *Army of None: Autonomous Weapons and the Future of War*, W.W.Norton, 2018.

Schwab, Klaus, "The Fourth Industrial Revolution: what it means, how to respond," World Economic Forum, 14 January 2016.

Schumpeter, Joseph, *Capitalism, Socialism, and Democracy*, 1942.

Sejnowski, Terrence J., *The Deep Learning Revolution*, MIT Press, 2018.

Shannon, Claude, "A Symbolic Analysis of Relay and Switching Circuits," Transactions of the American Institute of Electrical Engineers, 1938.

Singer, P.W., and Emerson T. Brooking, *Like War: The Weaponization of Social Media*, Houghton Mifflin Harcourt, 2018.

Smith, Adam, *An Inquiry into the Nature and Causes of the Wealth of Nations* (1776).

Solow, R.N., "Technical Change and the Aggregate Production Function," The Review of Economics and Statistics, August 1957.

Standage, Tom, "Telegraphy: The Victorian Internet," Chapter 14, Communication in History, David Crowley and Paul Heyer (editors), Routledge, 2011.

Topol, Eric, *Deep Medicine: How Artificial Intelligence Can Make Healthcare Human Again*, Hathette Book Group, 2019.

Turing, A.M., "Proposals for Development in the Mathematics Division of an Automatic Computing Engine (ACE)," presented to the National Physical Laboratory, 1945. Reprinted as Com Sci 57, National Physical laboratory, Teddington, UK, 1972.

Unal, Beyza, "Cybersecurity of NATO's Space-based Strategic Assets," Research paper, Royal Institute of International Affairs, July 2019.

Wang, Shuohang, et al, "Evidence Aggregation for Answer Re-Ranking in Open-Domain Question Answering," April 2018.

"Weapons of Mass Disruption: America is deploying a new economic arsenal to assert its power," The Economist, June 6, 2019.

Weinstein, Michael M., and Aishani Prem, et al, "FIGARO: An efficient and objective tool for optimizing microbiome rRNA gene trimming parameters", bioRxiv April 16, 2019.

Weng, Tsui-Wei, "Evaluating the Robustness of Neural Networks: An Extreme Value Theory Approach," Sixth International Conference on Learning Representations, January 2018.

Wikipedia, "Vertical farming," https://en.wikipedia.org/wiki/Vertical_farming.

Zuboff, Shoshana, *The Age of Surveillance Capitalism*, PublicAffairs, 2019.

Zuckerberg, Mark, "The Internet needs new rules," Washington Post, March 30, 2019.